Jewish Studies and
Holocaust Education
in Poland

Jewish Studies and Holocaust Education in Poland

Lynn W. Zimmerman
with Contributing Scholars

McFarland & Company, Inc., Publishers
Jefferson, North Carolina

LIBRARY OF CONGRESS CATALOGUING-IN-PUBLICATION DATA

Jewish studies and Holocaust education in Poland /
    Lynn W. Zimmerman with contributing scholars.
        p.   cm.
    Includes bibliographical references and index.

    ISBN 978-0-7864-7861-3
    softcover : acid free paper ∞

    1. Holocaust, Jewish (1939–1945)—Study and teaching—
Poland.   I. Zimmerman, Lynn W., editor of compilation.
D804.33.J49 2014
940.53′180710438—dc23   2013048081

BRITISH LIBRARY CATALOGUING DATA ARE AVAILABLE

© 2014 Lynn W. Zimmerman. All rights reserved

No part of this book may be reproduced or transmitted in any form or by any means, electronic or mechanical, including photocopying or recording, or by any information storage and retrieval system, without permission in writing from the publisher.

On the cover: artwork *Students*, 1920 (© 2013 PicturesNOW)
Manufactured in the United States of America

McFarland & Company, Inc., Publishers
   Box 611, Jefferson, North Carolina 28640
      www.mcfarlandpub.com

To my dear friend Katarzyna (Kasia) Kucharska.
Through her I encountered many of the people, events,
and institutions that are part of this book.

Table of Contents

INTRODUCTION	1
Culture, Identity and Stereotypes	7
The Historical Context	20
• *Jewish Student NGOs in Present-Day Poland (1999–2013): Being Here by Piotr Goldstein*	*38*
Jewish Studies and Holocaust Education at Polish Universities	49
• *The Center for Holocaust Studies at the Jagiellonian University in Kraków: Studies, Research, Remembrance by Jolanta Ambrosewicz-Jacobs, Elisabeth Büttner and Katarzyna Suszkiewicz*	*58*
Holocaust Education in Polish Public Schools	78
• *The Legacy of the Holocaust in Poland and Its Educational Dimension by Piotr Trojański*	*93*
NGOs and Their Role in Holocaust Education and Jewish Studies	117
• *Memory, Non-Memory and Post-Memory of the Holocaust: Coming Out of Amnesia in Post-Communist Poland? by Jolanta Ambrosewicz-Jacobs*	*121*
Museums: Their Role in Holocaust Education and Jewish Studies	140
The Role of the Arts in Holocaust Education and Jewish Studies	152
• *Teaching About the Holocaust through Music by Izabella Goldstein*	*159*
Jewish Culture Festivals in Poland	166
CONCLUSION	187
EPILOGUE	190
APPENDIX: FURTHER READING	191

REFERENCES	193
ABOUT THE CONTRIBUTORS	201
INDEX	203

Introduction

One evening in 2002 I was listening to *This American Life,* a public radio program in the United States. A young American woman who was Jewish was talking to Ira Glass, the host, about living in Kraków, Poland. She talked about Polish interest in Jewish culture and the Jewish cultural festival which has been hosted in Kraków since the early 1990s. This young woman said that she had mixed feelings about the interest in Jewish life and about this festival. She told him that on one hand she was happy that people in Poland were recognizing the contributions of Jews to their culture, history, and society. However, she was also slightly disturbed and, even, offended, by it. She said she felt uncomfortable because at times she felt like she was watching outsiders reenact a romanticized version of culture which no longer existed (Glass, 2002).

Her story piqued my interest. Even though I had been to Kraków several times, I had never been to the festival, partly for the reasons she had mentioned. I thought that it would feel odd going to see other people celebrating a culture that was not theirs, and that no longer existed in their country. I have never been to one of the popular American Indian festivals in the United States for the same reason. I had been to Kazimierz, the former Jewish quarter in Kraków, on several occasions and I felt that I was in a museum or in a place whose past and present did not match. Like this young woman, I felt some discomfort. I knew from reading and talking to others that most of the residents and shop and restaurant owners were not Jewish. However, Judaica and Jewish souvenirs were being sold, and there were several restaurants featuring "Jewish" food.

I did finally attend the festival in 2005. I had similar mixed feelings as the young woman whose story I had heard. The unease started with the Friday Shabbat service at the Tempel Synagogue. This formerly "progressive" synagogue has a women's balcony, so that men and women could sit separately during services, women upstairs and men below in the main sanctuary. This arrangement is more in line today with traditional and Orthodox branches of Judaism, so I assume that the Friday evening service I attended was organized with the requirements of the more orthodox Jews in mind. As a modern Conservative Jewish woman, it was strange to have to sit in the women's balcony since I am accustomed to egalitarian services in which men and women sit together and participate equally in the services. Not only was being segregated in this way strange for me, the set-up of the balcony was not comfortable. The panel on the front of the women's balcony in Tempel Synagogue is over a meter high, so although you can hear quite well while sitting, you can see nothing of what is going on down below. To see what is happening in the main sanctuary below, one must stand and look over the rail. Therefore, during the service—and it was a religious service, not a show—there were quite a number of women in the balcony, some sitting, but most standing looking over the rail. Although I was sitting with some Jewish women from the United States, most of the people were Poles who came to see what the service was like. Think about how you would feel if you were attending mass in your church or services in your mosque and there was a group of people there as curiosity-seekers—not just to see the building, but to see what you were doing. It is a disquieting feeling. The other American women I spoke to expressed that same feeling. Not only was I participating in a service in a way that was strange to me, but I also felt as if I was part of a spectacle.

Then one fall a couple of years later, I was in Warsaw during the Singer's Warsaw (referring to Isaac Bashevis Singer) Jewish festival. Out of curiosity I went one day. There were a few vendors set up in the narrow street near the Nożyk Synagogue. Some had old items for sale, such as menorahs and kiddish cups. I was a little disturbed, just as I had been in Kraków when I had seen such items for sale. I wondered, Whose family were these stolen from? Whose family was murdered in the concentration camps so that someone could steal their family heirlooms? Equally as disturbing was seeing the pictures that a young woman had for sale. They looked like typical mass-produced pictures, but they were all stereotypical portrayals of Jewish men—old men in skullcaps with long beards counting money or holding money in their hands. I was frankly appalled by these pictures. First of all, they were portraying a stereotype of what a Jew looked like—all had big noses and sad, sagging eyes. They were also portraying the stereotype of Jews and money being connected. Nowhere was there a picture of a modern Jewish man in jeans and a T-shirt or of a Jewish woman working on her computer, only the old tired stereotype from the pre-war years.

All of these experiences came together to make me ask, What is the purpose of these festivals? Who attends them? Who are they benefiting?

What are they trying to achieve? So I started thinking and researching information on cultural festivals. This project has evolved since then into this much broader look at Jewish studies and Holocaust education in Poland.

In 2009 I lived in Wrocław, Poland for six months and while there took the opportunity to continue the research and to present on this theme at two conferences in Poland to largely Polish audiences. At one conference where I presented some of my research into Jewish cultural festivals in Poland, the comment about a modern image of Jews not being presented at the festivals was challenged by a fairly young Polish academic. She told me that, of course, Poles would not represent Jews as looking modern because they had never seen a modern Jew, or at least not one they would recognize as Jewish. She said there had been a Jewish boy in her class at school for a while, but he moved away. How she knew he was Jewish was unclear. However, the implication was that if a Jew does not present as Jewish—peyes (side curls), tallit (prayer shawl), kippah (yarmulke), dark hair, etc.—he (and the image is almost always Orthodox and masculine) did not fit the Polish notion of what and who a Jew is.

At this same conference a young Polish woman commented on my remark about visiting Kazimierz, the former Jewish quarter in Kraków, and feeling as if I were in a museum. She said that she and her young daughter went on a visit to Kraków and went to the former Jewish quarter. She said that as they were walking around and looking at the buildings and talking about the people who used to live in this area, her daughter asked, "Why did all the people go away?" This question from her 6-year-old daughter made her realize that she did not have a good answer to that question. She vaguely knew about the Holocaust, but she did not know how she could tell this child that the people had been taken from their homes and murdered.

At another conference that same year, I was talking to a young Polish-Jewish woman after my presentation. This blond-haired, blue-eyed young scholar said that being Jewish in Poland was difficult because of the stereotypes that Poles have of Jews. When people found out she was Jewish, she would often get the comment, "You don't look Jewish," because she did not fit the stereotype of dark hair and eyes. She said her classmates would also say things like, "Oh, I wish I were Jewish. Then I would be smart in all my subjects like you are." She told me that she did not think being Jewish was the reason she was an excellent student, but her Polish classmates could not look beyond the stereotype of the bookish Jew.

Partly as a result of these experiences and partly as a result of my role as a professor teaching about diversity and multicultural issues to education majors, I also started looking into Holocaust education, which I wanted to integrate as part of my courses. I began using an article that I translated from Polish which had been written by a Polish secondary history teacher. He explained and reflected on why teaching about Jews and the Holocaust was so important to him and to his students. He is a regular presenter at the Jagiellonian University's Summer Holocaust Institute for Secondary Teachers, which I attended one summer with a Polish friend. Then in summer 2011 I was invited to present there as well and spoke to a number of the participants about why they were there. In the meantime, I had also attended some talks by Polish professors who taught in Jewish studies programs and/or about the Holocaust. My interest in the topic had grown from wanting to understand more about Jewish cultural festivals in Poland to wanting to see the educational implications of what was going on in Poland in regards to Holocaust education and Jewish studies, and how Poles view this part of their history, culture, and education.

Despite this growing interest in Jewish life and culture in Poland, one must realize that not everyone in Poland is eager to be reminded of the past, a fact brought to my attention when on a "Tour of 5 Shtetls" organized during the Jewish Culture Festival in Kraków. We were at the first stop, Działoszyce, looking at the unrestored ruins of a nineteenth century synagogue. One man on the street, who was probably drunk, shouted "This isn't a Jewish town any more. Forget about them." The guide knew that several of us spoke Polish and was obviously embarrassed by this outburst. She explained that many of the small towns, shtetls, where Jews lived before the war are now inhabited by Poles who re-located from other areas of Poland, and they do not have a connection to their town's past. That may be one explanation, but it does not explain all the overt and covert expressions of anti–Semitism that still appear in Poland.

All of these experiences came together for me and raised questions about what is the educational function and value of a Jewish studies program, of teaching young people about the Holocaust, of going to a cultural festival. How effective is each as an educational tool? What are they trying to teach? Are they perpetuating stereotypes or breaking them down? Who attends each and why? How does such education relate to Jewish identity? Polish identity? How does each reflect current trends in identity politics? In Holocaust education? Can these issues be the foundation for teaching about human rights in general?

I realized that I could not separate the three types of educational experiences and arrive at an answer that made sense. What is taught at universities reflects current social and political issues and shapes research and scholarship. Educational reform for public education is tied to what is going on at the university and in society. Museums, NGOs (non-governmental organizations) and cultural festivals reflect local interests and the views that society has of groups of people, including minority groups. Museums and NGOs may educate formally with courses and workshops or more informally through their other programs and projects. Cultural festivals, which usually focus on the arts, represent an informal way for people to teach other about their own culture or for others to learn about a culture or a people that they may not know much about.

In this volume, I bring these ideas together to examine and analyze educational experiences in this particular environment and context. After defining how I use terms such as culture, cultural marker, and stereotypes, I then briefly present the history of Jews in Poland to provide the background against which these events and experiences take place. An essay by a young Jewish-Polish man gives insight into what it is like to grow up in contemporary Poland. Next I look at education about Jewish history and culture and about the Holocaust at the secondary and university levels. Essays by Polish scholars who are active in Holocaust education and curriculum design for secondary teachers round out this section. Then I describe a few NGOs related to Jewish issues to show what is being offered through these organizations. An essay by a Polish academic gives a scholarly perspective of the role of NGOs in Holocaust education and in learning about Jewish history and culture. An examination of museums as educational institutions also offers insight into the how the Holocaust and Jewish life and culture are memorialized and taught about in Poland. A look at the arts and how they are used to inform and educate is followed with an essay by a Jewish-Polish woman who was musical director and conductor of the Jewish choir, Tslil, giving another view of learning through the arts. Then, I examine and compare Jewish festivals in several Polish cities to provide an overview of what they offer and how. One element of this section is identifying what these festivals do to perpetuate stereotypes and what they do to break them down. Finally, I analyze and reflect on how these elements come together to create an educational context about Jewish life in Poland, before, during and after the Holocaust.

Culture, Identity and Stereotypes

> "Whilst in the nineteenth century, and in the first half of the twentieth, more and more Jews assimilated into the majority culture, aspired to rootedness in it, and gave up their Jewish heritage, in the last two decades or so I and others like me have regained the Jewish identities and Jewish knowledge that our parents did not pass on to us. We do not need to aspire to being Polish, because we have been raised Polish."—Krajewski, 2005, p. 17

Cultural identity is taught and perpetuated through formal and informal educational experiences. We and others learn about our cultural identity through expressions and demonstrations of our culture markers, such as language, cuisine, and music. Generalizations and even stereotypes about a culture are often based on interpretations of the prevalence of these cultural markers and perceptions about them.

Culture and Cultural Markers

Culture in its broadest form can be defined as behavior, beliefs, values, and worldview which are associated with a particular group of people. Because we acquire our culture unconsciously as children we are generally unaware of its influences on our behaviors and attitudes (Gudykunst and Kim, 2003). Our culture shapes how we interact with those around us, whether they are part of our cultural group or not.

In 1976, Edward T. Hall proposed that culture should be portrayed as an iceberg with internal (below the water) and external (above the water) components (Weaver, 1997). The internal aspects are those that are generally implicitly learned, unconscious, and difficult to change, such as beliefs, values, thought patterns, and myths. The external aspects can be perceived with the senses and are explicitly learned, conscious, and more open to change. These include art and literature, as well as religious rituals and holiday customs.

Cultural is multidimensional and represents a complex and integrated system of these internal and external aspects.

Cultural markers, identified more with the above the waterline portion of the cultural iceberg, such as language, accent, ethnicity, cuisine, and attire, are important expressions of cultural identity (Weaver, 1997). They serve as tangible identification of membership in a cultural group or as not being part of that group. Cultural markers also play a role in creating national identity, one form of collective identity that can be culturally based. Taylor (1997) describes the connection between culture and collective identity as "that descriptive aspect of the self-concept that the individual shares with every other member of the group" (p. 174). An examination of identity and national identity is relevant at this point, because in the case of Polish-Jewish identity, national identity plays an important role.

Identity Formation

A thorough treatment of identity and identity formation is beyond the scope of this book. However, relevant background material is necessary to provide context for some of the issues that arise in this topic. Identity is the result of a complex combination of factors, including social, cultural, legal, geographical, environmental, and psychological, which come together to create and maintain individual and group identity.

By visualizing identity as a web, one can see how the various strands that make up the individual's identity are interconnected and interdependent. Most of the strands of identity are created by how that person makes meaning of her life and the world around her, through interactions with others. The strongest and most dominant strands are those that connect the individual to the larger world, creating "collective identity." The strands of collective identity, the part of an individual's makeup that shows the person as "an extension of the collective ... a distinguishable part of the whole" (Casey, 1996, p. 221), are created by the individual's interactions with family, friends, peers, teachers, television, books, culture, political conditions, anything in the world around her. Collective or group identity is also shaped by how we define those who are not like us, those that we may refer to as "strangers." This connection through difference provides the tension that gives shape to the web of identity.

Identity formation theory presents one way of examining how the modern world categorizes people. Erikson's (1963, 1968) work on identity formation examined stages of development, beginning with a lack of awareness of identity, then progressing to a stage or stages where identity is being examined, even questioned, which is often called an identity crisis. The final stage of identity development is gaining a sense of identity. According to Erikson (1968), "ego identity formation is particularly critical in young adulthood, specifically during the college years, because the extent to which the identity issue is resolved determines the success or failure of adult development" (St. Louis and Liem, 2005, p. 228). Erikson's stages of development have been used as the basis of some models of ethnic identity formation. These models, supported by existing research in the field (Arce, 1981; Aries and Moorehead, 1989; Phinney, 1991, 1992; Phinney and Tarver, 1988; Spencer and Markstrom-Adams, 1990; Streitmatter, 1988), support the notion that "the formation of a positive sense of ethnic identity is considered to be essential to the successful development and adaptation of ethnic minority youth in American society" (St. Louis and Liem, 2005, p. 230). The social aspects of ethnic identity formation theory (Tajfel, 1978) make it is a useful construct for an examination of the notion of "stranger" in the context of national identity, which is discussed more fully in the next section.

There are multiple definitions of "stranger," but the general perception is that a "stranger" is someone who is not of one's group. Gudykunst and Kim (2003) state that "[a]nytime we communicate with people who are different and unknown and those people are in an environment unfamiliar to them, we are communicating with strangers" (p. 19). Therefore, there are degrees to which someone can be a stranger, and these differences affect communication and interaction with others. As identity is formed, individuals learn to identify themselves in relation to others, those in their group and those who are not.

In general, there are three primary elements of identity, human, personal, and social. Our human identity is how we are like other humans. These characteristics are closely related to the elements at the bottom of Maslow's (1943) hierarchy of needs pyramid, physical needs and security needs. Humans eat, sleep, and try to protect and shelter themselves. Personal identity refers to those characteristics that are individual differences which separate one from others in their group. Social identity is related to the third tier of Maslow's hierarchy and is defined by group membership. These groups vary. They may be roles, such as student, teacher, mother, brother. They may be demographic categories, such as age, race, ethnicity, and gender. They can be organizations which individuals join or affiliate with such as political parties or a community choir. The situation or context affects which identity is foremost at a given time, and can govern behavior in a particular situation. At the same time, how different someone seems to be from another person, how much of a stranger someone seems to be affects behavior and communication with them and between them. The degree of perceived difference also impacts the degree of uncertainty and anxiety participants may feel in an interaction.

One other variable that impacts identity formation and interactions between groups is whether a group is characterized as individualistic or collectivistic. Although this variable is based in a cultural dimension it is influenced by and influences social, environmental, and psychological manifestations of identity and can influence how communicators "predict each other's behavior" (Gudykunst and Kim, 2003, p. 54).

A brief overview of the characteristics of individualism and collectivism provides insight into how group identity is formed and how it influences interactions with others, inside and outside one's group. Individualism is characterized by focus on the self and one's immediate family, making and meeting individual goals, valuing individual initiative and achievement, and promoting self-realization. Collectivism on the other hand focuses more on making and meeting goals for the in-group, group loyalty, belonging, and fitting in. Communication is influenced by these variables as well. Individualism tends to be connected to direct communication in which communication is likely to be explicit and detailed. Collectivism on the other hand relies more on indirect communication in which the exchanges tend to be implicit and even ambiguous and are often aimed at promoting and maintaining group harmony. Misunderstandings between interlocuters using different styles can result if one or both do not realize that the goals and process of communication is different between them. These types of misunderstandings can highlight the differences between groups, creating uncertainty and anxiety between them. An understanding of such differences is especially important for the "stranger" who is trying to fit into a new environment.

However, an individual, even though he tries to assimilate, may not be at home anywhere. According to Bauman (2001) he becomes a "universal stranger" who "is 'fully at home' only with himself" (p. 95). This status comes only with incredible effort and the ability to create a self-identity that is integrated and the ambivalence is integrated. The uncertainty of where one belongs can create feelings of loneliness and isolation in one who assimilates. Jacob Wasserman (Bauman, 2001) explains that it is characteristic of individuals crossing the margin between social groups that they are not only uncertain about their belonging to the group they are ready to enter, but also about their belonging to the group they are leaving [p. 118].

National identity is one important form of identity which confers a sense of belonging. A common culture in a nation creates an environment in which inhabitants feel they understand one another and they can reliably predict one another's thoughts and behaviors. In nations in which more than one culture exists, which is the case in most modern nations, the notion of a common culture may be more or less fulfilled. However, usually one culture dominates and those who of different cultures must either assimilate fully or partially or accept minority status.

National Identity

In *Modernity and Ambivalence*, Bauman (1991) asserts that modernity abhors ambivalence. The modern world seeks to classify and bring order to everything, including people. National boundaries, geographical, legal, social, and cultural helps define who is a member of a nation. Modern nations can tolerate those who are outside their definition of who belongs because these outsiders can be classified. However, "strangers," as Bauman calls them, people who are not so easily classified, people who do not neatly fit the description of insider or outsider, are treated with suspicion, and even hostility, because of their ambiguity.

Bauman (2001) contends that the scientific principles of the modern world seek to order and classify everything. These principles indicate that for a nation to be properly classed as such, it should have a homogeneous, i.e. easily classified, population. Although the nation may be comprised of one or more ethnic groups, national identity is an attempt to unify a population legally, linguistically, culturally, and ideologically (Steiner, 1995; Vertovec, 2011). The establishment of a national identity is an attempt to establish a shared history and a common culture so that the population has a "shared feeling of belonging together ... being different from all others" (Steiner, 1995, p. 307). This construction of a "collective consciousness" around economic, political, and geographical conditions creates boundaries which define a nation's citizenry, and does not allow or encourage deviation. By constructing these boundaries, this one "way of being" is legitimized, creating inequalities for those who do not conform to what becomes "the values of the dominant elite" (Bauman, 2001, p. 107). He says that these boundaries must "be both exclusive and comprehensive [so that] nothing left inside may be irrelevant to the total design" (p. 24). This kind of social engineering gives a sense of order and a sense of belonging for those who are included, but those who do not fit the pattern become the "other."

In his work, sociologist Bauman (1991) suggests that membership in a group provides at least a perception of comfort and security to those within the group, giving a sense of order and a sense of belonging for those who are included. Those who do not fit the pattern become the "other" or "stranger." When individuals move from one culture or nation to another, they will find that their socialization may have taught them social and cultural norms that are different from those they are experiencing living in another place. They have moved from being like those around them to being a "stranger." Native members of a community learn knowledge and attitudes about what is relevant and taken for granted in the community, so that they feel both security and assurance about their shared world-view within the community. When in-group characteristics are narrowly defined, as is common in collectivistic cultures, national identity can take on a narrow definition as well. National identity gives the individual the opportunity to develop a sense of belonging to something larger than herself. However, when national identity is narrow or even is essentialized so that there is only one "right" way of being an American or a Pole, for instance, the individual has little opportunity to develop and express a unique sense of self within this nationalistic context. It also limits who can be members of the in-group, in this case, citizens of the nation.

While immigrants and other "outsiders" can enrich the cultural fabric of a nation, they also change it and some see these changes as a weakening of national identity. The "alien culture" introduces other cultural markers such as different languages, food, customs, beliefs, and practices, which can create anxiety about cultural changes. In the twenty-first century with increased globalization and greater population shifts, there is an increase of what Vertovec (2007) refers to as transnational engagement. "The degrees to and ways in which today's migrants maintain identities, activities and connections linking them with communities outside Britain are unprecedented" (p. 1043). This phenomenon is not limited to Great Britain.

According to Bauman (2001), the "other" can consist of those who are totally outside the boundaries of national identity, but more often there are those within a nation he calls "strangers" whose identity is ambiguous, defying classification. They occupy an area of uncertainty between the "in" and "out," with characteristics of the "in," but cannot really be classified as "in" or only with uncertainty. For example, the individual may speak the language fluently but with an identifiably different accent. The stranger who assimilates rarely becomes an integral part of the dominant culture because she never gains full acceptance by the dominant culture. The native does not believe "that the stranger will [ever] become like the native and will never see the world though native eyes" (Bauman, 2001, p. 84).

In addition to social and economic concerns about immigrants, such as they take jobs, they are a burden on public services, or they are a risk to national security, there is often a fear among the "native" inhabitants of a nation that immigrants—the other—"erode the national culture" (Vertovec, 2011, p. 242). This cultural concern can become part of the political rhetoric. These cultural changes may be blamed for various economic and social problems because of this perception of erosion of the national culture. Oftentimes these "alien" cultures are essentialized through immigration policy, racial/ethnic profiling, or even labels such as "victims of..." Creating a schemata in which immigrants and other "outsiders" are represented as "problems" contributes to increased stereotyping and increased anxiety about the strangers.

Bauman (2001) asserts that nations are formed as an attempt to "eliminate the strangers" (p. 63). The nation extends the rights and privileges of citizenry to those it deems desirable, those it can classify. When a stranger comes into a nation, assimilation of that stranger is usually the goal, but depending on how different she is from the national "norm" and how rigid the rules of identity are, she may be stigmatized as "other, or "untouchable." The stranger also may be banished completely or placed outside the realm of normal social contact, as in a ghetto. Such separation makes it easier for stereotypes to be created and maintained which further separate the stranger from the citizen.

Stereotypes

How do individuals and groups identify those who are in their groups and those who are not? They often rely on stereotypes, especially when they first meet others, because they are trying to fit them into their cultural categories. Gudykunst and Kim (2003) define stereotypes as "cognitive representations of another group that influence our feelings toward members of that group" (p. 127). Hewstone and Brown (1986) state that people categorize individuals on the basis of an easily identifiable characteristic such sex, race, etc. A set of attributes is generalized to all members of the group having this characteristic, and is ascribed to any individual in the group. It is common to rely on stereotypes that are commonly seen in the media and in advertising. Hewstone and Brown (1986) assert that stereotypes kick in immediately on meeting a stranger, because stereotypes are based on mostly visual as well as unconscious perceptions. Although stereotypes are generally based on some external trait or traits, a group's self-conception may be based on intrinsic or other traits. Therefore, a group's image of itself may vary considerably from how others outside this group view the group and members within it.

Although identity is complex and multifaceted, having human, personal, and social aspects, stereotypes as representations of an identity ignore this complexity and suggest a one-dimensional view of an individual's or a group's identity. Because the human mind cannot process so much complexity accurately and comfortably, stereotypes are useful in interactions with others to reduce this complexity, helping create a perceived predictability to the interaction. Relying on stereotypes, particularly early in a relationship, can help reduce uncertainty so that communication can proceed and more meaningful interactions can develop. However, relying on stereotypes often results in errors in attribution, attributing certain characteristics or behaviors to the person based on the stereotype rather than on individual idiosyncrasies or the situation.

Based on Gudykunst and Kim's (2003) definition, stereotypes have a cognitive and an affective component, what one thinks and what one feels about the characteristics they are witnessing. Stereotypes consequently influence interactions with others. People make predictions on one's behavior and the interactions with them are based on expectations of behavior and interactions. However, because the boundaries between many groups are fuzzy, inaccurate predictions often occur. One may perceive a behavior incorrectly based on an inaccurate application of expectations. Additionally, when meeting someone, whether they are from the same group or another group, "we generally expect our perceptions of others to be slightly positive" (Gudykunst and Kim, 2003, p. 129). Therefore any negative or extreme behavior that they exhibit takes on greater significance and is generally attributed to stereotypes of that group. Generally, people ignore information that does not confirm their stereotyped perceptions. When they do start processing extra information, get to know the other better, stereotypes can change.

Stereotypes serve several functions related to identity. They "maintain division between ingroup ('us') and outgroups ('them')" (Gudykunst and Kim, 2003, p. 129) by providing some type of classification of characteristics and behaviors. Comparisons between groups can arise based on stereotyping, so they also help maintain ingroup bias, the belief that one's ingroup is better than other groups. In all countries and cultures there is a tendency to target outsiders as objects of insult or humor, routine expressions of prejudice that may or may not have malicious intent. Some languages, such as ancient Greek, Japanese and Chinese, even embed these stereotyped differences by using the same word for "foreigner" as they use for "barbarian" (Hoffman, 1997). Bar-Tal (1997) asserts that there is also a tendency to stereotype strangers over whom one has power. He says that background factors, such as the history of relations between the groups, economic conditions, political and social climate, and behavior of group members all impact the strength and content of stereotypes.

The process of stereotyping is related to several factors. Although stereotypes are used to categorize people in order to "reduce our uncertainty and increase our confidence in predicting strangers' behavior" (Gudykunst and Kim, 2003, p. 131), they are not really reliable predictors. The higher a person's anxiety in a situation, the more prone that person is to stereotype. One tends to rely on stereotypes to re-confirm what one thinks he knows about a group. One expects others to meet their expectations, so that the stereotype becomes a self-fulfilling prophecy. In order to improve communication with strangers, "we need to increase the complexity of our stereotypes (e.g., include a large number of traits in the stereotype and differentiate subgroups within the group being stereotyped) and question our unconscious assumption that most, if not all, members of a group fit a single stereotype (Stephan and Rosenfield, 1928)" (Gudykunst and Kim, 2003, p. 134).

The process of stereotyping can lead to more extreme forms of separation such as ethnocentrism and xenophobia. Ethnocentrism is based on "our tendency to identify with our ingroup ... and to evaluate outgroups and their members according to our ingroups' standards" (Gudykunst and Kim, 2003, p. 137). According to Rosenblatt (1964) nationalism and ethnocentrism can help maintain ingroup integrity through a variety of functions, such as increased homogeneity, greater ease of striving against outsiders, decreased social disorganization, increased tenure of leaders, and facilitation of learning. However, ethnocentrism and nationalism can be negative when they are too highly developed. They can lead to ideas of superiority, so that one group feels so superior to the other that they think it is their role to change the other groups to be more like them. In general, there are more "positive functions for the ingroup, but ... consequences for outgroups tend to be negative" (Gudykunst and Kim, 2003, p. 139) which can also create anxiety about interacting with strangers to the point of xenophobia. Xenophobia, which is literally "a fear of strangers" develops as the observer perceives "threats to the predictability and stability of our social worlds" (Gudykunst and Kim, 2003, p. 138).

In order to understand these issues, one must be aware of and understand the contexts in which stereotyping takes place. Cultural and societal contexts are created and can be traced historically through an examination of a society's past and/or a culture's traditions. These contexts are often related to group membership. Being part of a group influences how people think of themselves and others (Gudykunst and Kim, 2003). One's ingroups are those people that a person is taught to associate with. It includes the people they care about and cooperate with. Outgroups are groups that people are taught not to associate with. There is no feeling of meaningful connection, no real need to associate with people in that other group. However, members of different groups may create connections and "remain on amicable terms if their interests converge, or at least do not impinge on each other" (Hoffman, 1997, p. 44).

Individualist cultures and collectivist cultures tend to view ingroups and outgroups differently (Gudykunst and Kim, 2003). Therefore, their stereotyping process and interactions with strangers take slightly different courses. Because individualistic cultures focus more on the individual, ingroup connections can be looser and group boundaries more transparent and fluid. Differences are emphasized and group identity tends to be in large social groups giving more room for inclusion by a more heterogeneous mixture of people. Collectivist cultures tend to have tighter connections with ingroups than individualistic cultures, because they are focused more on the group. Their groups are smaller, more homogenous, and less inclusive. In general, therefore, differences would create a higher level of uncertainty and anxiety for members of a collectivist culture than for an individualist culture. There would be less porosity of boundaries and more conditions for being part of the group.

Anti-Semitism

One outcome of stereotyping is feelings of dislike or distrust of other groups, prejudice, and discrimination against groups based on these feelings. Prejudice and discrimination can be on the individual level or the institutional level. An individual may feel prejudice against a group. However, institutional prejudice and discrimination takes place at the policy level and is directed at minority or subordinate groups in a society. These can include discriminatory hiring or housing policies, or unequal access to education or healthcare, and may be overt or covert, intentional or unintentional. Examples of institutional racism are the apartheid system in South Africa and the "separate but equal" education in place in the United before the Brown vs. Board of Education decision in 1954 whose aim was to end racial segregation of schools. An examination of anti–Semitism, a prejudice experienced in the individual and institutional levels, is relevant as background for a discussion of Polish and Jewish relations.

Although there has been hatred of and discrimination against Jews throughout their history, the term anti–Semitism was coined in 1879 by German journalist Wilhelm Marr (USHMM, 2012). The nineteenth century was a time of increased nationalism and in Germany this manifested itself in the "voelkisch movement," an ethnocentric and xenophobic movement supported by the German intelligentsia using racial anthropology and social Darwinism to put forth the idea that Jews were a different race than Germans and had no place in the German national landscape. These ideas were politicized and legitimized when Hitler and the Nazis came to power in the 1930s enacting anti–Jewish legislation and a racist hierarchy based on the 1935 Nuremberg laws which "racially defined Jews by 'blood' and ordered the total separation of so-called 'Aryans' and 'non–Aryans'" (USHMM, 2012, para. 4).

The Anti-Defamation League (2001) identifies three primary ways in which anti–Semitism is expressed. Besides political efforts such as those enacted by Nazi Germany, there are also religious teachings which proclaim Jews as inferior or evil, as well as stereotyped images and prejudices against Jews.

Historically in Poland many Jews engaged in trade of one sort or another. As Hoffman (1997) found when she talked to a rural Pole in the mid–1990s, stereotypes and prejudices about Jews and trade persist. This man declared that when Jews lived in his shtetl, they were shrewd and always cheated the peasants in any way they could. When she asked him "What goes on in the market now, without the Jews?" [he laughed and responded] "Ours are just the same. Everyone always walks all over the peasants" (p. 79). He also confided to her that after the war everyone was worried about trade with no Jews to around to carry on, as though trading were some great mystery which required "devilish cleverness." He assured her, however, that "ours know how to do it, too" (p. 79).

Although anti–Semitism has decreased in parts of the world, it still exists, sometimes in different forms. The ADL (2001) states that issues such as policies toward the State of Israel which denounce "Zionism" and Holocaust denial are two ways in which anti-Semitism can be covertly and overtly expressed. In a 2012 report the ADL examined anti-Semitism in modern Europe and found that anti-Semitic stereotypes persist despite a decrease in overt acts of anti-Semitism. The project did find, however, that these stereotypes tend to persist more with older, less educated, and lower income participants in the study.

The one survey question that has particular relevance for this volume is whether the Jews are responsible for the death of Christ. "Nearly half of Polish respondents, 46 percent, agree with this statement—the highest percentage among all the countries surveyed" (ADL, 2012, p. 12). As will be shown in the next section, Poland's national identity is strongly connected to Catholicism which traditionally has taught that the "Jews killed Jesus."

Religion can be a strong cultural and personal identity marker with implications for those who belong to the majority religion and those who belong to a minority religion. Religion can influence people's traditions and customs, the holidays they celebrate, the way they dress and what they eat. However, on a deeper level, religion also shapes and influences its adherents' beliefs, values, self-concept, and worldview, internal markers which define who we are and how we fit into our environment. When these characteristics diverge, conflict can arise. The number of wars throughout human history which has been fought in the name of religion is evidence of how strongly attached people are to and influenced by religious views. In the case of Poland, Catholicism has been the majority religion since 966 C.E., when the first king of Poland declared it to be so. Historically, the largest religious minority in Poland has been the Jews, a group which has been rejected and even demonized by the Catholic Church throughout the centuries. "In folk pageants and Catholic morality plays, the Jew was often pictured as a frightened, cowering figure, speaking broken Polish and will to undergo any number of humiliations for financial gain" (Hoffman, 1997, p. 38). While there have been periods of religious tolerance in Poland, the stereotypes of Jews as Christ-killers, as shrewd financial manipulators, and as "not really Polish" have persisted. Therefore, it can be argued that while modern Polish anti-Semitism has connections to the political and social environment, its roots are in religious stereotypes and prejudices. The next chapter establishes the historical context for Polish culture and national identity and Jewish culture and identity in Poland.

For Further Information

Anti-Semitism, http://www.adl.org/anti-semitism/. The Anti-Defamation League's website, which posts updates and information about anti–Semitism around the world.

The Concept of Culture, compiled by George Dafoulas, http://www.swyaa.org/resources/handbook/Index/THE%20CONCEPT%20OF%20CULTURE.html. Designed for young people taking part in its program, this is part of SWYAA's *Handbook for Cultural Understanding.*

Culture Matters: The Peace Corps Cross-Cultural Workbook, http://files.peacecorps.gov/multimedia/pdf/library/T0087_Culture_Matters.pdf. Developed by the Peace Corps with readings and activities for cross-cultural training for Peace Corps volunteers and others

"Updated Maslow's Pyramid of Needs," http://psychcentral.com/news/2010/08/23/updated-maslows-pyramid-of-needs/17144.html. Compares Maslow's original hierarchy of needs with an updated version based on new findings and theories.

"Social Identity Theory: Tajfel and Turner 1979," http://www.age-of-the-sage.org/psychology/social/social_identity_theory.html. An overview of Tajfel and Turner's Social Identity Theory.

The Historical Context

> *Prawda, że się wywodzim wszyscy od Adama,*
> *Alem słyszał, że chłopi pochodzą od Chama,*
> *Żydowie od Jafeta, my szlachta od Sema,*
> *A więc panujem jako starsi nad obiema.*
>
> While it's true that we all from old Adam have come,
> Yet I've heard that the peasants are issue of Ham,
> Jews of Japhet, we gentry from eldest of brothers,
> Are of Sem, and as eldest rule over the others
> [from *Pan Tadeusz* by Adam Mickiewicz].

In this section, Polish national identity will be examined. By tracing the course of Polish history, one can see how group identity was formed in the Polish context and how Jewish identity in Poland plays out against this backdrop of a culture which is moderately collectivistic and which is rooted in a different religious tradition.

Polish National Identity

The history of Poland as a nation began in the tenth century when Mieszko I, founder of the Piast dynasty, became king of the group of West Slavic people inhabiting an area in Central Europe. In 966 CE he decreed that the people of Poland become Roman Catholics. Over the past 1000 years, the borders of Poland have shifted and altered with changing political conditions in Europe, but the identity of the people who call themselves "Polish" has remained defined by their Slavic ancestry, the Polish language, Roman Catholicism, and the many customs and traditions of their culture. According to Davies (1986) the Polish language "is the essential ingredient of Polish nationality" (p. 330). Volenski and Grzymala-Moszczynska (1997) assert that being Roman Catholic is such a part of the Polish identity that church membership was seen by many as not just a religious duty, but as a patriotic duty. Rituals and customs related to Roman Catholicism have contributed heavily to Polish culture, from celebration of Church holidays to baby naming conventions. Traditionally, Poles have been named after saints and that saint's name day is the individual's major celebration, rather than one's birthday which is the primary individual celebration in many European cultures.

In the mid–1500s, Poland, the largest state in Europe, was home to a diverse group of people. There were numerous languages, ethnic groups, and faiths represented in the country. A times "less than half the population was ethnically Polish" (Hoffman, 1997, p. 9), although the Polish language became the language of government, commerce, science, and culture. This diversity promoted tolerance and "encouraged a strong tradition of education" (Davies, 1986, p. 317) as the various groups shared with and inspired one another. The Jewish community became the largest in Europe, making up about 10 percent of Poland's population in the 1700s before the partitions. Especially during the Renaissance, Jews saw Poland as refuge, a place where they could live in relative peace and safety. Many Polish Jews "believed that the word 'Poland' was the same as the Hebrew *polin*, which means 'here thou shalt lodge' in exile" (Hoffman, 1997, p. 10). While some Poles and Jews advocated assimilation of the Jews into Polish society, there were others who recognized the strength of a pluralistic society in which "the Jewish legacy was an integral and enriching part of the national identity" (Hoffman, 1997, p. 11).

Despite this atmosphere of tolerance, the Poles "had a reputation for exaggerated pride in their country [believing] that traditional Polish ways were superior to those of all other nations" (Davies, 1986, p. 269). This notion was based partly on the desire of the Polish aristocracy to assert that their roots were not the same as the common people's roots. Group identity was tied to one's place in society and, as with many collectivist cultures, a culture of high-power distance developed. Power distance is "the extent to which the less powerful members ... accept that power is distributed unequally" (Gudykunst and Kim, 2003, p. 75). There is a distinct separation between those in power and those without power and the boundaries between the groups are not porous. This differentiation into classes helped solidify the collectivist nature of Polish society and culture. While this differentiation created social rigidity within the society, it also created a central ideology about Polish identity on which Poland during the Partitions depended.

In the 1700s, Poland lost much of its territory, and finally ceased to exist as a political entity. Its territory was partitioned among Germany, Austria, and Russia on three different occasions in 1772, 1793, and finally in 1795. Although Polish systems of education, government, military, and so forth were abolished under the Partitions, "many of the more intangible elements of old Polish life—their culture, languages, religions, social and political attitudes" (Davies, 1986, p. 316) survived. The suppression of their national rites and rituals resulted in a Polish patriotism which "became the object of an intense, secret, and highly developed mysticism" (p. 270). This "underground religion" of Polish patriotism was modeled after the Catholic Church, and those who followed it believed that it was something worth dying for. According to Davies (1986) the literature of that period, the Romantic Period, was a driving force in keeping this desire for freedom alive and representing this mission as a spiritual journey.

By the end of the nineteenth century, partitioned Poland was laying the groundwork for reunification. Many Poles rejected the notion of Pan-Slavism which came into vogue during the 1800s. They were afraid of being subsumed in Russia's history. They developed their own Piast Concept (based on the Piast Dynasty which began with King Mieszko I) of a Poland that was made up of Polish-speaking people; that was totally Catholic; and that was resistant to Germany. This movement established the Polish language and Catholicism as integral parts of the Polish national identity.

One example of the strength of this connection occurred during the third partition. A "children's strike" was staged in western Poland at the beginning of the twentieth century protesting the use of the German language in religion classes. Września is a small town located near Poznań, which was in the German partition. At the liceum (high school), classes were conducted mostly in German, except for religion classes which were taught in Polish. The German authorities decided that since Września was part of the German nation, all classes there should be taught in German. A small group of high school students went on strike protesting this mandate. They believed that something as personal as religion should be taught in one's home language, and as ethnic Poles they were not interested in giving up their language. With the support of their parents, they refused to go to classes. Their fathers lost their jobs, and despite being beaten and imprisoned, the students refused to give in. The author Henryk Sienkiewicz who was living in exile heard of their plight, and he and other Polish exiles brought international attention to this situation. Finally, after about two years, the German authorities gave in. When a new liceum was built in 1910, it was named about Sienkiewicz in honor of his support.

The writings of authors in exile, such as Henryk Sienkiewicz, also contributed to the view of Poland as a Christian nation. The link with the Catholic Church was strengthened at the beginning of the twentieth century as the Polish clergy struggled together with the Polish people to create a cohesive nation. However, there was not total unity, and friction continued to exist between the political and church arenas, even after Poland regained its independence after World War I. Then the horrors of World War II brought about "the undivided Catholicity of the Polish nation" (Davies, 1986, p. 342).

On September 1, 1939, Germany invaded Poland followed by an invasion by the Soviet Union on September 17, 1939. From 1940 to 1945 Poland was the site of many of the work camps and extermination camps set up by the Nazi regime. Enemies of the German state, a host of people defined as "undesirable" by the Nazis, and especially Jews, from all over Europe, were sent to these camps as slave labor and to be exterminated. In an attempt to cover up their crimes, the Nazis "liquidated" many of these camps in the closing days of the war, killing the inmates, attempting to destroy the camps, and remove evidence of their existence.

The Holocaust did not begin with the onset of World War II. The persecution of the Jews began with Hitler and the Nazi's rise to power in 1933. Although other groups such as the Roma, people with disabilities, Jehovah's Witnesses, the Polish intelligentsia, Communists, and homosexuals were victims of the Nazis, the Jews were the primary target of their "systematic, bureaucratic, state-sponsored persecution and murder" (USHMM, 2012, para. 1). Through a progressive set of measures, Jews were first marginalized in German society, then segregated from the general population in ghettos, and finally sent to work camps and death camps. By the end of World War II, about only one-third of the Jews living in Europe prior to the Holocaust survived.

A full discussion about the Holocaust is beyond the scope of this book. However, the facts that most of the death camps were located on Polish soil and that the largest Jewish population in Europe lived in Poland prior to the Holocaust are relevant. Poles did not plan and carry out the Holocaust. However, there were Poles who were complicit, either by being passive witnesses, through indifference or fear for their lives, by collaborating with the Nazis, or by perpetuating crimes against Jews themselves. In contrast, there were Poles who hid and rescued Jews either on their own or as part of a group such as Żegota (the Council for Aid to Jews). For example, in the shtetl of Bransk, in eastern Poland, villagers "were responsible for the deaths of thirty-two Jewish people" (Hoffman, 1997, p. 246) but on the other hand nine families, about 40 people, "have been honored as Righteous Gentiles by the Yad Vashem memorial in Israel" (Hoffman, 1997, p. 246) for saving Jewish lives. Many survivors believe "righteous" Poles were not the norm, while many Poles contend the opposite. What part anti–Semitism played in Polish response to the Holocaust, what role human nature played, how conscience and morality came into play are all part of the complexity of the tragedy known as the Holocaust. Because of the lacuna of memory caused by the policies of the post-war Soviet era, Poles and Jews alike are trying in the twenty-first century to learn about and teach about this catastrophe which took place on Polish soil.

After World War II, Poland's boundaries changed again, and its population became fairly homogeneous. This homogeneity was the result of two occurrences. The first was the destruction of minority groups, such as Jews and the Roma, in Poland and other Eastern European countries by the Nazi regime during the Holocaust. Of the few Jewish survivors, most did not return to Poland. The records of the number of Jews in Poland after the Holocaust vary widely but generally is thought to be somewhere between 250,000 and 500,000 people (Hoffman, 1990). There are several reasons for the inability to accurately report these figures. One reason is determining who is counted as a Jew. Jewish communities and synagogues keep records of their members, but someone not registered with a community or synagogue is not included in the count. Another reason is that there were people who did not want to be identified as Jews, either from fear of their Polish neighbors or because they considered themselves Polish and wanted nothing to do with their Jewish roots. There were also children whose families did not survive the Holocaust who had been hidden by Christian neighbors; many of these children did not know they were Jewish.

The other occurrence which contributed to the homogeneity of post-war Poland was the re-formation of the state which changed the borders. People from other ethnic and national groups were relocated to areas in the Ukraine and Belo-Russia, in particular, and ethnic Poles were re-located to Polish territory. For example, a large population of ethnic Poles was relocated from the eastern part of Poland which became the western Ukraine to Wrocław, the former German city of Breslau in the western part of the new Polish territory. Others made the journey voluntarily, "so they could remain within their old nationality even at the cost of leaving home" (Hoffman, 1990, p. 8). To further solidify this homogeneity, the Communists under the Soviet regime, with the support of the Catholic authorities, adopted the Piast Concept. When borders were re-drawn after the war, "recovered territories" placed the Polish state approximately where it was during the Piast dynasty and established Poland's historical legitimacy to the territory. This concept represented the Poles as more than merely Russian puppets, but as a separate people with their "distinct ethnic composition and its own national territory" (Davies, 1986, p. 326).

Despite the influence of the Soviet Union and its attempts to create a classless society through Communism, the upper classes in Poland and the peasant class, by and large, maintained their identity. "[C]ollectivization succeeded on only a small percentage of the land, and many farms remained privately owned" (Hoffman, 1990, p. 53) leaving landowners and peasants to engage in small-scale private enterprise. "In most people's minds, coming from an old lineage counts for more than high position in the Polish People's Republic (Hoffman, 1990, p. 43). These attitudes are still in place in the twenty-first century. One summer when I was teaching at an English language camp in Poland, the Polish directors of the camp were quite pleased to be able to claim the descendants of two noble families, Potocki and Rzewuski, among the campers. My status was also elevated by the fact one of these was the son of a friend of mine.

Another effect of the Soviet's repressive economic regime was that a fairly well-developed black-market economy developed in Poland. For Jews and Poles alike this was often a necessity for living above the subsistence level, but it was also a form of resistance. As Hoffman (1990) states, "[n]ose-thumbing the system is a national pastime" (p. 58). A distrust of the political system and politicians was also part of the Polish landscape.

Another form of resistance which occurred during this time took place in schools. The Russian language was compulsory starting in the fifth grade. Oftentimes teachers and students alike were lackadaisical about Polish students learning the language of the oppressor. In the same way, the history presented in the Soviet-approved texts was taught, but oftentimes with an underlying message of the greatness and heroism of the Polish people throughout history and the importance of Catholicism to that history.

As Davies (1986) points out, Poles define their national identity primarily by language and religion. Even those who do not actively practice Catholicism acknowledge its influence on their lives. Even under the Soviet system, the Catholic Church was able to exert its power. In 1957, they were able to reinstitute prayers and religion classes in the Polish schools. The election of Karol Wojtyla, a Polish cardinal, as Pope John Paul II on October 16, 1978, helped solidify the role of Catholicism in Polish private and public life. The Constitution of the Republic of Poland adopted on April 2, 1997, recognizes religious freedom but emphasizes Poland's Christian (and *de facto* Catholic) heritage.

Poland's admission to the European Union in 2004 has also influenced Polish national identity. On the one hand, Poles identify with the broader European framework in areas such as economy and higher education, and they want to participate as individuals and as citizens in European unity. However, they also depend on Polish identity to create their basic sense of self as a people within this larger framework.

Poles tend to distinguish between their in-group and out-groups in a collectivist manner, in the ways they define their group and in their perceptions of others. They feel a responsibility and moral duty to one another, and Poles extend this no matter where they live. For instance, the Polish community in Chicago which has the second largest Polish population outside of Poland maintains ties to one another and to Poland through church, through language classes for adults and children, celebrations, food, and Polish language media. Poles in Chicago continue to have a voice in Poland by voting in Polish elections. When the airplane crashed in Smolensk in April 2010, killing all aboard, including the Polish president and his wife, outpourings of grief and outrage reverberated through Polish Chicago. Therefore, even for those who no longer have close ties to Poland itself, their Polish-American community provides them with Polish identity separate from their American counterparts, a separateness with historical roots in the partitions.

The partitions influenced a people to make the effort to maintain their identity through clinging to the cultural markers of religion and language. Davies (1986) contends that their history has taught the Poles to anticipate enmity from those who not speak their language or practice Polish Catholicism. According to Bauman (2001), the "anticipation of enmity is indispensable in the construction of enemies" (p. 54), the "other." Therefore, those outside their language and religious sphere are often treated with suspicion, distrust, and even contempt. The importance of this collectivist worldview toward language and religion is evident when examining the history of minority groups in Poland, specifically the Jews, who have historically been viewed as a national minority, as much as a religious or ethnic minority.

Jews in Poland—Then and Now

Although Jews traveled through Poland before that time, the first recorded permanent Jewish settlements in Poland were in the twelfth and thirteenth centuries. In 1264, the Statute of Kalisz, signed by Prince Bolesław the Pious, conferred a number of rights and privileges on Jewish inhabits of the Wielkopolska (Greater Poland) region. These expanded freedoms made Poland a more attractive place to live than the repressive regions of Germany and France. In the fourteenth century, King Kazimierz Wielki (Casimir the Great) eased immigration restrictions against Jews and many Ashkenazi Jews from western European countries settled in Poland and became part of Polish society. "[T]he degree to which Jewish people were incorporated into daily Polish life came as a surprise to visitors from Western Europe" (Hoffman, 1997, p. 32).

After the 1492 expulsion of Jews from Spain, many Sephardic Jews from Spain, Portugal, Italy, and Turkey also moved there. Jewish settlers were valued because they stimulated trade and urban development. Jewish-controlled businesses and other economic and political endeavors grew. However, the teachings of the Catholic Church, and economic rivalry with Christian burghers created hostile relations in many areas of Poland. Despite these problems and various restrictions on where they could live and work, Jews had relative freedom, even having their own parliament. This parliament, the Vaad, met twice a year and while it served subordinate to the Polish crown, it had a degree of autonomy in how it represented the Jewish communities across Poland. This autonomy worked for and against the Jewish population in Poland creating an insider-outsider position for them in Polish society and Polish culture.

Bringing their own religion, traditions and language with them also helped create an outsider position for Jewish settlers. Yiddish, which combines Hebrew, Aramaic, German, and some Slavic elements and is written with Hebrew characters, remained the home language of most Ashkenazi Jews, and was adopted with variations by Sephardic Jews who immigrated later. Few Poles learned Yiddish, and depending on their circumstances, Jews did not learn Polish if it was not needed in their business dealings or everyday life.

The Jewish community in Poland was not homogeneous. Not only did they come from different backgrounds and traditions, but people lived in cities, in towns, and in the country, each environment creating distinctive communities. In most Polish cities, there was a separate Jewish quarter but it was not uncommon for Jews to live intermingled with the Poles. Shtetls, small towns or villages, varied in their makeup. Some were predominately Jewish while others were a mixture of Jews and Poles. However, as is often the case in rural areas, shtetl dwellers, both Jewish and Polish tended to be conservative, traditional, and even insular, living in close proximity but maintaining separate lives. As Catholicism became a stronger force in Polish society and as Jews established stronger religious institutions, there was less intimate contact among them. Jews, in general, did not want to and saw no need to assimilate to Polish culture and society. Conversely, there was little pressure on them to do so from the Polish side. "The Polish polity continued to develop in a fashion conducive to the possibility of simultaneous coexistence and separateness" (Hoffman, 1997, p. 46). The Polish ruling elite exhibited some democratic tendencies and "contributed to the climate of tolerance that prevailed in Poland" (Hoffman, 1997, p. 48) prior to the partitions.

As with any society, there were also various social classes in Jewish communities, including those who were wealthy and powerful, industrialists, and professionals, as well as merchants, craftsmen, scholars, and peasants. Class distinctions were important in Jewish relationships with Poles. In Polish society, there was a feudal-like class system with an elite, noble class, burghers who were the equivalent of Poland's middle class, and the peasants who lived in serf-like conditions. Polish aristocrats and nobles had the most cordial relationships with Jews. Their self-assuredness about their own position in society and the advantages they saw of doing business with Jews overrode the cultural and religious differences that existed. The burghers, however, tended to resent the privileged position that they perceived the Jews held with the noble class.

> Jews were often perceived as dangerous competitors who looked out exclusively for their own interests and attained their wealth and success at the expense of native Poles—who, in contrast, were pictured as hard-working, sincere, and too honest to achieve much in the world [Hoffman, 1997, p. 42].

The illiterate and poverty-stricken peasants' views of Jews were usually much more simplistic. One the one hand, the peasants usually saw the Jews, who often served as estate stewards collecting dues and taxes from the peasants, as exploiters against whom they felt fear and loathing. On the other hand, the peasants perceived the Jews as alien with supernatural powers and unnatural customs and regarded them with superstitious awe and fear.

As well as differences in social class among Jews, there was also a wide variety of religious conviction and observance among Jews in Poland, from those who were completely secular to Orthodox. In the 1700s and 1800s, the Age of Enlightenment, a number of Polish Jews embraced Hasidism and others joined the new Progressive (Reform) movement which came out of Germany in the 1800s. Jews were also members of various political factions, from those which supported a monarchy to those which advocated a more democratic form of government. The more religious Jews tended to favor a political system which did not upset the status quo, while secular Jews embraced the new nationalism that was sweeping Europe. During the partitions, some Jews were satisfied with adapting to life in this altered circumstance while others actively fought for Polish independence.

The seventeenth and eighteenth centuries were a time of turmoil and war in Poland, finally resulting in its partition at the end of the eighteenth century (Davies, 1986). During the 1600s and 1700s a series of wars destabilized the economy, the wholesale destruction creating poverty, famine and epidemics throughout the country. Allegiances between Jews and the Polish nobility were strained and broken and distrust of Jews grew among burghers and the peasant class. The Vaad was dissolved. During this time, the Counter-Reformation also brought on a period of religious intolerance supported by the Catholic Church, against Protestants as well as Jews. The existence of a large minority group, about 10 percent of the population, and how would it fit into the Polish nation, became the "Jewish question." There was a growing number of Poles who thought that "as long as the Jewish community remained separate, it did not deserve equal rights" (Hoffman, 1997, p. 71). At the same time, the Jewish community was also debating how they would fit into Polish society. Some leaders advocated for becoming more integrated into Polish society, learning Polish and dressing in the Polish style. Others argued that Jewish traditions and religious customs prevented them from any type of assimilation. However, most agreed that it was important for Jews to retain the rights and privileges they had enjoyed in Poland for centuries. By 1795 all these arguments became moot.

Despite the passing of the Constitution of May Third in 1792, the third partition of Poland occurred in 1795 and Poland as a country was dismantled and divided into three parts. Prussia (Germany) took control of the western portions, while the Austria-Hungarian Empire had control over the south. Russia annexed the eastern section. The partitions had a detrimental effect on the Jewish population for several reasons. Under the partitions, Jews lost the autonomy they had enjoyed under Polish rule. In addition anti–Semitism grew across Europe during the nineteenth century and pogroms (violent attacks by mobs against Jewish settlements often at the instigation of local authorities) became more frequent.

For Jews, the period following World War I in which Poland once again became an independent state, reflected the pre-partition autonomy as well as the anti–Semitism of the partitions. Although they paid taxes, Jews were denied first-class citizenship in the new state. However, they had a fair amount of autonomy and freedom. They were able "to have their own newspapers, their own schools and theatres, libraries, sports clubs, youth movements, and charitable organizations" (Webber, 2010, p. 29). Hasidism and Zionists alike were free to organize their own activities and associations. Many Jews became secularized, speaking Polish rather than Yiddish, considering themselves Polish rather than Jewish. Even the *Tanakh* (the Hebrew Bible consisting of the 5 books of the Torah, the writings of the prophets, and assorted other writings such as Psalms and the book of Ruth) was translated into Polish for those Jews who wanted to read the Bible in Polish. However, as the 1930s came to a close, many of these freedoms were taken away, and discrimination, anti–Semitism, and pogroms increased.

Despite these problems, before World War II, Poland was home to the largest Jewish population in Europe contributing to the diversity of pre–War Polish society, and to the culture of pre-war Poland. In some ways, Jews were part of the greater society, and in other ways separate from it. "[B]eing a Jew or a Pole meant different religions, different holidays, different languages, different cultures, and different nationalities" (Gold, 2007, p. 76). He goes on to say that they even dressed differently. Gold (2007), who grew up in pre–World War II Poland explains the tension in this way:

> As religious Jews, we conceded that Poland belonged to "them" and that we were in exile, waiting for God to redeem us. We were a nation "sojourning," living in Poland only temporarily. But being "strangers" in a country where our ancestors had lived for centuries produced complex feelings about ourselves and about Poles [p. 76].

The Jewish experience in Poland has always been one of insider-outsider and of contending with the lure of and/or demands for assimilation. Even assimilated Jews and those who had converted to Christianity often were not accepted as Polish nationals by their fellow Poles. Despite feeling like outsiders and exiles in many ways, many religious and secular Jews still considered Poland their home. Hoffman (1990) whose family left Poland in 1959 claims that she still feels a love of Poland "despite knowledge of our marginality, and its primitive, unpretty emotions" (p. 74).

In many Polish cities and towns, Jews lived alongside their Polish neighbors. However, there was usually a predominately Jewish area, too, traditionally built up around the synagogue, and other places of study. Kosher butcher shops, delicatessens, and bakeries, as well as shops which sold religious articles, clothing and other items provided for the Jewish population. Jewish elementary schools (cheders) prepared young people for Jewish life, teaching them holiday rituals and customs, as well as Hebrew, liturgy, and religious and ethical tenets from Jewish holy texts. Yeshivas, institutions of higher

Jewish learning, flourished in many cities and towns. On Shabbat (sundown Friday to sundown Saturday), the Jewish quarter would close down. However, life would go on as usual in the Polish parts of town, even shops with Jewish owners might stay open.

Polish-Jewish communities were controlled by the kehilla, an appointed or elected Jewish community organization usually headed by the rabbi. The organizations played an important role in "sustaining a strong collective Jewish identity" (Hoffman, 1997, p. 52) and exercised almost complete religious and secular power over its community, serving as tax collector, administrator of the community's finances, and even as a court. In his memoir about life in Radom, Poland in the inter-war period, Gold (2007) points out that the kehilla in his community in Radom was made up of elected officials who were extremely religious as well as completely secular. Dues paid to the kehilla were intended to pay the rabbis' and other religious and community leaders' salaries, as well as support the Jewish hospital, homeless shelters, homes for orphans, and other community services. However, during this period, some institutions, such as cheders, previously regulated by the Jewish community, came under Polish governmental regulations. One such regulation was that the Polish language must be taught in cheders.

Education for Jewish children followed gender lines. Boys generally attended cheder, a sort of elementary school to learn the basics of Hebrew, Yiddish (and in the inter-war period, Polish) and math as well as Torah (the first five books of the Bible) studies. Around age 8 they began studying Talmud, a compendium of commentaries on the Torah. If a boy showed promise in Talmudic studies, he was sent to a yeshiva for more advanced Talmudic study. By the sixteenth century, Polish yeshivas were renowned throughout the world for their high quality.

Traditionally, education for Jewish girls was limited. However, in the new period of independence during the 1920s and 1930s, secular and religious schools were established for girls. The classes in secular schools were often conducted in Polish, so that the girls who attended became fluent in that language as well as Yiddish which was used at home and in their religious instruction. Between 1927 and 1937 about 250 religious schools for girls opened which were part of the Beis-Ya'akov (House of Jacob) movement. Gold (2007) credits these opportunities for secular and religious schooling with his sisters' ability to become economically and socially independent, something which was unheard of for Polish women, much less Jewish women, before this period, while strengthening their ties to Jewish tradition. "It became a religious movement of young women that liberated its members from the inferior status that tradition had assigned them, turning the gender difference from inferiority to distinctiveness" (p. 56). He opines that if Jewish life had not ended so tragically in Poland when it did, that this movement towards what he calls "enlightened Orthodoxy" would have changed the future of Polish Jews in a positive direction.

According to Gold (2007) less than one third of the three and a half million Jews who lived in Poland prior to World War II were religious. Many young Jews in particular wanted to be part of secular society seeking solutions to Jewish problems through political and practical means. "They were attracted to Zionism, to the Jewish Socialist Bund, or to Communism, the groups that were competing successfully for the allegiance of the younger generation (Gold, 2007, p. 16). These allegiances would come back to haunt many Jews later as they were accused of trying undermine the Polish nation in various ways, before, during, and after World War II.

Although "[l]ess than 5% of Polish Jews actually immigrated to Palestine between the wars" (Zolynia, 2011, sect. Zionism and Jewish Nationalism in Zolynia, para. 3) Zionism grew during this period. Zionism, a movement which flourished in the nationalistic fervor of the 1800s, was aimed at maintaining Jewish identity and reclaiming the Jewish homeland in Palestine. The most obvious reason for its growth was dissatisfaction with the conditions in Poland. Religious and non-religious Jews alike began to take active part in the international Zionist movement. The Balfour Declaration of 1917 and the support of the League of Nations strengthened the Zionists' position for a Jewish homeland in Palestine. The rise of Hitler and the Nazi party in Germany also provided impetus for immigration to Palestine.

Gold (2007) identifies the death of Marshal Joseph Piłsudski as a turning point in Jewish-Polish relations. Piłsudski in November 1918 had "invited representatives of the largest Jewish parties for consultations on forming the Republic's government. Jewish deputies and senators were part of the sovereign state's legislature, shared in making laws, and took part in the debates" (Tomaszewski, 2005, p. 19). Polish Jews believed that Piłsudski would continue to treat them fairly. They also believed that his policies and presence held back Polish anti–Semitism. Upon his death, anti–Semitism did begin to rise under openly anti–Semitic leaders.

As stated earlier, one of the roots for anti–Semitism in Poland was the Catholic Church. Priests often spoke against Jews from their pulpits, then in 1936 a pastoral letter from the primate of Poland, Cardinal Hlond, denounced Jews as a blight upon Polish society and encouraged an economic boycott of Jewish businesses. At the same time, the Polish government began supporting economic boycotts, institutional discrimination that was embraced by many Poles. Jewish students at Polish universities were attacked and segregated from their Polish classmates. Pogroms were unleashed in several towns. Anti-Semitic graffiti appeared in public places. While there were Poles who did not feel these pressures to discriminate against their Polish neighbors, they were a minority. The prejudice ran both ways; however, for Poles there were no consequences attached to Jewish prejudice. Many traditional Jews were contemptuous of the "idolatrous" Catholic faith and stereotyped Poles as drunkards, lechers, and wife-beaters (Gold, 2007; Hoffman, 1997).

Gold (2007) also points out the inter–Jewish prejudice that traditionalists and secular Jews often felt for one another. He said that religious Jews "felt that they [assimilated Jews] had lost their self-respect as Jews and were still treated by Poles with contempt" (p. 80). Another area of contention among Jews was between Hasidim (a charismatic branch of Judaism) and other Jews. Orthodox and secular Jews alike were dismayed and troubled by the Hasidic lack of concern for practical "earthly" matters which often caused a drain on the community finances.

After World War II, Poland's pre-war diversity was dismembered because most minority populations in Poland had been destroyed in the Holocaust or removed through resettlement due to the borders' changing after the war. The Polish population became almost homogeneous. The number of Jews left in the country was less than 10 percent of the pre–War numbers. In the years following the war, these numbers dropped even more.

Acts of violence against Jews after the end of the war created feelings of unrest and unease, so that those who returned to their homes were not comfortable and even feared for their lives. After the war about 6,000 Jews returned to Kraków, but anti–Semitic attacks, including one which resulted in the death of a Jewish woman on August 11, 1945, and the massacre of Jewish citizens in Kielce on July 4, 1946, convinced many Polish Jews that they were neither welcome nor safe in this country. Such pogroms were often carried out with the knowledge of and even at the instigation of the local militia and police (Zaremba, 2012). Some were able to gain exit visas, while others were deported. Of the Jews that were left, some actively pursued their lives as part of the small Jewish religious community within the larger community, while others lived lives as secular Jews, and others assimilated. Overall, Jewish life was subsumed by the larger society.

In her memoir, Eva Hoffman (1990) tells how her parents, although Jews who were somewhat assimilated to Polish culture maintained an awareness of being Jewish partly as a connection to their past and to those they lost during the war. For Eva, being told she was Jewish at age 7 was no surprise. "Of course, I've known we're Jewish as long as I can remember. That's why everyone died in the war" (p. 29). Eva's parents, who reacted to the anti-Semitism they experienced in post-war Poland with anger, taught her to affirm her Jewishness with dignity.

Under Soviet policy, any forms of nationalism, whether by majority groups such as Poles, or minority groups such as Jews, were repressed. These policies also included an "anti-religious indoctrination [as] part of the official ideology" (Pinchuk, 1986, p. 164) which impacted the religious life of Jews and Christians alike. However, this ideology had more impact on Jewish life since Jewish religious and cultural activities are cultural markers that separate them from other groups, so that "it became apparent that the true goal remained the complete assimilation of the Jewish community within the surrounding population" (Pinchuk, 1986, p. 164). Religious holidays were particular targets since they are central to Jewish religious life and culture. "It was obvious that the communist rulers understood well the educational value of the holidays and their contribution to strengthening Jewish national identity and consciousness" (p. 164).

In the late 1950s, after the death of Stalin, there was a slight relaxation in the political environment. During that period, immigration restrictions on Jews in Poland were lifted. Many immigrated to Israel and others went to other parts of the world. The ones who stayed could not face leaving their homes, thought they had nowhere to go, or were entrenched in Polish life and the Polish system.

Some of the Jews who remained became functionaries in the Communist regime. They were especially exposed to "hostility and rejection from much of society at large" (Gebert, 2010, p. 44), often seen as infiltrators and Communist agents, and treated with dislike and distrust. In 1968, "party hardliners resorted to mass use of anti-Semitism in a bid to seize power" (p. 45). Jews were driven out of positions of power and over 20,000 emigrated over the next two years. By the early 1970s, fewer than 12,000 Jews remained in Poland. Most of those remaining were assimilated Jews who has chosen a Polish identity and considered themselves Poles, not Jews. According to Gebert (2010) taking on a Jewish identity at this point "would mean not only adopting an alien identity, but confirming the accusation hurled against them by the anti-Semites, namely, that they were not 'really' Polish. They could not do it" (p. 45). Young people during this period were caught in the difficult situation of having "Jewishness thrust upon them by the outside world" (p. 46) when they felt their identity was as Poles. The shame and self-hatred that many of these young people felt stayed with them throughout their lives.

In the period after the war until the fall of communism, pre-war Jewish life and the Jewish experience during the Holocaust was largely ignored, and even taboo. Even public libraries were "forced to remove Jewish materials from their shelves" (Webber, 2010, p. 27). One Polish woman recorded by Einhorn (Glass, 2002) said:

> I was taught on communist history books. And you had no mention about Jewish people living in Poland. You just said one word about the king Casimir the Great, who invited Jews in the fourteenth century, then big nothing, and then the Holocaust.

According to Miles (2000) in Communist-era Poland the Holocaust was "de-judaised." Rather than acknowledging the systematic persecution and extermination of the Jews, the Holocaust was viewed from the perspective of anti-fascism, implying that all groups were equally victimized by the Nazis. Under the Communist regime, "Auschwitz was a symbol not of Jewish oppression but of Polish persecution" (Miles 2000, p. 36). Until the 1980s, the Polish government continued to uphold the notion "that during the war Poles were uniformly sympathetic to the plight of the Jews" (Miles 2000, p. 36). Despite the Solidarity-led government's commitment to Holocaust remembrance, since the early 1990s there has been ambivalence among Poles about the Holocaust and "the proper role of Jews, within Polish history and consciousness" (Miles 2000, p. 38). Despite changes in society and in the educational curriculum, this ambivalence toward Poland's role in World War II and the Holocaust is still evident in twenty-first century Poland.

Houwink ten Cate (2010) points out that there are changes as evidenced by the number of well-known scholars in Poland such as "Waclaw Dlugoborski, Czeslaw Madajczyk, Feliks Tych, Franciszek Piper, and Jan T. Gross [who] have been doing distinguished work since the 1980s" (sect. Division of Labor, para. 1). At the secondary level, since 1981, textbooks in Poland have been moving away from the anti-fascist treatment of World War II and the Holocaust. In addition, new curricula were implemented in Polish secondary schools in 1999 which expose students to issues related to the Holocaust. However, they may not address the issues with any depth for various reasons.

In the transition period after the fall of communism, there has been a revival of interest in Jewish life in Polish society in general. Although there is a small number of Jews living in Poland, who have, perhaps, covertly celebrated who they are, there are many more Jews who either did not openly acknowledge who they were, who denied who they were, or did not know who they were (Krajweski, 2011). Hoffman (1997) points out, however, that this revival of interest in Jewish life has also come with "a resurgence of anti–Semitic rhetoric ... which is particularly insidious in that it is rhetoric without a real object ... as if ... the prewar prejudices have reemerged from their Pandora's box in an unreconstructed—because unprocessed—form" (p. 15).

According to Krawczyk (2010) another aspect of this issue is the difficulty of returning property to pre–Holocaust owners. Jews who left, or are descendants of those who were murdered during the Holocaust or left afterwards, often have had nowhere to which to return. Despite attempts at creating a compensation or restitution plan in Poland, fewer than half of the claims have been resolved and most of these were for public property, such as synagogues or cemeteries, but fewer for private property, which has often changed hands several times in the years since the end of the war.

Because there was a dearth of religious leaders in Poland during the period following World War II, Polish Jews had to look outside Poland for leadership in these early years of openness. Rabbi Michael Shudrich (2012), the Chief Rabbi of Poland in the early years of the twenty-first century, is an American who first came to Poland in 1973 for a visit as part of a program for young people which visited Eastern Europe then went to Israel. He returned to Poland in 1979 and he met young Poles who were exploring their Jewish roots and they asked for his help in learning about Jews and Judaism.

These young Jews had begun questioning the official line about Jews and wanted to make sense of the taboo topics, as well as of their own heritage as Jews. They were not trying to establish a collective Jewish identity such as had existed before the Holocaust. They wanted to figure how they as individuals could have a future in Poland as Jews, Poles of Jewish origin. Gebert (2010) says, "What we wanted was to be able to make sense of that experience, to be prepared to cope with the dangers it entailed, and possibly to transform it into something more positive" (p. 47). As they learned more about "Jewishness" some focused more a secular Jewish identity while others moved to a religious identity. This creation of a modern Polish-Jewish identity often brought these young people into conflict with Jews who had survived the Holocaust. First of all, the older community members were worried that these younger people would attract the unwanted attention of state authorities. Gebert (2010) says that another issue that arose was that "[f]urthermore, our Jewishness, self-made and often contradictory, did not strike them authentic" (p. 48). The older Jews also wondered why someone would take on this identity in a country that had little or no room for them if they did not have to. This attitude was held by many people who did not want to reveal their Jewish background for fear of anti–Semitism or other forms of discrimination. This new generation of Jews did find that despite their active involvement in Polish life during the 1980s, when the Solidarity movement succeeded in bringing down the Communist regime in 1989, anti–Semitism sometimes was used as a weapon in the ensuing power struggles.

In 1990 Shudrich accepted a position in Poland as part of the wave of Jewish educators and religious leaders who came and were sent to Eastern Europe after the fall of communism. One major initiative from this period was the establishment of the Lauder-Morasha School in 1994, the first Jewish day school in Poland since the end of World War II. Shudrich (2010) says that in recent years the median age of the Jewish community in Warsaw "has declined from over 65 to about 45, and new members are all under the age of 40" (p. 57). Some of those embracing their Jewish heritage are the children of those young people that Shudrich met in the 1970s. Others are just now learning of their Jewish pasts and may be looking for someone like Shudrich to guide them.

Shudrich (2012) admitted that in order to effectively lead and educate Jews in Poland one of his struggles was to overcome his own stereotypes about Poles and Polish anti–Semitism. Once he grappled with that, it was easier for him to see that what he really had to share was his almost innate sense of his Jewishness which had been created by a strong Jewish education and had a warm Jewish home life. Shudrich believes that the most important function he serves as Chief Rabbi of Poland, a position he has held since 2004, is being there and listening and helping when a Polish person comes to him and says "I think I'm Jewish." Shudrich (2010) points out that fear often plays a role in the reluctance of some people to acknowledge their Jewish roots, "not so much concern [about] current anti–Semitism, but mainly [about] what might happen again" (p. 58). Therefore, he also recognizes that it is important to identify potential allies and friends among Poles, learning about them and from them, and supporting them when they advocate for the preservation of Jewish memory.

Helise Lieberman, Director of the Taube Center for the Renewal of Jewish Life in Poland, and founding director of the Lauder-Morasha School, agrees with Shudrich, that as an American coming to Poland in the early 1990s, her strong sense of Yiddishkeit helped her connect with Jews in Poland on the individual and community levels. In that way she was able to discover what they wanted and needed to create their own sustainable community and create a strong infrastructure. Jonathan Ornstein, director of the Jewish Community Center (JCC) in Kraków believes that steps have been taken so that the next leaders in the Jewish community, the next chief rabbi, the next director of the JCC, will be local, a true sign of permanence and sustainability in Jewish communities in Poland.

For Jews and non–Jews, especially, this "discovery" of Jewish identity in Poland is a burgeoning field of study at the university level in post-communist Poland. Polish secondary schools are now teaching about the Holocaust, although the role of Jews in Polish history is still a largely unexamined area at that level. Along with the scholarly explorations there are also social explorations of Judaism and Jews. Since 1989 there has also been an increase in the amount of literature, particularly novels, which demonstrate a shift in the portrayal of Jews as "Others" who are part of Polish society not outside it. There has been a renewal of interest in Jewish culture, Jewish customs, Jewish music, and Jewish life as evidenced by a variety of museum exhibits and cultural festivals.

The following essay is from the perspective of a young man who grew up in Poland in the post–Communist era. He looks at Jewish identity in twenty-first century Poland and what kinds of organizations are available for Polish-Jewish young people to strengthen their identities and to create bonds with other young people. He closes with reflections on what the future holds for the children of the next generation.

Jewish Student NGOs in Present-Day Poland (1999–2013): Being Here
by Piotr Goldstein

> All the world is a very narrow bridge, and the most important thing is not to fear at all.—Reb Nachman of Bratslav

This essay addresses three key issues. Firstly, it gives a general overview about how being a Jewish student in Poland is different from being a Jewish student elsewhere. Secondly, it shows examples of several student and semi-student Jewish organizations in present-day Poland. Finally, it presents a brief analysis of changes in these NGOs in the given period (1999–2013). The essay is entirely based on participant observation and in particular autoethnography (Marechal, 2009): the author was for a number of years a Jewish student in Poland and was—or in some cases still is—a member of several of the mentioned organizations and through friends or other channels is exposed to the functioning of those organizations to which he does not belong himself.

How Is Being a Jewish Student in Poland Different from Being a Jewish Student Elsewhere?

Three specific aspects of the Polish-Jewish student's existence have been identified for the purposes of this essay: (a) being the constant subject of attention; (b) living with (the memory of) the Holocaust; (c) having limited "Jewish infrastructure" in and around campus.

Being the subject of attention: A Polish-Jewish student studying in Poland can easily feel under constant observation and may often be approached as a "living example" of a member of a once huge and incredibly significant—but today supposedly practically non-existent (Serraf, 2010; Smith, 2007)—Jewish minority in Poland. This attention, and often not hidden surprise, is augmented by the fact that between 1968 and 1989 Jews were practically non-visible in Polish public life. After the Holocaust and the post-war experiences of 1946 pogroms, followed by the official anti–Semitic propaganda of 1957 and 1968, the few Jews left in Poland were in most cases very cautious about revealing their Jewishness. It was not uncommon for parents not to tell their children about their Jewish roots and few of those knowing of their origins would make this knowledge public. As a result, many of today's young Poles have never had the opportunity to meet a person who is openly Jewish. Their knowledge about Jews, therefore, is often limited to whatever can be found in the textbooks, the Internet or the media.

Many young people also doubt that there is anyone ever willing to openly say "I am Jewish." Some even think that the word "Jew" is offensive and will try not to use it in conversation with someone who is possibly Jewish. Because of this, a Polish-Jewish student will hardly ever be asked "Are you Jewish?" by his or her classmates. The question "Where did your ancestors come from?" is posed instead. The author of this chapter would usually answer, "from Egypt," trying to bring the asker's attention back to the absurdity of the question. Similarly, a Jewish student may notice that their last name is believed to be nothing else but a synonym of the word "Jew." "What is Goldstein's last name?" would be asked by those who always thought that "Goldsteins" and "Rosenfelds" could only exist in Israel or America, assuming instead that such surnames would only be used in Poland in order to avoid saying "my Jewish friend."

On the other hand, a Jewish student's teachers may also be (positively) surprised by a Jew in their class. One then becomes a living example of those Jews who came to Poland 1000 years ago, selling fish in medieval markets, contributing to the growth and prosperity of Polish towns, and of the many other Jews they know only from textbooks. More than that, since it is thought that no one can know better about Jewish things than the Jews themselves, one is often believed to be an expert on everything Jewish: Hebrew, Yiddish, Torah, Talmud, Hasidism, traditions, the history of the Jews here—the history of the Jews there.... Finally, a Polish-Jewish student in Poland is the subject of attention of local and international media, as well as of researchers and tourists. To date, a huge number of newspaper and magazine articles on "Jewish Revival in Poland" have been published in English, Polish, Hebrew, French and many other languages (Easton, 2012; Ingram, 1997; Liège, 2000; Tzur, 2013). TV and radio interviews have been recorded as well as documentary and semi-documentary films. Some of these intend to give a general overview, while many others focus on personal stories. In any case, the number of productions is so large that probably each Jewish student in Poland who is involved in the community has participated , or has at least been asked to participate, in several newspaper/magazine/radio/TV/film interviews/productions on the subject.

As well as such interviews, the Jewish student may also be asked to participate in academic research (both Polish and international) or to tell one's story to tourists. Some of this research is without doubt of a very high standard (e.g. Bilewicz, 2007; Fleming, 2003; Gudonis, 2003; Krajewski, 2005; Reszke, 2013) and many of the visitors to Poland are well informed. Yet there is also some ignorant research and ignorant tourism. For some tourists a synagogue in Łódź or Warsaw is just one more sight on a long list of things to see in Europe. A Polish-Jewish student photographed inside or outside the synagogue building may then be fairly sure that his or her picture will later be shown alongside the noble company of a zebra from the Berlin zoo, or the Charles Bridge in Prague. The label "the last Jew of Poland" may also be there underneath the photograph.

Living with (the memory of) the Holocaust: Along with the many researchers, journalists and tourists often comes astonishment about the possibility of living "so close to Auschwitz" or "so close to the ghetto." The astonishment is even greater when it is found out that there is a Jewish student living in the very city of Oświęcim (on the outskirts of which stands the infamous camp), or that some of us live not close but *in* the areas of former ghetto or even *in* former ghetto houses, something which is not difficult when you live in Łódź where the ghetto occupied a large part of the city and where most buildings survived the war.

How this is possible, or how this is difficult, is very personal and there is no one good answer to the above questions. One thing to consider is that despite the internationally announced economic boom in Poland (Dougherty, 2009) deciding where to live is not an option for everyone. People who live in the old ghetto houses in Łódź, Jews and non–Jews, would probably not mind moving with their families to Miami, Florida (or at least to some more modern housing within the city), but this is hardly ever an option.

In this case, is a Polish-Jewish student, upon waking up, thinking about living in, or close to, a ghetto, or is the student instead swearing at whoever scheduled his or her class at eight in the morning? We do live with the memory and many of us feel to be its "guardians" (an issue explored in the section by Izabella Goldstein). It is hard to say, however, whether this feeling is in any respect related to distance. After all, is a Jew who lives five thousand miles from Auschwitz less responsible for remembering it than one who lives in the city next door?

"Jewish Infrastructure" in and around campus: It should first be noted that many, if not most, Polish universities do not have campuses. For example, Łódź University has its departments and institutes spread across the city. Yet, for the Jewish student, the biggest difference between universities in places like the USA or the UK and their own in Poland is what could be called "Jewish life on campus." Institutions like Hillel do not exist in Poland. Events like a "bagel lunch"—the chance to meet fellow Jewish students between one class and another—do not happen. Kosher, or even "kosher friendly" (e.g. vegetarian) food is either not available or hard to get. Jews are not visible at university the way they are in countries with larger Jewish communities. A chance to run into a fellow Jew on the way from a classroom to the library is very small.

It would be wrong, however, to say that Jewish student life in Poland is non-existent. There are Jewish students at Polish universities, as there are also Jewish teachers. The existence of Polish-Jewish students has been acknowledged by Polish law, which now allows Jews not to take exams during Shabbat and other Jewish holidays. These legal changes and the related politics were analyzed by Fleming (2002) who suggested that these issues are related to a minority community's ability to express its concerns in politically strategic ways.

Jewish (Student) Organizations

One expression of Jewish community life is a variety of organizations and initiatives run by, and for, local Jewish students. The following Polish-Jewish student and semi-student organizations will now be considered: PUSZ, ZOOM, Czulent, Yalla! and Tslil.

PUSZ (Polska Unia Studentów Żydowskich—the Polish Union of Jewish Students) is the only one of these organizations with "Jewish students" in its name. It was a member of the European Union of Jewish Students, and was for several years the only Jewish student organization in Poland. In 2000 it had approximately 300 members all around the country. The Union organized summer and winter camps, which often involved cleaning Jewish cemeteries or exploring the remains of Jewish communities in Polish towns and villages. It also brought together members from different cities during Shabbatons (an educational event or program held during a weekend, including the Jewish sabbath), conferences, leadership training, and other meetings organized centrally or by local branches, in places like Wrocław, Łódź, Kraków, Bielsko Biała, Poznań or Gdańsk. Many of the leaders of today's Jewish communities and other Jewish organizations and initiatives around Poland originated from within PUSZ, which existed between 1992 and 2007.

ZOOM (Żydowska Ogólnopolska Organizacja Młodzieżowa—The Polish Jewish Youth Organization) is considered to be the successor of PUSZ. Certainly, it was started soon after PUSZ was dissolved, and many PUSZ members joined ZOOM. One of the main differences between the two organizations, however, is that ZOOM seems to have much less desire than PUSZ to operate outside Warsaw. Its summer and winter camps are attended by young Jewish people, mostly students, from around the country, yet its everyday activities are mostly Warsaw-based. Another difference is that it relies on Jewish sponsorship much less than PUSZ did: its office is not located in the Jewish community buildings in Warsaw and many of its projects are funded by EU sources rather than by Jewish ones.

Czulent and Yalla! are local organizations operating in Kraków and Łódź respectively. Czulent is a well-established NGO with an office, a professional website, good PR and a significant budget. It has run projects which are large-scale and highly visible. The organization even has its own library. Yalla! is the opposite—it has no office, is not very well known and operates on zero budget. Members communicate through a mailing list and Facebook, project initiatives are irregular and often spontaneous, and most of the programs are not externally visible. Yet Yalla! should not be seen as insignificant. Its simple get-togethers, Jewish cooking, Israeli dance classes or Yiddish film nights help create a form of Jewish student life in the city.

Tslil Jewish Choir of Łódź and Warsaw is not a student or youth organization per se. The age range of the singers is from 16 to over 75. Nevertheless, many of Tslil's members are students. In its short history, the organization has already proved to be an important link between the Jewish community and those Jews who are not in any way engaged in Jewish communal life. The choir, which includes both Jews and non–Jews, is a safe way-in for people who, having lived their lives in non–Jewish settings, would feel overwhelmed by membership in a Jewish community or some other uniquely Jewish organization. It is also important as a truly inter-generational organization where young people have the chance to work on an equal basis with the peers of their parents and grandparents.

As well as the larger Jewish student or semi-student organizations (of which this essay does not intend to list all) there is also a number of smaller short- or long-lived Jewish student-run initiatives, some of which maintain their status as an informal group, while others are legally established NGOs. It should not, therefore, be a surprise to hear about the existence of Polish-Jewish Scouts, a pan–Baltic Jewish student union, an association of young Jewish women or a local Jewish film club.

It would probably not be too much of a generalization to say that there are three main elements in the work of all of the above-mentioned organizations: recreation, integration and education. All three are tightly interlaced. These NGOs and informal groups bring people together and make sure that, while they have fun and get to know each other, they also learn, usually about Jewish things. In this respect it is easy to see the similarity in all these organizations. At the same time one could probably say that the wide spectrum of Jewish student opportunities is valuable. Why would a young Polish Jew not do traditional kosher cooking with Yalla! on Monday, learn Yiddish and Hebrew songs with Tslil on Wednesday and celebrate Shabbat with ZOOM on Friday, meeting fellow Jewish students from all of these places?

What Is Changing?

The author of this essay has noticed four important factors that changed the nature of the operation and existence of Jewish student and semi-student organizations between 1999 and 2013. These are:

- The on-going change in attitude towards Jews in Polish society;
- A trend in the organizations to diversify their funding sources by including non–Jewish sponsors;
- The rapidly growing level of access to cheap Internet and mobile communication, as well as the popularity of community portals;
- Birthright-Taglit (sponsors of heritage trips to Israel).

Changing attitudes towards Jews: The situation described earlier, that many young Poles have never had the chance to see a "real Jew" and that many may consider the word "Jew" offensive, is fortunately changing, for various reasons. As Polish society becomes re-accustomed to the existence of Jewish life in Poland, Jewish student organizations are more and more confident in their existence. One visible example of this is the inclusion of photographs of members on organizational websites. In the late 1990s and early 2000s PUSZ, as well as other Polish-Jewish organizations, had a strict policy of not publishing photographs of its members on the Internet. Today the websites of most, if not all, Jewish organizations are full of sharp-focus photographs of local Jewish faces. This shows how the Jewish community in general, and Jewish student organizations in particular, have become less and less insolated and are becoming more often understood as a normal element of the Polish social landscape or, in the case of the student NGOs, of university life.

Funding: Some level of non–Jewish sponsorship has always been visible in the budgets of Jewish student NGOs in Poland. Yet for many years their finances depended mostly on the handful of international Jewish foundations that were well-established in Poland. Today, however, Jewish student organizations have widely diversified budgets. Polish government programs, European Union schemes, and foreign Jewish and non–Jewish foundations, along with local Jewish and often non–Jewish sources, all sponsor the various activities of Polish-Jewish students. This improved funding contributes to an increased independence and, again, to the confidence of these Jewish student associations.

Cheap Internet, Cellphones and Facebook: Back in the late 1990s and early twenty-first century, communication within organizations, particularly on a national scale, was one of the biggest challenges of Jewish students in Poland. The Internet was expensive and not available to everyone, and the same was true of cellphones. PUSZ needed a significant investment of time and money by its leadership and volunteers just to inform its members of new activities, to send out letters, or to make phone calls, which were also quite expensive at that time. It is no secret that huge phone bills were one element of the "financial problems" that led to the dissolution of PUSZ.

Unlike PUSZers in the 1990s, today's members of ZOOM not only have the Internet at home but usually are able to check for new messages on their handheld devices also. Tslil, established in 2003, also has never had this kind of problem. Since its very beginning it has communicated with members mostly through text messages (SMS) sent by the board of directors from special websites either for free or for very little money. For ZOOM even this expenditure is not necessary—it has a Facebook group which is all it requires for effective communication. This change in availability of Internet and cheap mobile communication also has made it possible for Yalla! to operate on a zero-budget. A Yahoo group, text messages and Facebook were all used to arrange get-togethers with no extra cost or serious time investment for anyone.

Birthright: In the past, recruiting new members was another major challenge of Jewish student NGOs in Poland. As noted before, not only were many young people afraid to disclose their Jewish origins, many did not even realize they had them. For Jewish student organizations to rely on such a small group of active members was often a problem. Although Jewish student leaders would recruit new members for their organizations through appearing in the Polish media or through personal contacts and "marketing" within the Jewish community, the influx of new members was slow.

The establishment of the Taglit-Birthright Israel program and its introduction to Poland has changed these dynamics. Nowadays, groups of "newly discovered" young Jews depart from Poland for Israel every winter and summer. They return home with new Polish-Jewish friends and often with the desire to stay engaged in Jewish student life in Poland. These young people fill the ranks of existing Jewish student organizations and enrich them with their fresh enthusiasm.

Conclusion

Jewish student life in Poland is still not comparable to Jewish student life in countries with larger Jewish communities. It is unique not only because of the small size of the Jewish minority in Poland but also because of the level of attention it receives both within and outside the country. Jewish students in Poland are associated with a range of organizations which differ in size, budget, target group, etc. Yet, it can be said that all these organizations complement each other and contribute to the common goal of integrating and educating (in a Jewish sense) young Polish Jews. Globalization and the spread of new technologies have had a visible impact on the functioning of Jewish student and semi-student NGOs. The wide accessibility of the Internet, cheap mobile communication and Facebook are some of the factors which make these organizations more efficient and at the same time visible and accessible. The Birthright program has also been significant for the Polish-Jewish student NGO scene as it has guaranteed a regular influx of new members and new energy into these associations.

Jewish education, remembering, and teaching, both about the vivid prewar Jewish life in Poland and about the Holocaust, are important elements of lives of young Polish Jews. They are shaped through work of Jewish NGOs, such as *Tslil*.

Post-Scriptum—Growing (Up)

According to the recently announced results of the 2011 Polish census, the number of Jews in Poland grew from 1,133 in 2002 to 7,508 in 2012. The announcement, the analysis of which often fails to acknowledge that the change in the way the question about ethnicity was asked could be responsible for the rise (in 2002 respondents were able to choose only one ethnicity, i.e. either Polish or Jewish, while in 2011 they could choose two), was the impetus for another wave of press articles about the "generation unexpected" of Polish Jewry (e.g. Connolly, 2013). While such numbers should not be taken as an indication of the growth of the Jewish community of Poland, this community is growing, not only by new "hidden Jews" joining, but also it is experiencing natural growth. Student activists of PUSZ of the early 2000s have grown up and many of them are now parents of two, and in some cases, three little "new Polish Jews." If a list of first names of members of PUSZ and other Polish-Jewish student and youth organizations operating in the 1990s and early 2000s was created, it could serve as a catalogue of Christian names with names of the evangelists (John, Matthew, Mark and Luke) and the apostles (especially Peter and Paul) accompanied by Christopher, Christina, and the like. At that time some Marias became Miriams, some Matthews became

Mordechais or Matans and many Saras became Sarahs. However, the children of these Jewish university graduates, shaped by their experience in Jewish organizations, will not be able to hide, will not need to change names, and are unlikely to be asked "where did your ancestor come from?" Now children, with names like Bela, Lea, Natan, Joel, Benjamin or David, will form their own, probably very different, Jewish Student Organizations. Will they be dubbed "generation very-unexpected," or maybe "we are here!"?

(A shorter version of this essay was originally presented at "Poland: A Jewish Matter" a symposium in London on May 30, 2010, and was published by Adam Mickiewicz Institute in the proceedings of this symposium [Goldstein, 2010].)

References

Bilewicz, M. (2007). History as an obstacle: Impact of temporal-based social categorizations on Polish-Jewish intergroup contact. *Group Processes & Intergroup Relations, 10* (4), 551–563.

Connolly, K. (2013, April 20). Poland's "generation unexpected" leads resurgence of Jewish culture. *The Observer*. Retrieved April 23, 2013, from http://www.guardian.co.uk/world/2013/apr/20/generation-unexpected-poland-jews?INTCMP=SRCH.

Dougherty, C. (2009). Despite the downturn, a Polish city thrives. *New York Times*. Retrieved April 23, 2013, from http://www.nytimes.com/2009/09/01/business/global/01zloty.html?pagewanted=all&_r=0.

Easton, A. (2012, April 20). Jewish life slowly returns to Poland. *BBC News*. Retrieved April 21, 2013, from http://www.bbc.co.uk/news/world-radio-and-tv-17741185.

Fleming, M. (2002). The new minority rights regime in Poland: the experience of the German, Belarussian and Jewish minorities since 1989. *Nations and Nationalism, 8*(4), 531–548. doi:10.1111/1469–8219.00064.

Fleming, M. (2003). *National minorities in post-communist Poland*. London: Veritas.

Goldstein, P. (2010). Jewish Student NGOs in present-day Poland (1999–2010): An insider's view. In K. Craddy, M. Levy, and J. Nowakowski (Eds.), *Poland: A Jewish Matter* (pp. 65–73). Warsaw: Adam Mickiewicz Institute.

Gudonis, M. (2003). New Polish Jewish identities and a new framework of analysis. In Z. Gitelman, B. Kosmin, and A. Kovács (Eds.), *New Jewish Identities: Contemporary Europe and Beyond* (pp. 243–261). Budapest: Central European University Press.

Ingram, J. (1997, September). Restitution helps fuel Jewish revival, but fans fear of prejudice. *Los Angeles Times*. Retrieved April 21, 2013, from http://articles.latimes.com/1997/sep/07/news/mn-29634.

Krajewski, S. (2005). *Poland and the Jews: Reflections of a Polish Polish Jew*. Kraków: Austeria.
Liège, C. (2000, January). Timide renouveau du judaïsme en Pologne. *Le Monde diplomatique*. Retrieved April 21, 2013, from http://www.monde-diplomatique.fr/2000/01/LIEGE/13314.
Marechal, G. (2009). Autoethnography. In A. J. Mills, G. Durepos, and E. Wiebe (Eds.), *Encyclopedia of Case Study Research* (pp. 43–45). London: Sage.
Reszke, K. (2013). *Return of the Jew: Identity narratives of the third post–Holocaust generation of Jews in Poland*. Brighton, MA: Academic Studies.
Serraf, H. (2010, July). Cracovie invente le philosémitisme ... sans juifs. *Le Monde.fr*. Le Monde. Retrieved April 21, 2013, from http://www.lemonde.fr/idees/article/2010/07/03/cracovie-invente-le-philosemitisme-sans-juifs_1382310_3232.html.
Smith, C. S. (2007, July 12). In Poland, a Jewish revival thrives—minus Jews. *New York Times*. Retrieved April 21, 2013, from http://www.nytimes.com/2007/07/12/world/europe/12Kraków.html?pagewanted=all&_r=0.
Tzur, N. (2013, March 27). Passover in Kraków: Jewish revival in Poland. JPostwww. Retrieved April 21, 2013, from http://www.jpost.com/Jewish-World/Jewish-News/Passover-in-Kraków-Jewish-revival-in-Poland-307811.

Websites for Further Information

"Bais Ya'akov Schools," by Deborah Weissman and Lauren Granite, http://jwa.org/encyclopedia/article/bais-yaakov-schools. An overview of the history of the Bais Ya-akov schools for girls started in Kraków, Poland, in 1917 by Sarah Schenirer.
Historical Maps of Poland, http://info-poland.buffalo.edu/classroom/maps/task4.html. Maps of Poland from past times until the present.
Jewish Community Centre of Kraków, http://jcckrakow.org/. (Click the Union Jack icon for English version). Official website of the Jewish Community Centre of Kraków.
Lauder-Morasha School, Warsaw, Poland, http://www.lauder-morasha.edu.pl/. Official website of the Lauder-Morasha School (website in Polish).
Taube Foundation for Jewish Life and Culture, http://www.taubephilanthropies.org/. Official website of the Taube Foundation for Jewish Life and Culture, which supports projects related to secular and Jewish life.
Yiddish Language and Culture, http://www.jewfaq.org/yiddish.htm. An overview of Yiddish language and culture.
Żegota, http://zegota.org/. Website under construction in 2013; directs viewer to www.projectinposterum.org/docs/zegota.htm which explains the underground movement in Poland in during World War II.

Jewish Studies and Holocaust Education at Polish Universities

> "Prospsutudects for future generations of trained Holocaust scholars appeared dim indeed. Where were they to be educated? Would they be self-educated, as were those of my generation and the scholars on whose shoulders I stood?"—Dwork, 2009, p. 190

Jewish Studies and Holocaust Education are fairly new programs of study at most Eastern European universities. According to Dr. Viktoria Sukovata (2009), a Ukrainian scholar, the teaching of the Holocaust and Jewish Studies at schools and universities of the former Soviet Union is problematic for many reasons based in the past and in the present. She points out that although Holocaust studies arose as an independent academic discipline with practical and theoretical goals in Western European and North-American higher education after World War II that did not happen the former Soviet Union. The Holocaust and Jewish Studies were neither systematically studied nor taught in schools and universities during the Soviet period. In addition, during that time, the archives in the Eastern Bloc countries relating to the Holocaust were mostly closed to researchers and to a wider audience.

The Development of Jewish Studies at Polish Universities

Michał Galas (2012) of the Institute of Jewish Studies at Jagiellonian University explained that in Kraków, Poland, Hebrew was taught in Polish universities since the Renaissance usually as part of Christian theological studies. In the nineteenth and early twentieth centuries the first Jewish Studies programs were established in Warsaw by scholars who were Jewish and were interested in learning and teaching about Jewish culture and history.

These courses were most often taken by students who were Jewish. Immediately after World War II and the Holocaust the Jewish Historical Institute (JHI), an outgrowth of the Central Jewish Historical Commission, was established in 1947 in Warsaw and was the only institution which offered opportunities for research, education, and publication in the general area of Jewish Studies. Although it is housed in the same building as the pre-War Institute of Judaic Studies, the goals and purpose are not the same. One major aspect of the JHI is that it is the central depository for the vast archives of Jewish life from all over Poland. The Institute is an important resource for researchers on all aspects of Jewish life in Poland.

During the 1950s, departments of theology were removed from Polish public universities resulting in the loss of courses in Hebrew, Jewish literature and so on. Only the Department of Hebrew Studies at Warsaw University survived this purge. There was also little access for Polish scholars to publications and research from abroad. Therefore, until the 1980s there were few opportunities for Polish scholars to explore aspects of Judaism and Jewish life.

However in the 1980s, the winds of change began to blow in Eastern Europe and in Poland. Scholars and academics were beginning to feel more freedom to explore previously forbidden and unavailable topics. During the 1980s several conferences focusing on Jewish-Polish relations provided the spark for the revival of Jewish Studies in Poland. As result of some of these conferences Jagiellonian University even offered courses and lectures in the history of Jews in Poland during the 1982–83 academic year.

According to Galas (2012), a conference at Oxford University in England was the real watershed. It was the first important meeting of Jewish and Polish academics where all aspects of Jewish life in Poland were discussed. They not only talked about the history of Jews in Poland, but also addressed the more difficult issues of the Holocaust and post-Holocaust in Poland. This conference sparked numerous initiatives including other conferences, collaborative projects between Polish and Jewish scholars, and the publication of *Polin: Studies in Polish Jewry,* an annual journal of academic interests which was first published in 2004. These initiatives were seen as opportunities which promoted better understanding between Polish and Jewish scholars by helping break down stereotypes from each side.

A conference in 1984 was another watershed moment. For the first time a group of Israeli scholars and students met with Polish scholars. Then in 1986 another conference on Jewish-Polish relations focused on relations during the Polish partitions and produced publications in Polish and in English.

During that same year, 1986, Jagiellonian University in Kraków, Poland opened a center focusing on the history and culture of Jews in Poland, the first center of its kind ever established in Poland. It original purpose was to organize bibliographies for research and to provide an archival inventory. Out of the work of this center arose courses about Jewish history and culture which were offered to students from all departments. Galas (2012) was a student at Jagiellonian at that time and he says that these courses were his introduction to the history of Jews in Poland.

In addition to academic interest in Jewish history and culture, the general population began expressing interest in this unknown topic of Polish history. As a direct result of the establishment of the center, the first Jewish cultural festival was organized in Kraków in 1988 by students at the center. This festival was primarily a film festival focusing on Jewish topics. The Center for Jewish Culture in Kraków also had its inception through the influence of the center at the Jagiellonian.

Throughout the 1980s and 1990s there were numerous conferences across Poland which explored many aspects of Jewish history and culture as well as the Holocaust. In 1996 the Polish Association for Jewish Studies was established in Kraków by scholars from several Polish institutions. Its primary goal was to offer a centralized point to promote scholarly research of Jewish history and culture and to help foster and develop cooperation with Polish and other institutions and associations.

Although there are various institutions which offer courses and programs for individuals who are interested in different aspects of Jewish Studies in Poland, as of 2012, there are five universities which offer programs for students. These universities are Adam Mickiewicz University in Poznań, Jagiellonian University in Kraków, Maria Curie-Skłodowska University in Lublin, Warsaw University, and University of Wrocław. While several other universities offer some courses or programs in the Holocaust or Jewish Studies, including the University of Białystok, University of Bydgoszcz, the University of Śląsk (Silesia) in Katowice, and Opole University, only three other universities are considered Jewish Studies research institutions. These are University of Łódź, University of Rzeszów, and University of Gdańsk. These programs grew out of centers and institutes started by Polish academics who were not Jewish. As well as these centers, there are two institutions that bring scholars together. The Polish Association of Jewish Studies is based in Kraków while The Polish Center for Holocaust Research is based in Warsaw.

The Polish Association of Jewish Studies was established in Kraków in 1996, and is now affiliated with the European Association for Jewish Studies.

It is dedicated to Jewish studies and research, and through lectures, seminars, and conferences aims to bring together scholars and institutions, both in Poland and abroad, that are involved in Jewish studies. While the association promotes all aspects of Jewish studies, they focus on the history and culture of Jews in Poland specifically. The Association publishes books and the journal, *Studia Judaica*.

The Polish Center for Holocaust Research which was established in 2003 is part of the Institute of Philosophy and Sociology of the Polish Academy of Sciences in Warsaw. It is dedicated to Holocaust studies and research which include academic/scholarly research; documentation, specifically of the Warsaw Ghetto; educational seminars and lectures; conferences; and publications, including books and a journal, *Zagłada Żydów. Studia i Materiały*. The Center provides an interdisciplinary environment for researchers and scholars who are interested in the Holocaust.

This section will look at the five Polish universities which offer programs for students, what they offer and how they present it. The programs are presented in alphabetical order. These programs are multidimensional and are fairly comprehensive, and represent different geographical areas of Poland.

Adam Mickiewicz University, Poznań: Adam Mickiewicz University (AMU) is located in Poznań, a city in the western part of Poland. Poznań, one of the oldest cities in Poland, has a population of around 550,000. Although, historically Poznań was home to large numbers of Jews, many had immigrated and left the region before and after World War I (Witkowski, 2012). Therefore by the outbreak of World War II, Poznań was home to about 2,000 Jews. The university, founded in 1919, is named after the Polish Romantic poet, Adam Mickiewicz. It currently employs around 3,000 academic staff and has around 52,000 students. AMU offers degrees in a wide range of fields, including mathematics and sciences, humanities, and social sciences.

Adam Mickiewicz University offers a program focusing on Hebrew and Judaism which is housed in the Asian Studies Department of the Oriental Studies Institute. This department was formed in 2008, and as of 2013 about 200 students are enrolled at the master's and doctoral levels in Arabic, Hebrew, Turkish, and Chinese studies.

Many of the courses in the Hebrew Studies area focus on religious aspects of Hebrew and Judaism, such as Biblical Hebrew and Aramaic, Greek, Aramaic, and Hebrew translations of the Bible, and the history of Judaism. The offerings also include studies of Hebrew and Jewish history, literature, art, and culture in the Middle East context as well as in Poland and Eastern Europe.

Jagiellonian University, Kraków: Jagiellonian University is located in Kraków, Poland, one of the oldest cities in Poland with a population of about 750,000 inhabitants. Prior to World War II, Kraków was an important cultural and spiritual center for Polish Jews. At that time about 60,000 Jews lived in Kraków, approximately 25 percent of the city's population. Founded in 1364, Jagiellonian University is the second oldest university in Central Europe. It has changed and evolved through the centuries, and currently has 15 schools, offering a full range of degrees from including mathematics and sciences, humanities, social sciences, and medicine.

Jagiellonian University offers a comprehensive program of Jewish Studies and Holocaust Studies. The History department houses Jewish Studies while the Center for Holocaust Studies is part of the Faculty of International and Political Studies.

The Institute of Jewish Studies evolved from the Research Center for Jewish History and Culture in Poland, which was organized in 1986. As it was originally called, the Department of Jewish Studies was established as an autonomous unit in the History department in 2000. With more than 150 students at all levels, it is one of the largest programs in Europe. Each year 40 students are accepted of the 80 or so who apply. The scope of the research in the department ranges from Polish-Jewish cultural heritage in Kraków and the Małopolska (Smaller Poland) region to the history and culture of Jews during the time of the Second Temple. The program offers three areas of study: Jewish history; Jewish culture; and Jewish literature and Judaism. The department offers bachelor's, master's, post-diploma, and doctoral degrees in these areas, offering coursework in Polish and in English. The bachelor's and master's degrees offer a specialization in Jewish studies and can include such courses as history and culture of Jews, the history of anti–Semitism, and the study of Hebrew and/or Yiddish. The post-diploma program which can be used as the basis for a doctorate requires 160 contact hours in courses such as the history of Jews, their religion, culture and language and can focus on Jewish Kraków. In 2012, this program became independent and rather than students receiving a degree in history with Jewish Studies specialization, they can now receive a degree in Jewish Studies, the only degree of its kind in Poland at this time.

The Center for Holocaust Studies, part of the School of International and Political Studies, was inaugurated in 2008. It was the outgrowth of the Research Group for Holocaust Studies which had been established in 1996 in the Centre for European Studies of the Jagiellonian University. The Center's mission is to conduct research about the Holocaust and to educate, both formally and informally, about it. The Institute's team includes professors from various disciplines as well as doctoral students at Jagiellonian University who have research and teaching interests related to the Holocaust.

Maria Curie-Skłodowska University, Lublin: The Maria Curie-Skłodowska University was established in Lublin, Poland in 1944. Lublin, a city in the eastern part of Poland, has around 350,000 residents. In the sixteenth century, Lublin became a center for Jewish learning, and had a large, active Jewish community until World War II. In the 1930s 35 percent of Lublin's population was Jewish and many of them lived in the Jewish quarter located around Lublin's castle hill. During World War II, the Nazis destroyed most of the buildings and they were never rebuilt. Lublin is also the site of Majdanek Concentration Camp where 59,000 Jews were killed during its 34 months of operation. The university, which focuses on the arts and sciences, employs about 1,700 academic staff and has over 34,000 students enrolled at undergraduate and graduate levels.

Prior to 1939, there had been some research on Jewish life in this region by Jewish and non–Jewish scholars alike. Beginning in 1944 and continuing after World War II, the Central Jewish Historical Commission of Poland (which later became the Jewish Historical Institute) began a project to create memory books, memorial books which included pictures, letters, survivors stories, newspaper articles from before the war, legends, and many other types of materials to commemorate communities destroyed during the Holocaust. Their purpose was to serve as "tombstones made of words" (Kubiszyn, 2012) to preserve and honor the everyday lives of everyday people. These memory books became one of the foundations on which Jewish scholarship was built at Maria Curie-Skłodowska University.

Around 1994, there were attempts to create a Center for Jewish Studies at Maria Curie-Skłodowska University based on the American university model. Finally it was established in 2000 as an independent unit in the Humanities department. One of the original aims was to offer academic studies and research, but also to make Jewish studies accessible to the general public. Local secondary school teachers were especially interested in participating in activities at the center. In 2004 it became part of the Cultural Studies department. In the meantime, the center moved away from offerings for the general public and now its courses are available only for students in the university. The Center offers courses in Jewish history and culture and also offers a focus on Jewish life in the Lublin region. Their offerings are as diverse as literature and art of the Holocaust, and Hebrew language studies. They also organize presentations, workshops, etc. in coordination with programs in Israel and the US. Since 2010, they have offered a PhD in Jewish Studies.

University of Warsaw: The University of Warsaw is located in Poland's capital city, Warsaw, which has over 1,700,000 inhabitants. Prior to World War II, Warsaw was home to almost 400,000 Jews, about one-third the city's population. The University of Warsaw was established in 1816. In the 1920s topics related to Jewish history and culture began to be taught and studied by Jewish and non–Jewish scholars in the Institute of Jewish Studies. At present, it employs over 3,000 academic staff. More than 55,000 students are enrolled in undergraduate and graduate programs, in a wide range of fields, including mathematics and sciences, humanities, and social sciences.

There are three programs related to Jewish Studies at the University of Warsaw. The Department of Hebrew Studies is in the Institute of Oriental Studies. This program focuses on the Hebrew language, Judaism, and Jews in Israel and around the world. The Mordechai Anielewicz Center for the Research and Study of the History and Culture of Jews in Poland focuses on Polish-Jewish history and culture, as well as Hebrew and Yiddish. The university also offers a post-graduate program in the History and Culture of Jews in Poland through the Historical Institute of the University of Warsaw.

The Department of Hebrew Studies was established in 1977 as part of the Division of Ancient Near East and Hebrew Studies. In 1990 it became part of the Institute of Oriental Studies. At the end of the 5 year program, students receive a Master of Arts in Hebrew Studies. The program includes compulsory Modern Hebrew courses; general history courses, such as history of Judaism; History of Ancient Israel; History of Jews in the Diaspora; and History of Modern Israel; and specialized major courses in focusing on history, sociology, literature and linguistics.

The Mordechai Anielewicz Center for the Research and Study of the History and Culture of Jews in Poland was established in 1990. Since 2001 it has been part of the Institute of History in the History Department. The Center offers a 2 year program, The History and Culture of Jews in Poland. This program is available not only to students who are part of the Historical Institute, but to students across the university. The program requires 120 hours of study of Hebrew or Yiddish language and 240 hours of other coursework.

A two-semester post-graduate program in the History and Culture of Jews in Poland is offered to college graduates who are interested in Polish-Jewish cultural heritage and the modern Jewish experience in Poland. Courses include the history of Polish Jews from the Middle Ages to today, modern history of Israel, as well as Jewish philosophy, literature, film, and theatre.

University of Wrocław: The University of Wrocław is located in Wrocław, Poland, the fourth largest city in Poland. This city of over 630,000 inhabitants is located on the Oder River in Lower Silesia, the southwest corner of Poland. Before World War II, Wrocław was Breslau, Germany and was home to about 30,000 Jews. After the war, about 80,000 Jews settled in Wrocław because there were jobs and housing available there. However, due to conditions in Poland, most of them immigrated over time. The university was originally established in the 1700s as a small college run by Jesuits, focusing on philosophy, Catholic theology, evangelical theology, law and medicine. After World War II it expanded and became a comprehensive university with schools in all disciplines. There are over 40,000 students enrolled.

In 1993 the Research Centre for the Culture and Languages of the Jews was established in Wrocław. In the fall of 2003 the University of Wrocław changed the name to the Centre for the Culture and Languages of the Jews and created a program of Jewish Studies. Students can receive an M.A. or a PhD. in Jewish Studies. The aim of the program is to educate about Jewish traditions, Jewish culture and history, and to revive the tradition of the Breslauer Theologisches Seminar. The two-year program consists of 20 courses (or 600 contact hours) which cover Jewish history, culture and literature; introduction to Judaism; introduction to the Jewish Studies; and Hebrew and Yiddish language courses. The Center also organizes conferences, seminars, public lectures, and other activities. In October 2010 the University began offering an Individualized Interdisciplinary Humanities Study Specializing in Jewish Studies.

Summary of Jewish Studies and Related Programs

A comparison these various programs shows the breadth and depth of Jewish Studies and Holocaust Education at the university level in Poland. Based on information about these selected programs, it is evident that Jewish Studies and Holocaust Education are fairly recent programs of study at the university level in Poland. The Department of Hebrew Studies at the University of Warsaw is the only one that was established during the Communist period. All of the other programs were established in the post–Soviet era, and several since 2000. This delay in starting such programs is not surprising when one considers that the Holocaust and Jewish Studies, in general, were neglected in the former Soviet-bloc countries of Eastern and Central Europe. It is also not surprising that the majority of scholars and students are not Jewish. Many of the young Polish scholars are curious about this gap in their country's history.

In comparing these programs to Bauer's analysis (1999) one sees similarities in how the programs are organized. Bauer pointed out that oftentimes Holocaust education is part of the Jewish Studies program, and he cautioned that serves to make the subject seem to be only a "Jewish" topic without wider implications. Of the programs highlighted here, all of them are embedded in Jewish or Hebrew studies, except for the Center for Holocaust Studies in the Faculty of International and Political Studies which is a research center than a degree program. Bauer (1999) also pointed out that making the subject a "Jewish" topic without wider implications impedes implementation of an interdisciplinary approach. Only the program at the University of Wrocław seems to offer interdisciplinary studies and that began as recently as 2010.

Most of the programs also offer, and even require, courses in Hebrew and Yiddish, the languages related to Jewish culture. In some cases, it is unclear from the websites whether the Hebrew courses are Biblical Hebrew or modern Hebrew, although some do differentiate. It is also unclear whether the Yiddish courses cover Polish/Galician Yiddish or the more Germanic/Western European Yiddish in which much of Yiddish literature is written.

As Houwink (2010) pointed out there has been a move in recent years to look at the Holocaust as local history. This trend is certainly apparent in the programs offered by Jagiellonian University in Kraków and the Maria Curie-Skłodowska University in Lublin. Each offers courses in Jewish history and life in their respective regions.

According to Galas (2012) such programs in Poland are moving toward being independent scholarly disciplines rather than being embedded in other programs or departments. He pointed out that there are about 100 books per year published in this field in Poland and about 1,500 scholarly articles are published by Polish scholars each year. Polish scholars are beginning to move to the top of the fields in Holocaust Studies, Yiddish, history of Chasidism, and social and local history of places in Poland. Because many of these programs offer and even may require that the students study Yiddish, there has been a revival of interest in Yiddish and Yiddish literature in Poland.

One challenge that Galas (2012) sees with the variety of courses and programs in a country the size of Poland (38 million inhabitants) is that there are not enough specialists to go around. He suggested that centralization of Jewish Studies programs would address that issue as well as the issue of decreased enrollment that many universities are facing.

Although these programs offer a wide array of courses, it does not appear that any of them are aimed at secondary school teachers specifically. The courses are content courses which provide information about Jews and the

Holocaust without providing information on how to teach about the Jewish history and culture or the Holocaust. Programs such as the one at the Center for Holocaust Studies of Jagiellonian University, the Summer Holocaust Institute for Secondary Teachers, have been established to meet that need and fill that gap. This one-week institute offers workshops for 60 secondary teachers and focuses on Jewish culture and history, the Holocaust, teaching strategies, and includes visits to Auschwitz and the Kraków Jewish Cultural Festival. However, at this point the institute, like many others, does not have one dedicated source of funding and has depended largely on grants from abroad which are not guaranteed each year.

In the following essay the Director of the Center for Holocaust Studies and two of her doctoral students expand on the Center's mission and what the Center offers. As the first university institution in Poland whose sole objective is to carry out research on the Holocaust, Holocaust education and commemoration, the Center engages in a wide range of activities. In addition to the aforementioned Institute for teachers, programs range from research on the Holocaust to courses and degrees for university students to lectures for the local community by noted Holocaust scholars. The Center also sponsors and participates in events such as the sixty-fifth anniversary of the liquidation of the Kraków ghetto to programs to panel discussions at the Jewish Cultural Festival in Kraków. As Dr. Ambrosewicz-Jacobs and her students point out, their work and the work of the Center are steps on the way to a deeper understanding of the tragedy and the legacy of the Holocaust.

The Center for Holocaust Studies at the Jagiellonian University in Kraków: Studies, Research, Remembrance

by Jolanta Ambrosewicz-Jacobs, Elisabeth Büttner, and Katarzyna Suszkiewicz

"Why continue a line of research that is so disturbing and leaves so many questions unanswered? The question contains a partial answer: since the subject disturbs us, it must be pursued."—Bergman, 2009, p. 281

For Professor Józef Gierowski, who founded the interdisciplinary Interfaculty Department of the History and Culture of the Jews in Poland at the Jagiellonian University in 1986, the history and culture of the Polish Jews was an integral part of the history and culture of Poland. Recognition and remembrance of the role Jews played in the history and culture of Poland can be demonstrated in various ways. In recent years, many young Poles have taken an interest in abandoned Jewish cemeteries, cleaning them up and trying to find out about the families who are represented in these places. Frequently cooperating with the Foundation for the Protection of the Jewish Heritage and other organizations, they commemorate the Jewish residents of their towns, their onetime neighbors, telling about the history and culture of those who cannot speak for themselves.

Collective memory in Poland is created and maintained in part by training sessions for teachers on the subject of teaching about the Holocaust, curriculum programs, packages, and textbooks, Holocaust memorial museums, plaques on the walls of houses where people died, and ceremonial observances of the anniversaries of the liquidation of the ghettos and the liberation of the camps. Yet this facade of collective memory, approved or even created by state institutions and non-governmental organizations, perpetuated in large part through rituals, continues to be accompanied by a collective lack of memory in Polish families. The mass murder of 10 percent of the citizens of prewar Poland, those with Jewish origins, generally has gone unnoticed in the family memory of Poles, even though Jews sometimes accounted for the majority of the population of towns and villages, communities in which these Polish families may have lived for generations.

This collective lack of memory is perhaps influenced by the fact that all Poles were Holocaust bystanders, but some of them profited from the events that happened around them. Do the subsequent generations know about this? How much do they know? Do they want to know at all? Should they know? As individuals, we are not responsible for what our parents, grandparents, and great-grandparents did. If this is so, why do we have so many defensive reactions, so much resistance to being informed about the unworthy behavior of members of the group we belong to—even such a large group as a community or nation?

In the domain of groups larger than the family, especially in the domain of the community, the absence of neighbors cannot be a matter of indifference, even if no one wants to remember them. Sometimes, this remembrance is done by individual people—a sudden interest in *matzevot* (gravestones) in an abandoned cemetery nearby, or students traveling to Kraków and suddenly discovering Jewish Kazimierz without the Jews about whom their teachers "forgot" to tell them. Which memories are revived and how they are recognized and made part of the collective memory is a role of that education can play. The mission of the Center for Holocaust Studies of the Jagiellonian University in Kraków, Poland is to help education at all levels and in different forms, play that role effectively.

Background of the Center for Holocaust Studies

On January 17, 2008, the inauguration of the Center for Holocaust Studies of the Jagiellonian University (CHS), an independent unit at the Faculty of International and Political Studies, took place in the Libraria room of Collegium Maius. This historical building is the site of the original university, dating from the fourteenth century, and now serves as a museum. The significance of this event taking place in this historical site cannot be ignored.

The Center is not the first academic institution in Poland which is focused on the subject of the destruction of the Jews; it is continuing the work of the small Research Section for Holocaust Studies created in 1996 at the Chair of European Studies (now the Institute of European Studies) by Professor Zdzisław Mach. There are also other academic centers in Poland which carry out studies of the Holocaust; however, the CHS at Jagiellonian University is the first university institution whose sole objective is to conduct research on the Holocaust, Holocaust education and commemoration.

The goals of the CHS at Jagiellonian University are to conduct research and education concerning the Holocaust, and research in areas directly connected with it. It accomplishes these goals through a variety of activities, including: disseminating knowledge about the Holocaust and other genocides through the organization of conferences, seminars, summer schools, congresses, lectures, meetings, exhibitions and through the publication of its own materials; creating electronic databases; introducing innovative teaching methods and creating teaching materials which serve the purpose of combating anti–Semitism, racism, xenophobia and discrimination; documenting Holocaust studies in Polish academic centers; and documenting formal and non-formal educational projects. The CHS has established working relationships with international and national institutions which have similar missions and goals, including the International Center for Education about Auschwitz and the Holocaust at the State Museum Auschwitz-Birkenau, the Pedagogical

University in Kraków, the House of the Wannsee Conference, Centropa, the Foundation for the Preservation of Jewish Heritage in Poland (FODZ), the Jewish Historical Institute, the Jewish Community Center (JCC) in Kraków, the Jewish Museum Galicia and many other institutions, museums, sites of commemoration, publishing houses, and academic journals.

Of the goals which the founders of the Center for Holocaust Studies have set, the most significant are research and teaching. The CHS draws attention to academic research areas where more scientific inquiries are called for and proposes creative methods of education about the Holocaust, in cooperation with institutions working in the field of anti–Semitism and the preservation of Jewish heritage. The Center wants to have a strong presence in the public space of the city and works towards the strengthening the memory of the Shoah among the wider community, and not only among specialists and academics. Therefore, in addition to these academic challenges, the Center strives to develop activities in which the results of academic research are accessible not only through specialist publications (though such publications are being produced and more are planned in the future), but also through lectures, and discussion panels for the wider public in the city of Kraków.

Why the Work of the Center Is Necessary and Important

Education serves as a prism through which attitudinal changes toward the Holocaust can be analyzed. This perspective shows that there is a long path which leads from silence and taboo in the past to efforts to recognize and face the trauma of the disappearance of neighbors with whom ethnic Poles had shared a homeland for almost 1,000 years. This silence is being broken with the asking of "difficult questions" and the process of integrating unwanted and detached memories has begun with the initiatives of numerous intergovernmental, governmental and civic agencies. These steps are the way to developing a deeper understanding of the tragedy and the legacy of the Holocaust.

In the autumn of 2008, Dr. Jolanta Ambrosewicz-Jacobs, director of the CHS, initiated a long-term research project called "Researching Attitudes towards Jews and the Holocaust among Polish Youth." The project, sponsored by the Center, had a nationwide scope, and undertook research on anti-Semitism and attitudes towards the Holocaust among Polish youth (funded through grants from the Fondation pour la Memoire de la Shoah and the

International Task Force). This project had an educational component carried out in cooperation with academic institutions and NGOs. The objective of the project was to ascertain the current attitudes of Polish youth towards Jews and the Holocaust and to produce an analysis of civic activities related to the memory of the Holocaust. The first part of the project consisted of research on the changing attitudes of young people in comparison with similar studies carried out among young people ten years earlier. The second part of the project envisaged an in-depth analysis of educational programs in Polish schools and those carried out by non-governmental organizations.

In the 2008 survey, 38 percent of participating students responded "I don't know," and 34 percent responded affirmatively to the question "Did Jews live in your town before the War?" One in five students answered that they were not interested in this subject, and about 50 percent claimed that Jews once lived in their town and left various things behind. A considerable proportion knew nothing about, nor was interested in, the topic.

The results indicate that while understanding of the Holocaust is increasing, reaching 33 percent of young Poles in 2008, a large proportion of students are ignorant of the Holocaust. Knowledge of the number of Polish Jews killed was very low (14 percent) although there was almost universal agreement that it was important to know about the Shoah. The research data showed that sensitivity to the Holocaust was increased in those who had received specific education about the Holocaust.

A number of educational initiatives, including exhibitions related to the Holocaust, have appeared in Poland in recent years and are a factor in increasing Holocaust awareness in Polish youth. Annual competitions to increase awareness of the Shoah have been arranged by organizations such as the Shalom Foundation. In addition much more attention has been given recently to the previously ignored Righteous Among the Nations, a term coined by Yad Vashem in Israel, to honor those who helped save Jews during World War II. However, since Polish youth think of national identity in national rather than civic terms, the Holocaust is not considered part of their collective memory, and there is the risk of over-idealizing Polish actions to enhance national self-esteem.

As recent research demonstrates, there are some positive changes in knowledge about and attitudes toward the Holocaust. However, there is the danger that students' consciousness with regard to the Holocaust may become limited to bare historical facts or to the repetition of certain general statements without deeper understanding of the essence of the phenomenon and the losses to Poland and Polish culture. Despite numerous initiatives in local communities, a considerable number of young people did not seem to realize that Holocaust victims, apart from the Jews deported to death camps in Poland from other European countries, were also Polish citizens living in Polish cities, towns and villages.

Despite an increase in growth of education about Jewish life and culture and the Holocaust, anti–Semitic attitudes persist in organizations such as All Polish Youth and many other fiercely nationalist parties and organizations. Anti-Semitic literature continues to be produced by the media group controlled by Fr. Tadeusz Rydzyk, who is the producer of the conservative, and controversial, radio station, Radio Maryja (Mary), as well as via websites and occasional magazines. These vehicles of nationalism and anti–Semitism form a syndrome of closed memory, denying Polish anti–Semitism as a fiction fabricated by the enemies of "Polishness." In answer to a question on the project's questionnaire, 78 percent of the youth surveyed in 2008 thinks that anti–Semitism exists in Poland. Because of the strong influence that the Catholic Church has in Poland, the active involvement of the Church is essential in educating about and solving the problem of anti–Semitism in Poland.

Projects and Programs

Research projects, university degrees, educational activities, websites, various types of publications, seminars, workshops, and presentations are a few of the types of activities and projects initiated and supported by the Center. The activities and projects are varied in scope and in form. Some of them are described in this section.

In addition to the *Internet Guide to Tolerance Education* which was established early in the twenty-first century, the book *Why Should We Teach About the Holocaust?* (edited by Jolanta Ambrosewicz-Jacobs and Leszek Hońdo) was published in 2005. It is still offered free of charge for distribution among teachers, thanks to the financial support of the Office for Democratic Institutions and Human Rights of the Organization for Security and Cooperation in Europe (OSCE). *Why Should We Teach About the Holocaust?* is a collection of essays written by outstanding Polish specialists in the field of Holocaust education. It also includes descriptions of institutions with appropriate educational tools. The volume was created with a wide range of readers in mind, not necessarily limited only to the dichotomy of teacher—student, but also for those for whom the educational process has more open boundaries. The book is addressed both to people who are aware of and not indifferent to the murder of 10 percent of Poland's pre-war population, as well as to those who may not be aware that this destruction took place. The essays were written by academics, influential figures in public life and specialists from various academic fields: Jerzy Tomaszewski, Zdzisław Mach, Ireneusz Krzemiński, Stefan Wilkanowicz, Olga Goldberg-Mulkiewicz, Monika Adamczyk-Garbowska, Stanisław Obirek, Robert Szuchta, Tanna Jakubowicz-Mount, Stanisław Krajewski, Sergiusz Kowalski, Sławomir Kapralski, Hanna Węgrzynek, Andrzej Mirga, Natalia Aleksiun, Leszek Hońdo and Jolanta Ambrosewicz-Jacobs. The Center has been responsible for the distribution of this free publication, distributing about 75,000 copies in two languages, Polish and English.

In 2008 in Wasilkow (Podlasie region) workshops led by experts from the CHS were carried out for teachers and local leaders. The workshop sessions were devoted to intercultural dialogue and the religion, history and culture of Polish Jews. The workshops were organized by the Foundation for the Preservation of Jewish Heritage (FODZ) in cooperation with the local government in Wasilkow as one of the activities in the project "Examining attitudes towards Jews and their heritage, in cooperation with local partners in fifteen chosen localities and tolerance education" which was supported by the Stefan Batory Foundation. By 2008 workshops had been organized in the following localities:

- the Lubelskie region: Frampol, Krasnik, Leczna, Tarnogród, Zamosc
- the Podkarpacie region: Dynów, Medyka, Niebylec, Sieniawa, Sokolów Malopolski
- the Podlasie region: Milejczyce, Przerosl, Suchowola and Tykocin.

Also in 2008 the Center for Holocaust Studies initiated a project in cooperation with the Polish Ministry of Foreign Affairs which consists of creating a map of Poland showing sites of education and memory related to the Holocaust. The Center is collecting information, materials, statistical data, summaries and reports from previous seminars, conferences, teacher-training workshops, seminars and conferences for students, exhibitions, performances and a variety of other events relevant to the history and remembrance of the Holocaust which have taken place since 1989.

A significant publication of the Center, in cooperation with Austeria Publishing House, was *The Holocaust: Voices of Scholars* (edited by Jolanta

Ambrosewicz-Jacobs) and published in 2009. This book presents the reflections of many prominent scholars and public figures whose work involves the subject of the Holocaust. They were asked to write about difficulties they have faced, and several questions were posed to them:

- Do the analytical tools of the scholar, the researcher, the philosopher, the sociologist, the artist, prove weak or ineffective in dealing with the Holocaust?
- More than sixty years after the liberation of Auschwitz, are we intellectually and emotionally baffled by the genocide the Nazis committed there?
- If so, what are the paths taken to overcome this?
- How and why continue work on this most perplexing subject?

The invited contributors are a diverse international group, each one representing a significant dimension of engagement with the problem of the Holocaust. Among them are distinguished professors, researchers and psychotherapists, and the heads and co-founders of important institutions from Canada, Germany, Great Britain, Israel, Poland and the United States, including Yehuda Bauer, John K. Roth, Ian Kershaw, John T. Pawlikowski, Zdzisław Mach, Michael R. Marrus, Charles S. Maier, Omer Bartov, Shimon Redlich, Dan Michman, Maria Orwid, Krzysztof Szwajca, Jonathan Webber, Nechama Tec, Dalia Ofer, Feliks Tych, Debórah Dwork, Robert Jan van Pelt, Michael Berenbaum, Stanisław Krajewski, Moshe Zimmermann, Wolfgang Benz, Jan Woleński, Eleonora Bergman and Elie Wiesel. Many of their writings are known as foundational works in their fields of study and in the study of the Holocaust.

A very important function of the Center for Holocaust Studies is higher education; it offers masters' and PhD degrees, and in 2013 had 55 MA and 12 PhD students. In 2011/2012 the CHS launched an MA program in Holocaust and Totalitarianism Studies. This new program does not limit itself to historical perspectives within the boundaries of twentieth century European totalitarianism but also addresses the sources of national and religious conflicts throughout the contemporary world, different mechanisms of the creation of totalitarian states and their structures, and problems of racism and anti–Semitism which are still present in contemporary Europe. The program of study contains one of the most comprehensive approaches to the question of the Holocaust and totalitarianism available at this time in the European system of higher education. Apart from perspectives of history, political science, philosophy and cultural studies, they also contain the basis of pedagogical education and practical aspects of teaching about the Holocaust and totalitarianism.

The Center for Holocaust Studies and the Institute for European Studies offer courses taught by visiting professors who aim to provide a better knowledge of the Shoah and other aspects connected with the subject. One of the instructors was Wolf Kaiser PhD, deputy director for education of the House of the Wannsee Conference in Berlin. He taught a 30 hour course in May 2008 at the Jagiellonian University entitled "Aspects of the Holocaust." During the class two primary thematic strands were examined. Historical themes presented a chronological timeline of the Shoah (Hitler's policies, the ghettos, camps, persecutors and victims). The other strand involved examining questions pertaining to commemoration of the Holocaust and the perception of the Holocaust by various social and national groups using oral history, memories of survivors, Holocaust museums and memorials. The course was interactive, and demanded that the students participate actively in the classes—their task was to prepare selected source materials and texts and to present their own opinion during the discussion of the various issues.

Another series of lectures organized by the Center were presented in May 2009 by Professor Moshe Zimmermann, a renowned Israeli historian from the Hebrew University of Jerusalem whose research interests include the history of German Jews and anti-Semitism. His 30 hours of lectures on the subject "Anti-Semitism, Nazism and the Holocaust in German and American Movies" examined how two societies, German and American, presented anti-Semitism, Nazism and the Holocaust, and how they used film to shape attitudes and collective memory. It included films representing the phenomena in real time (Germany: *Triumph des Willens, Grosse Liebe, Jud Suess*; and America: *The Great Dictator, Mortal Storm* and others) and in historical retrospective (Germany: *Die Moerder sind unter uns, In jenen Tagen*; and America: *Gentlemen's Agreement, Crossfire, Schindler's List* and others). The course reflected on how film can be used as a historical source or an interpretation.

The Center is also a partner in the program for *Fellowships at Auschwitz for the Study of Professional Ethics* (FASPE) organized by the Museum of Jewish Heritage in New York. This is an innovative program for university students, designed to address contemporary ethical issues through the unique historical context of the Holocaust. Since 2011 each year two participants from Jagiellonian University have joined their American colleagues on a trip to New York, Berlin and Auschwitz to explore the Holocaust through the lenses of their major study area such as law, journalism, business and medicine. Among other activities, they tour the core exhibit of the Museum of

Jewish Heritage in New York City and participate in seminars and workshops with German and Polish scholars.

Since its establishment the Center has organized many gatherings which have included professors, lecturers, diplomats, authors and representatives of non-governmental organizations. In 2008, the Center for Holocaust Studies of the Jagiellonian University took part in the commemoration events for the 65th anniversary of the liquidation of the Kraków ghetto by organizing several events. One of the events was the retrospective "The Holocaust in Polish Cinema" which included a meeting with Andrzej Wajda, a well-known Polish film director, on March 12, 2008, to commemorate the 65th anniversary of the liquidation of the Kraków Ghetto. The meeting drew a crowd to Przegorzaly Castle, the primary location for Center activities, where the event took place. Attendees included students and members of the public who wanted to take part in a discussion with a master of Polish cinema. Wajda spoke of the difficulties and dilemmas during the making of his films and also about the varied reception which some of his films, for example *Korczak,* received in different countries.

Another event for the commemoration was a panel discussion, chaired by Piotr Weiser PhD, entitled "Past-Present: Remembering the Kraków Jews." The meeting took place at Przegorzaly Castle on March 15, 2008. Among the participants were Professor David M. Crowe, author of Oscar Schindler's biography: *Oscar Schindler: The Untold Account of His Life, Wartime Activities, and the True Story Behind the List*; Professor Maria Orwid, a pioneer of research on the effects of the events of the Shoah on the survivors; Professor Aleksander Skotnicki, author of the book *Oskar Schindler in the Eyes of Cracovian Jews Saved by Him*; Katarzyna Zimmerer, author of the book *A Murdered World. The History of Kraków's Jews*; and Robert Gadek from the Jewish Culture Festival in Kraków. The discussion also included twenty-five survivors, who, in part, owed their rescue to Oscar Schindler. The discussion focused upon the memory of the Jews of Kraków and the tragedy of the Shoah, and on the figure of Oscar Schindler.

Professor Shimon Redlich, a historian at Ben-Gurion University in Negev, Israel gave a lecture at the Institute for European Studies in May 13, 2008, under the auspices of the CHS. The title of the lecture was "Autobiography in a historical context: How I wrote *Together and Apart in Brzezany: Poles, Jews and Ukrainians 1919–1945*." Professor Redlich's book *Together and Apart in Brzezany: Poles, Jews and Ukrainians 1919–1945* describes the co-existence of three groups of different ethnicities, religions and cultures in a small town on the Eastern Polish border, Brzezany, which was interrupted by the war and the Holocaust. The author recalls childhood memories, but also does not neglect his duties as a historian, and thoroughly documents facts as well as scrutinizes archival materials. *Together and Apart* depicts the collective memory of the three nations and the life of a community which ceased to exist.

On May 29, 2008, along with Galicia Jewish Museum, the CHS organized an open lecture and meeting with the renowned specialist in the field of European and Jewish history, Professor Robert Wistrich, director of the Vidal Sassoon International Center for the Study of Anti-Semitism (SICSA). Professor Wistrich, a lecturer at the Hebrew University in Jerusalem, presented a lecture regarding anti–Semitism in the Middle East. After the lecture Professor Wistrich answered questions from the young people who participated in the meeting.

The next year, on January 12, 2009, the Center organized a meeting at Galicia Jewish Museum with Professor Michael Berenbaum, Professor of Jewish Studies at the American Jewish University in California, and an expert on the Holocaust. Prof. Berenbaum, instrumental in the founding of numerous Holocaust museums, is president of the Berenbaum Group, a consulting firm specializing in the conceptual development of museums and the production of historical films. He is also Director of the Sigi Ziering Institute: Exploring the Ethical and Religious Implications of the Holocaust.

The following year, the festive opening of the new academic year (2010–2011) took place on October 11, 2010, at the Center for Holocaust Studies at Jagiellonian University. The guest of honor was Thomas Toivi Blatt who with 300 other prisoners participated in an uprising in October 1943 and escaped from Sobibor death camp in eastern Poland near Lublin. He delivered a moving lecture illustrated with clips from the movie *Escape from Sobibor*, a 1987 film about this event. After his lecture, for which he received a standing ovation, he answered questions. His impact on the audience, mostly young people, was enormous. Short speeches were also made by the late Professor Michał du Vall, the vice-rector of the Jagiellonian University, Professor Wiesław Kozub-Ciembroniewicz, the chairman of the Academic Council of the Center for Holocaust Studies and Dr. Jolanta Ambrosiewicz-Jacobs, the director of the Center. The vice-rector of the Jagiellonian University, Professor Andrzej Mania, also participated in the ceremony.

Another event co-sponsored by the Center for Holocaust Studies, Institute of European Studies and Yad Vashem: The Holocaust Martyrs' and Heroes' Remembrance Authority took place that same week on October 13, 2010, at the U.S. consulate in Kraków. Prof. Yehuda Bauer, a distinguished

Israeli historian, retired professor of Hebrew University of Jerusalem, an authority in the Holocaust studies, anti–Semitism and Jewish resistance during the Second World War, and author of numerous publications, participated in a videoconference. His publications include: *Anti-Semitism in Western Europe* (1988), *The Holocaust, Religion and Jewish History* (1991), and *Rethinking the Holocaust* (2001). His lecture, "The Holocaust and Genocide," was published on the Internet site of Yad Vashem in acknowledgment of Israel's being chair of the Task Force.

The Center has organized and co-organized several conferences, seminars and panel discussions also, as well as participating opening ceremonies of the European Association for Holocaust Studies. These activities include:

- Auschwitz and the Holocaust—Dilemmas and Challenges of Polish Education (October 20–24, 2008)
- Anti-Semitism and Racism in Europe—Fascist Ideology and Practice (November 9–10, 2008)
- First Conference in Memory of Rev. Stanisław Musiał (March 5, 2009)
- Seminar in Memory of Henryk Sławik and Other Righteous among the Nations (November 19–20, 2009)
- Holocaust Studies Today: The Research and Pedagogic Challenges of a Developing Field (June 12–15, 2011)
- Religion and Ideologies: Polish Perspectives and Beyond (July 3–6, 2011)
- Faces of Justice. The World in view of Holocaust and other genocides in twentieth century (July 27–30, 2011)
- How to teach about Holocaust younger generations? (July 1, 2011)—a panel discussion as part of the Jewish Culture Festival

The Center is not just focused on activities which are aimed at scholarship or reaching out to the local community. An important part of their function relates to the students who are taking courses and majoring in programs through the Center. The students are encouraged to participate in these activities and to create their own which meets their needs and interests.

In 2012 the MA students in the Center for Holocaust Studies established the Student Association, "Memento." Members of the group are engaged in the process of developing their knowledge about the Holocaust as well as dissemination of it in many ways. For instance, they participated in two study trips in 2012. In March 2012 they went to Lublin and Zamość with the Student Association from the Pedagogical University in Kraków. Then in April 2012 they visited former concentration camps with students of the political science program from Oświęcim. They also organized several study trips. In October 2012 they visited the Lublin district and studied the history of Jews in Lublin and in November of that year, they visited Auschwitz-Birkenau. "Memento" has also co-organized a few events with the CHS, such as a videoconference with Miami Dade College during Genocide Awareness Week in April 2012 and the lecture "Genealogy has more than one sense: The Jewish Genealogical Society" by Kamila Klauzińska in June 2012. The students also participated in the promotion of new specialization, "The Holocaust and Totalitarian Systems" in May 2012 during the Festival of Science and during an academic event called "Be a specialist—good places are waiting."

As these activities, events, and programs show, the Center plays an important role in researching, informing and educating about the Holocaust in Poland as well as abroad. A final important educational program that the Center organizes each year is the Summer Institute for Polish Secondary Teachers.

The Center's Role in Holocaust Education for Young People

Are educational initiatives in Poland after 1989 reconstructing or constructing the memory of the Holocaust? Even more than two decades after the fall of communism, crucial questions still remain: what is the place of the Holocaust in the education of Polish youth; how is it taught; what kinds of difficulties do teachers face; and how do they overcome them?

Teachers play a key role in education about the Holocaust. Teacher training seminars are provided not only by the Ministry of National Education and institutions working under the auspices of the Ministry (such as the National In-Service Teacher Training Center in Warsaw and regional teacher training centers) but also by other institutions and organizations such as: the Jewish Historical Institute, the Institute of National Remembrance, universities, memorial sites and NGOs. In 2000, the National In-Service Teacher Training Center (CODN) in Warsaw, in cooperation with the Yad Vashem Institute, initiated teaching about Holocaust and Polish-Jewish history to prepare Polish and Israeli teachers for youth meetings in Poland. CODN is currently called the Center for Regional Education

(ORE). The Institute of National Remembrance (IPN) provides education about the Holocaust and post-war history of Polish Jewry, developing conferences and seminars, educational workshops, outdoor and indoor exhibitions, and publishing teaching materials for teachers and students.

The Center has organized a "Teaching about the Holocaust" Summer Institute each year since 2006. Since its inception, it has operated with the cooperation of partners from Poland, Israel, and the United States. Among the many partners the two of major importance are the Illinois Holocaust Museum and Education Center in Skokie, Illinois, USA and Yad Vashem, Jerusalem, Israel. All experts invited to the Summer Institute are recognized academics and scholars from the United States, Poland and Israel. The Institute in July 2012 was co-sponsored by the Conference on Jewish Material Claims Against Germany, the Elizabeth Morse Genius Charitable Trust, the Michael H. Traison Foundation for Poland, Mrs. Shirley and Mr. Yossi Sagol and the Michael Arkes Family.

The objective of this project is to provide Polish teachers with up-to-date information on the Holocaust, familiarize participants with new educational materials, methods and strategies of teaching about the Holocaust, as well as to sensitize them to the dangers of prejudice, discrimination, racism and anti-Semitism. The partners' intention is to create a common ground for Polish teachers and educators to share ideas and strategies with other colleagues, as well as with university teachers and researchers from the USA, Israel and Poland.

Each year 50 to 60 participants take part in the Summer Institute, among them middle and high school teachers from different cities, towns and villages from all over Poland, educators from NGOs, consultants and evaluators, experts from the Teacher Training Center and university students. Since its inception in 2006, the Center has served 360 participants. Altogether there have been more than 1000 applicants demonstrating how necessary this project is.

The program of the Summer Institute includes a variety of activities, teaching strategies and methods such as lectures, presentations, workshops, discussions, Question and Answer sessions after each lecture, film viewings, and meetings with Holocaust survivors. Participants also spend one afternoon in Kazimierz, taking a guided tour around Kraków's old Jewish quarter, and the former Jewish ghetto in Podgórze. One full day is allowed for a study visit to the State Museum Auschwitz-Birkenau, a visit to the International Youth Meeting Center in Oświęcim/Auschwitz and the Auschwitz Jewish Center in Oświęcim where they tour the site and participate in lectures and presentations.

A survey of teachers who graduated from the Institute revealed some information concerning education about the Holocaust in Poland and about the effectiveness of the Institute. The subjects in which the participants teach about the Holocaust are shown in Figure 1.

While history and Polish are the most frequently mentioned subjects, the column "Others" contains a variety of initiatives and occasions such as extracurricular activities and educational projects or voluntary afternoon classes.

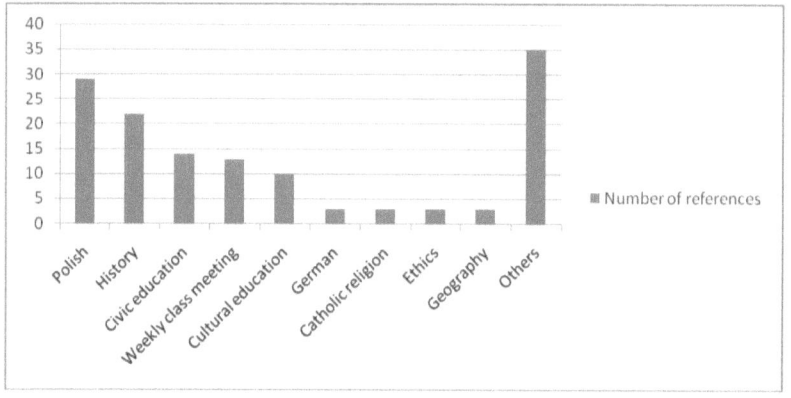

Figure 1. Subjects during which the Holocaust is taught.

Of the respondents who were surveyed, 30 had only one to five lessons (45 minutes each) within a three-year cycle at his/her disposal to cover the Holocaust. Only 10 out of 73 respondents were able to dedicate between 10 and 20 hours, while six could devote more time. An issue mentioned among respondents (16) was the negative attitude of students towards lessons on the Holocaust. Among the problems listed were anti–Semitic attitudes, lack of acceptance, and even denial, of Polish co-responsibility (especially in the local context), negative stereotypes and general lack of interest. The lack of willingness among students to face up to the negative behavior by some elements of Polish society towards Jews during World War II was revealed by a number of the teachers who participated in the study.

In order to have a short and clear indication whether teachers found their participation in the Summer Institute helpful, even from the perspective of several years after completion, we asked them to answer the following question: Did the content and didactic material offered at the Summer Institute provide you with new ideas for your daily work with students in the field of teaching about the Holocaust and Human Rights? The overwhelming majority of respondents (63 out of 75) agreed that they enriched their knowledge thanks to their participation in the Institute.

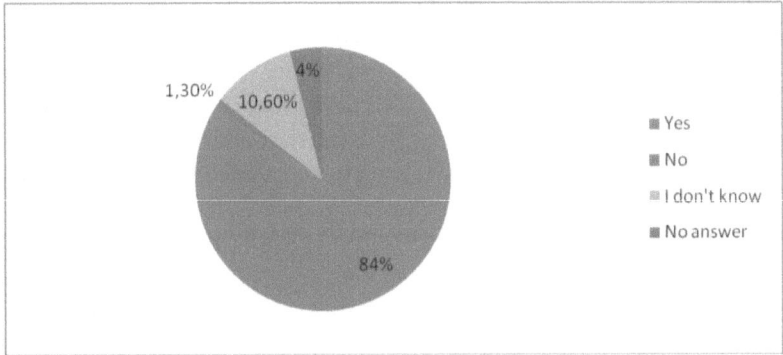

Figure 2. Usability of the material offered at the Summer Institute.

The outcomes of empirical studies related to teaching about the Holocaust clearly show the need for education, education which must not be reduced to facts and figures, but which needs to be embedded in the broader context of anti–Semitic attitudes, antidiscrimination, tolerance and respect. For that reason, the Center was created and continues it work.

Plans for the Future

One step for the near future is the preparation of a proposal for a Postgraduate Studies about the Holocaust for Professionals program at the Center for Holocaust Studies. Among the target audiences are: educational policy makers, public administration officers, teachers, teacher trainers, multipliers (those involved in train-the-trainer work), museum and memorial sites staff, NGO activists, PhD students, and academics. The rationale of the Project is to create a professional studies program for young adults, included, but not limited to teacher trainers, multipliers, university teachers and, ultimately, to create a permanent network of educators and multipliers involved in teaching, research and remembrance of the Holocaust. The main objectives of the postgraduate program are: to create opportunities for teachers, educators, employees of the memorial sites and museum and NGO activists to acquire knowledge, competence and skills in the field of research, remembrance and education about the Holocaust; to teach about preventive strategies against genocides in the context of the human rights context; and to facilitate sustainable cooperation with local non-governmental and governmental organizations in the field of education and memory of the Holocaust. One of the priorities are to use instructional technology in education about the Holocaust (distance learning, e-learning courses, create websites and database on the Internet, etc.). The students will learn how to develop the web portals, websites with ready-made e-learning lessons, educational applications available for mobile devices, as well as to construct and publish multimedia content on the web. The graduates of the program will be better prepared to organize their own courses and trainings related to the history and consequences of the Holocaust and dealing with contemporary anti–Semitism, ethnic and religious intolerance, xenophobia, extremism, neo–Nazism etc. They will improve their teaching skills by using sources, materials, methods and ideas they have been acquainted with during the program.

Conclusion

Analyzing attitudinal changes toward the Holocaust through the prism of education shows a long path leading from silence and taboo to efforts to face the trauma of the disappearance of the neighbors of ethnic Poles, with whom they shared the homeland for almost 1,000 years.

However, first we have to incorporate the Holocaust into the national collective memory, as in the case of the Henio Żytomirski project of Lublin's Grodzka Gate/Theatre NN Association, a governmental institution whose objective is to reconstruct the memory of Jewish Lublin for its contemporary non–Jewish inhabitants. Every year since 2005, the memory of the Holocaust in Lublin has had the face and name of nine-year-old Henio Żytomirski to whom school children write letters on Holocaust Memorial Day. The letters sent by the children are returned to their homes stamped with either "addressee unknown" or "no such address." The letters are collected at the entrance to the PKO S.A. Bank at 64 Krakówskie Przedmieście St. where the last known photo of Henio Żytomirski was taken in 1939. Henio was murdered in the gas chambers, probably in November 1942. This educational project is a continuation of the "Letters to the Ghetto" project, also initiated by the Center.

In Myślenice, Jews are remembered in various ways. There is a plaque on the town square, unveiled by Wspólnota Myślenice, a local NGO, after two years of conflict with the City Council. There is also a database of Jews from the towns surrounding Myślenice, Dobczyce, Sułkowice and Wiśniowa, who were murdered in the Holocaust. At the beginning this civil institution had problems persuading local city council members that deportation of Jews, Polish citizens, from Myślenice needs to be commemorated in a visible, honorable place. Recently, the attitude of local leaders has changed from indifference or opposition to active support of commemorative actions.

Numerous intergovernmental, governmental and civil society initiatives indicate that the process of asking "difficult questions" has begun, and that it may help to integrate unwanted and detached memories. An interest in Jewish culture and the memory of the Holocaust in Poland, noticeable since the 1980s, more visible after 1989 and significant from 2000 onwards, is an indicator in of an attempt to loosen the borderlines of one's own culture to incorporate the culture of the Jewish minority, as absent, intriguing, and valuable, a missing component of the past culture. However, in many towns and villages there is still an absence of memory. Recognizing and re-creating these memories are steps on the way to a deeper understanding of the tragedy and the legacy of the Holocaust. The Center for Holocaust Studies at the Jagiellonian University in Kraków is already undertaking those steps through research, education and remembrance of the Holocaust.

Websites for Further Information

Adam Mickiewicz University, Poznań, http://amu.edu.pl/en. Official website of the university; offers a program focusing on Hebrew and Judaism housed in the Asian Studies Department of the Oriental Studies Institute

Jagiellonian University, Kraków, http://www.uj.edu.pl/ (click the Union Jack icon for English version). Official website of the university; offers a comprehensive program of Jewish Studies and Holocaust Studies, including Jewish life in the Malopolska region.

Institute of Jewish Studies at Jagiellonian University, Kraków, http://www.judaistyka.uj.edu.pl/. Offers bachelor's, master's, post-diploma, and doctoral degrees in three areas of study: Jewish history; Jewish culture; and Jewish literature and Judaism (website in Polish).

    Centrum Badań Holokaustu Uniwersytetu Jagiellońskiego (Center for Holocaust Studies, Jagiellonian University), http://www.holocaust.uj.edu.pl/. Conducts research and educates, formally and informally, about the Holocaust (website in Polish).

Centrum Badań Holokaustu Uniwersytetu Jagiellońskiego Szkoła Letnia (Center for Holocaust Studies, Jagiellonian University Summer Institute), http://www.holocaust.uj.edu.pl/szkola-letnia. Displays information on the most recent Institute (website in Polish; however, there is a link at the bottom which brings up the information in English).

Maria Curie-Skłodowska University, Lublin, http://www.umcs.lublin.pl/ (click the Union Jack icon for English version), http://www.umcs.lublin.pl/articles.php?aid=1113. Official website of the university; offers courses in Jewish history and culture, and a focus on Jewish life in the Lublin region.

Center for Jewish Studies at Maria Curie-Skłodowska University, Lublin http://www.eurojewishstudies.org/redirect.php?url=http://www.umcs.lublin.pl/jednostki.php?id=1445 (Click the Union Jack icon for English version). Offers courses in Jewish history and culture with focus on Jewish life in Lublin region; offers a PhD in Jewish Studies.

University of Warsaw, Warsaw, http://www.uw.edu.pl/en/. Official website of the university; offers three programs related to Jewish Studies.

Department of Hebrew Studies at University of Warsaw, Warsaw, http://www.hebraistyka.uw.edu.pl/ (click the Union Jack icon for English version). Offers Master of Arts in Hebrew Studies.

Mordechai Anielewicz Center for the Research and Study of the History and Culture of Jews in Poland at University of Warsaw, Warsaw, http://www.ca.uw.edu.pl/ (click the Union Jack icon for English version). Offers a two-year program, the History and Culture of Jews in Poland

History and Culture of Jews in Poland University of Warsaw, Warsaw, http://www.jewish.org.pl/index.php?option=com_content&task=view&id=2558&Itemid=57. Offers a post-graduate diploma in Polish-Jewish cultural heritage and the modern Jewish experience in Poland (website in Polish).

University of Wrocław, Wrocław, http://uni.wroc.pl/ (click English for English version). Official website of the university; offers Masters' and PhD in Jewish Studies and an Individualized Interdisciplinary Humanities Study Specializing in Jewish Studies.

Centre for the Culture and Languages of the Jews at University of Wrocław, http://www.judaistyka.uni.wroc.pl/judaistyka/index.php?option=com_content&view=article&id=37&Itemid=35. Aims to educate about Jewish traditions, Jewish culture, language and history, and to revive the tradition of the Breslauer Theologisches Seminar.

University of Łódź, Łódź, http://uni.lodz.pl. Official website of the university; Jewish Studies research institution (website in Polish).

University of Rzeszów, Rzeszów, http://www.univ.rzeszow.pl/ (click English Version). Official website of the university; Jewish Studies research institution.

University of Gdansk, Gdansk, http://www.ug.gda.pl/en/. Official website of the university; Jewish Studies research institution; offers post-graduate diploma in Jewish Studies.

Centropa.org (Central Europe Center for Research and Documentation), http://www.centropa.org/. Offical website of the NGO based in Vienna and Budapest which relies on technology to preserve and disseminate information about Central and Eastern European Jewish communities.

European Association for Jewish Studies, http://eurojewishstudies.org/. Official website of an umbrella organization representing Jewish Studies programs in Europe.

Fellowships at Auschwitz for the Study of Professional Ethics (FASPE), http://www.mjhnyc.org/faspe/. Contains information for fellowships for students in professional programs designed to examine the role of various professions in Nazi Germany and the Holocaust and how this information can be used to tackle contemporary ethical issues.

Website Guide to Tolerance Education, Centre for European Studies, Jagiellonian University, Kraków, http://tolerance.research.uj.edu.pl/?lang=en. Designed for educational policy makers as well as teachers; provides educational tools, methods and approaches, a guide to programs that already exist; network for teachers and students to participate in joint projects, seminars, e-seminars and discussion lists.

Polish Association for Jewish Studies, Kraków, www.jewishstudies.pl. Offers a centralized point to promote scholarly research of Jewish history and culture; helps foster and develop cooperation with Polish and other institutions and associations.

Polish Center for Holocaust Research, Warsaw, http://www.holocaustresearch.pl/. Provides an interdisciplinary environment for researchers and scholars who are interested in the Holocaust.

State Museum at Majdanek, Lublin, http://www.majdanek.eu/?lng=1. Official website of the museum located on the site of Majdanek Concentration Camp.

House of the Wannsee Conference: Memorial and Educational Site, http://www.orte-der-erinnerung.de/en/institutions/institutions_liste/house_of_the_wannsee_conference_memorial_and_educational_site/. Official website of the museum with a library, educational programs, and the permanent exhibit "The Wannsee Conference and the Genocide of the European Jews."

Holocaust Education in Polish Public Schools

> "Today the problem with knowledge of the Holocaust is not the state of research but the scope of its dissemination: to make sure, in the interest of our civilization, that it is not niche learning for students of the teaching elite, but a part of general historical awareness."—Tych, 2009, p. 182

Since the mid–1990s the Holocaust and Holocaust education have become part of public and academic discourse in Poland. However, Ambrosewicz-Jacobs (2010) asserts that there is a lack of "effective cooperation between academia, school, and NGOs in education about the Holocaust" (p. 80) so that there is not a systematic curriculum of Holocaust and Jewish Studies pedagogy for secondary social studies teachers on how to teach these topics. Instead, there are a number of extracurricular programs which offer workshops and seminars providing Polish teachers with updated knowledge and understanding of these issues as well as up-to-date teaching methodology. This lack of a systematic Holocaust education curriculum is a result of post–World War II educational policies put in place during the era of Soviet domination.

What Is Holocaust Education?

Before looking more closely at Holocaust education in Polish schools, it is useful to look at what Holocaust education is and how it has been implemented in other places, specifically in the United States, Canada, and the United Kingdom. The Holocaust is a complex subject and is not easy to teach in any context, but the context is important in teaching about the Holocaust—who is being taught about it and why. The contrast of teaching about the Holocaust in the country in which much of it took place does and must present some different challenges and opportunities than teaching about it in other places.

As with most educational issues and topics there are differences of opinion about what should be taught and how it should be taught. Some are philosophical differences about what the outcomes of the curriculum should be while others are pedagogical differences about what constitutes effective teaching and learning. Still others question whether the topic should be taught at all. One issue that is agreed on by almost all educators of the Holocaust is that it not a developmentally appropriate topic for young children except in the most superficial way. Most school curricula are designed for middle school and/or high school students.

While Holocaust education became part of Jewish schools in the United States in the 1960s, it was slower becoming part of the public school curriculum. Interest in the Holocaust by public school teachers in the United States actually became part of a grassroots movement which led toward mandating Holocaust education in public schools in many states. However, researchers have found that even when Holocaust education is mandated, the teachers who are most interested in the topic are interested in it despite the mandate. Ironically, these teachers may not be any more effective than those for whom the Holocaust is just another subject (Fallace, 2008). The reasons for this are unclear; however, how the subject is taught, how clear the educational goals and objectives are, and to whom it is being taught, the context, may be as important as a teacher having knowledge and interest in the topic.

Holocaust education in the United Kingdom and Canada followed a slightly different path than in the United States. Antiracist education, which developed in both countries throughout the 1980s and 1990s, by and large ignored the Holocaust. Short and Reed (2004) attribute this omission to several social and political reasons, among them were post-war feelings related to British war experiences, post-war anti–Jewish sentiments, and the reluctance or inability of survivors to speak up. Holocaust education as a separate topic gradually emerged in the United Kingdom and Canada, and a strong interest in the Holocaust and Holocaust education was sparked by public interest in new events in the 1990s, such as the discovery of several Nazi war criminals, controversy over several books, including Goldhagen's book about "ordinary Germans," and popular films such as *Schindler's List* (Short and Reed, 2004). While Short and Reed (2004) point to a number of reasons for teaching about the Holocaust in their respective countries, their argument comes down to "learning about the Holocaust can constitute an educational experience that allows the democratic majority to protect itself against the consequences of racist discourse, demagoguery, and propaganda" (p. 4).

Most Holocaust educational curricula in the United States are based on using multiple approaches to meet two goals: understanding how and why the Holocaust happened, and how to prevent future genocides (Totten and Feinberg, 2001). In order to accomplish these two goals effectively, teaching of the Holocaust should not be so broad that it becomes superficial nor so narrowly focused that it loses meaning in the larger context. Since time is usually a critical factor in planning a unit, "an in-depth study of [selected] topics is generally preferable to superficial coverage of a plethora of topics" (Totten and Feinberg, 2001, p. 8), being careful not to water down the content. It is important that students understand how political, social, and economic factors came together to create this historical context and how these factors can and cannot be generalizable to other situations.

Because of the nature of the issues and events involved, teaching about the Holocaust involves cognitive as well as affective levels of learning. What is taught and how it is taught is often influenced by what the teacher knows, is interested in, and thinks is most important, as well as "the levels and the abilities of the students, the time allotted for the study, the type and amount of resources, and/or a combination of these concerns" (Totten and Feinberg, 2001, p. 6). To be the most effective, student input on what and how to study the Holocaust creates a meaningful exploration of the issues. Student-centered active engagement can help students think critically and creatively about the issues and make direct connections which help "them examine the broader historical themes in a more personal dimension" (Totten and Feinberg, 2001, p.14).

Strategies, activities, and materials must be carefully selected to be thought-provoking and to avoid oversimplifying and trivializing the Holocaust. Personal accounts contribute to an overall understanding of the Holocaust as being more than statistics or historical facts and create a connection to the real people who were affected by and who participated in the Holocaust. However, the people and groups involved should not be overgeneralized nor presented as one-dimensional. Totten (2001) is an opponent of teachers using games such as word puzzles which tend to trivialize these complex issues and simulations or role plays which he says oversimplify the issues (Totten and Feinberg, 2001; Wieser, 2001). There are other Holocaust educators who contend that "in the right hands, they [simulations] can be a powerful and effective pedagogical tool" (Fallace, 2008, p. 157). In addition, just as teachers need to be careful not to romanticize aspects of the Holocaust, bombarding the students with images of horror can have the effect of their shutting it out "to protect themselves from the ghastly images" (Totten and Feinberg, 2001, p. 17). British and Canadian teachers who were interviewed about teaching the Holocaust also expressed concern about the possibility of causing distress when exposing students to the horrors of the Holocaust (Short and Reed, 2004).

Short and Reed (2004) point out that besides the issue of traumatizing students, there are several other ethical issues that must be considered when teaching about the Holocaust. First, educators must be careful in how they present the materials so that they do not overtly or unintentionally foster anti–Semitism. Care must be taken not to imply that all of Jewish history is based in suffering and persecution. When teaching about Nazi stereotypes of the Jews, it is important that students understand "the fraudulent nature of anti–Semitic beliefs, and, more generally, to teach them about the nature of stereotyping" (Short and Reed, 2004, p. 51). An examination of the Nazi ideology of Jews as an inferior race of people, not as a religious group, who are "alien" is also important to address so students can see the fallacies of this type of prejudice and discrimination. Secondly, they point out that the amount of freedom to speak for and against the issues, whether by the teacher or the students, is governed by ethical as well as legal considerations. If the teacher remains neutral in a debate, that may imply that he/she condones what is being said or that he or she cannot make up their mind about the issues. On the other hand, if the teacher freely expresses his/her opinion, it may be perceived as coercion to believe as they do. While freedom of speech is valued in these countries, there are limits to what a teacher can say in a classroom. There have been several cases in Canada where teachers have been fined and/or dismissed for openly endorsing Nazi and anti–Semitic viewpoints. Short and Reed (2004) also view the decision on how to handle Holocaust denial as an ethical issue. Some of these ethical issues are addressed in the way in which Holocaust curricula are developed.

In a survey of British and Canadian teachers of the Holocaust, many of the respondents said that they focused on racism rather anti–Semitism (Short and Reed, 2004). However, Totten and Feinberg (2001) point out that "[t]here is a critical need to examine both the uniqueness of the Holocaust as well as its universal nature" (p. 18). They contend that it is important to teach about anti–Semitism specifically not just using the general terms racism, prejudice, and discrimination when teaching about the Holocaust. "[C]onnections between the historical and moral issues of the Holocaust and contemporary life" [are important to make, but] "it is pedagogically unsound to equate the Holocaust with any and all civil and human rights violations" (Totten and Feinberg, 2001, p. 19). Other educators contend that teaching about the Holocaust should be presented in a social justice and social activism framework which is relevant to the contemporary world. Some educators acknowledge that it may not be possible to eliminate hatred, racism and anti–Semitism, but that Holocaust education can "inoculate the generality of the population against racist and anti–Semitic propaganda and thereby restrict its appeal to a disaffected and politically insignificant rump" (Short and Reed, 2004).

In addition, there are those who contend that Holocaust education has no place in the public school curriculum (Short and Reed, 2004). Lionel Kochan, a British historian, asserts that study of war and violence does nothing to prevent them. Furthermore, he contends that teaching about the Holocaust in schools gives young people, Jewish and non–Jew alike, a sense that Jews are perpetual victims. His final contention is that future perpetrators of such atrocities will see the Holocaust as a precedent to be followed. Peter Novick (1999), an American historian, also spoke out against teaching about the Holocaust in schools. One of his arguments is that the barbarity of the Holocaust is too far removed from normal life for meaningful lessons to be learned from it, and he contends that many of the lessons taught in Holocaust education are "empty" and "useless." He also argues that by setting the Holocaust as the "benchmark" against which oppression and barbarism are measured, it trivializes any other kind of violence and atrocity as not being "as bad" as the Holocaust. Short and Reed (2004) respond to these critics of teaching about the Holocaust by saying that their arguments reinforce the need for good and effective Holocaust education. What that looks like and how it is implemented depends on the context and the goals and objectives which best meet the needs of that context.

Wieser (2001) is a Holocaust educator from the United States who agrees with Totten and Feniberg (2001) about the importance of basing the curriculum on teaching about anti–Semitism. In his curriculum, he identifies five topics that should be included in any serious study of the Holocaust. He states that a proper introduction of the topic would begin with an examination of the roots of anti–Semitism in Christian doctrine and how these teachings created a climate in which the Nazi policies were created and carried out. He identifies the second topic as post–World War I, specifically 1918 to 1933, which gives students the necessary historical background information to understand how Hitler and the Nazis gained power. The third area to cover is 1933 to 1939, what he calls "Toward the Final Solution," so that students can see how "the destruction of Europe's Jews evolved through stages and that it involved much more than an attempt to simply eliminate Jews from the German economy and society" (Wieser, 2001, p. 65). The next topic, the Final Solution, is the one that is most often covered in studies of the Holocaust. This section should cover not only the camps, but the roles of the perpetrators and the actions that led up to the implementation of the Final Solution. Wieser (2001) says that the final topic that should be covered is the role of bystanders, those who lived in the countries where the atrocities took place and other countries which did or did not act to prevent and/or stop the Holocaust.

In the United Kingdom, a packaged curriculum which is often used, *Lessons of the Holocaust,* follows a similar pattern (Short and Reed, 2004). It includes content material, lessons, and various types of supplementary materials. The first section of the curriculum looks at pre-war Jewish communities in Europe, the origins of anti–Semitism, and its role in Nazi ideology. The second section, "Nazi Germany's Anti-Jewish Policy: From Exclusion to Expulsion, 1933–1939" covers topics such as the Nuremberg Laws of 1935 and attempted Jewish emigration from Germany. The third part focuses on the years 1939 to 1942 and on the establishment of the ghettos and death camps. The final section is called "The Final Solution, 1942 to 1945" and includes the Allies' role related to the Holocaust, "the Nazi obsession with annihilating the Jews of Europe ... and the complicity of the German people" (Short and Reed, 2004, p. 91). The curriculum ends with some information about the aftermath of the Holocaust and some connection to more recent genocides.

In addition to identifying the topics which he thinks are the most important to cover, Wieser (2001) also addresses materials selection and pedagogical considerations. He points out that in the United States there are a wide variety of books, films, and other supplementary materials, as well as packaged curricular materials available. There is also a wide range of primary documents which are easily accessible, including memos, letters, political cartoons, other artwork, and photographs. However he cautions that the teacher must be selective and choose materials that are accurate, appropriate, and relevant for their teaching situation, and choose appropriate strategies for using each type of material.

One controversial aspect of content and materials selection is whether or not to include information on Holocaust denial. One group of educators says "absolutely not" (Novick, 1999; Totten and Feinberg, 2001). They assert that doing so gives credence to a group of "kooks." However, another group of educators, especially outside the United States, point out that Holocaust deniers are not just fringe groups of neo–Nazis. Holocaust denial is not uncommon in Europe (Bruchfeld, 2000; de Laine, 1997; Leigh, 1997; Short and Reed, 2004) and has spread throughout the Arab and Muslim world (Matar, 2001, Short and Reed, 2004). These educators think that ignoring the Holocaust deniers is a failure to address this serious issue.

Wieser (2001) suggests that the most effective way to teach about the Holocaust is through integrating it into other coursework, such as civics classes or English literature, an approach endorsed by Drew (1991). She states, "The integration of history and literature, by placing the individual story within its historical framework, can further the understanding of the difficult concepts involved in the study of atrocity" (p. 128). The skillful use of literature and poetry from or about the Holocaust can provide opportunities for students to engage with the issues of the Holocaust in a way that promotes critical thinking and reflection. An advantage to integrating history and literature is that it can provide more time to cover the topics in more depth so that students can engage in a meaningful way. Using primary source material in a variety of ways, examining the impact of laws passed by the Nazis, analyzing language used in Nazi documents, using dramatic works and music of the time which contextualize the history, analyzing the messages in Nazi propaganda posters and patriotic music, and contextualizing the events through extensive use of timelines are all strategies that can help students gain a meaningful understating of the events leading up to the Holocaust and the Holocaust itself (Chartock, 2001; Werb, 2001; Wieser, 2001, Zatzman, 2001).

Many Holocaust educators (Drew, 1991; Totten and Feinberg, 2001; Wieser, 2001) agree that using first-person accounts, such as diaries and letters from the time, or survivor accounts, written after the war, are one of the most powerful and effective ways of teaching about the Holocaust. To give students a well-rounded understanding of the Holocaust, a variety of accounts in a variety of formats should be used. However, they caution that the accounts must be contextualized in the historical events of the time, should avoid creating or perpetuating stereotypes, and they should not be used for shock value or exploitation of the students' emotions. Open discussion and debriefing are important aspects of teaching about the Holocaust. Totten and Feinberg (2001) say that "[o]pportunities to discuss and vent their thoughts and feelings should be interwoven throughout the study" (p. 117).

With the advent of the Internet, access to materials about the Holocaust, like to other topics, has increased. The most commonly accessed by teachers of the Holocaust are the numerous websites for organizations, links to lessons plans and materials and films on *YouTube*. As with all materials, there are sites which are well done and others that have serious shortcomings. In addition, the Internet has created a venue for a proliferation of sites maintained by hate groups and groups which deny the Holocaust. All materials, including those found on the Internet should be subjected to careful scrutiny for accuracy and appropriateness before using them with students.

In addition to Holocaust education which is presented in schools, Holocaust museums and memorials around the world also provide educational opportunities for school age children, offering exhibits and presentations which supplement what they are learning in school. Displays and exhibits vary from museum to museum and the quality of their educational value should be carefully examined by teachers before taking their students on such a field trip (Short and Reed, 2004). The European Union Agency for Fundamental Rights (FRA, 2010) suggests that there are seven questions to ask when deciding to visit a site, whether memorial site or museum.

- What kind of pre-visit preparation and follow-up activities does it offer?
- Does it use participant-oriented approaches?
- Does it use victim biographies?
- Does it use multiperspective approaches?
- What role does authenticity play in the educational process?
- What are the role and quality of guides and other educational staff?
- How much time is available for educational activities?

These questions were based on information gathered from focus groups made up of students and teachers.

As this overview of Holocaust education illustrates, teaching about the Holocaust is complex. Considerations of content, materials, and strategies have to all be made whether creating a curriculum or one lesson, and the choices must be made with the educational context in mind.

Holocaust Education in Poland

Despite being home to many European Jews prior to World War II and in spite of the brutal genocide of the Holocaust being especially severe in the territories of Eastern Europe such Poland, the Ukraine, and other republics of the former Soviet Union, the Holocaust was a "blind spot" in Soviet-era textbooks (Zimmerman and Sukovata, 2009). Sometimes traditional school texts mentioned that 11 million Soviet citizens were killed in the Nazi death camps, but they never specified that 6 million were Jews. Soviet schools did not teach about the Nazi policy of state anti–Semitism and the systematic destruction of the Jews. Soviet state policy on the Holocaust was to ignore it or to report it with falsification and distortions which supported their agenda. This state-induced ignorance about the history of Jews in Eastern Europe and the Holocaust created a climate in which people were reluctant to talk about and ask questions about events they knew had taken place in their communities and in their countries. Into the 1990s, textbooks often inferred that only the criminal element collaborated with the Nazis, and that the Jews were passive participants, nonresistant victims, in the Holocaust.

The end of Soviet domination and communism in Eastern Europe in the late 1980s and early 1990s brought with it political and economic changes, altering society and culture in those countries. No longer isolated behind the Iron Curtain, and with the promise of access to greater resources offered by European Union (EU) membership, these countries have been vying to take their places in the global marketplace of the twenty-first century. Educational reforms have been one of the priorities for gaining this access. Updated methodologies and pedagogic strategies have been part of the educational reform, as well as a shift of focus on content.

This end to isolation also opened inquiry into historical events that had been previously ignored. Before World War II, most of these countries had sizable Jewish populations, as well as other minority groups targeted by the Nazis. Many of the extermination camps were located in these countries, particularly Poland. After World War II, most of these countries either ignored the Holocaust, treating it as a side note to World War II, or used it as a means of educating about the communist struggle against fascism. Although more than 60 years have passed since the end of World War II, the foundations of the Holocaust, ethnocentrism, racism, and anti–Semitism, have not disappeared.

The forced amnesia about the Holocaust by the Soviet-controlled government in Poland has had the added effect of placing Polish anti–Semitism as an essential part of the Polish character in the minds of many who lived outside the Iron Curtain. By suppressing the role that Poles played in the Holocaust as well as the struggles they underwent and the immense losses they suffered during the war, Poles and non–Poles alike have an unclear view of what happened in Poland during World War II. An increased examination of and exposure to the events, people, and places can clarify what happened and why and what the implications for the future are. Educational policy makers in Poland have realized that education about the Holocaust is essential and can be the basis for teaching a fundamental understanding of what creates and maintains such hatred and abuse, so they have reconsidered how they address Holocaust education in their primary and secondary schools, as well as at the university level.

As mentioned earlier, since the mid–1990s the Holocaust and Holocaust education have become part of public and academic discourse in Eastern European countries due to increased availability of the Soviet archives, more openness in society, and academic and cultural contacts of Eastern European scholars with colleagues from American and Western European universities. As discussed in the previous section, several independent centers and programs of Holocaust Studies have emerged. However, in some Eastern European countries, programs on the Holocaust or genocide studies, or Jewish studies, in general, are still being established. Even in those areas where there are programs, scholars assert that many teachers in these former Soviet-bloc countries do not have the necessary knowledge and experience to teach about the Holocaust.

Since 1999, Holocaust education has been required at the secondary level in Polish public schools in the eighth grade and twelfth grade. Since that time a number of curricula and textbooks have been published which address World War II and include references to subjects such as Polish collaboration. In 2003, a textbook, *The Holocaust: Understanding Why?* was published for use by Polish teachers, and a number of schools sponsor visits to memorial sites and death camps for their students. In 2009, the curriculum was reformed so that the Holocaust as a separate topic is no longer taught in middle school, but it is integrated into the Polish language and literature curriculum and the civics curriculum.

Despite being required to teach about the Holocaust, many teachers are unsure how to approach the subject, because they were never taught about it themselves. In addition, while the Holocaust is covered in the curriculum to some degree, the role of Jews in Polish history is still a largely unexamined area at the secondary level. According to Kubiszyn (2012) the explanation of Jews in Polish history is limited to their role as a minority which impacted the Polish economy throughout its history, a narrow stereotypical perspective of a diverse and influential group.

Programs for Secondary Teachers: An Overview

While university students who want to be secondary social studies teachers have access to a range of content courses, including courses covering the roles of Jews in Polish history and the Holocaust, there is little available in Holocaust and Jewish Studies pedagogy, how to teach these topics. To fill this gap, however, there are numerous special programs offered for teachers which are often financed by grants and outside groups rather than the school or the Polish educational system. Teacher workshops and seminars which provide Polish teachers with updated knowledge and understanding as well as up-to-date teaching methodology help teachers better address the issues. Through workshops and conferences, teachers receive training which provides them, not only with new knowledge and understanding of the Holocaust and its causes and results, but have also helped them incorporate interactive teaching strategies into their practice. The Auschwitz-Birkenau State Museum and the Pedagogical University in Kraków offer a postgraduate program called "Totalitarianism, Nazism, and the Holocaust" which focuses primarily on content. However, it also teaches some strategies for teaching about countering stereotypes and prejudice. A few other organizations that have developed educational activities that teachers have found useful are: the Polish Institute of National Remembrance, the International Centre for Education on Auschwitz and the Holocaust, the Centre for Education Development (CED), and the Summer Holocaust Institute for Secondary Teachers at Jagiellonian University.

The Polish Institute of National Remembrance is one such organization. Established in 1998 by an act of the Polish Parliament, it began operations in 2000. One of its goals is public education which is accomplished through a variety of activities aimed at supporting and disseminating historical knowledge, including publications and exhibitions as well as seminars, lectures, and workshops. The Public Education Office of the Institute of National Remembrance is located in Warsaw, and it coordinates the work of eleven sites in cities across Poland.

The International Centre for Education on Auschwitz and the Holocaust was created by the Polish government in 2005 and is located at Auschwitz. Its mission is to provide a wide range of educational activities. The activities range from online courses to teaching young people about the Holocaust through hand-on activities. Conferences, seminars and lectures aimed at a broad audience also provide a variety of educational experiences.

The Centre for Education Development (CED), located in Warsaw, is a national teacher training institution was established in 2010. The Centre has two main objectives:

- providing educational support to schools to ensure quality assurance in education
- providing professional development for teachers to help them stay up-to-date with changes in the educational system

They have supported numerous projects and activities related to Holocaust Education. For example, in 2011 they organized a joint project with Yad Vashem for Polish teachers. In 2012 they coordinated a joint project for Polish with the Holocaust Museum in Washington, DC. In March 2012 they organized a four-day conference in Paris for regional coordinators and Polish teachers, "How Do You Teach the Holocaust?"

These and other such programs have provided much-needed curricular support to Polish teachers of the Holocaust. The final program that will be looked at here is the Summer Holocaust Institute for Secondary Teachers offered through the Jagiellonian University in Kraków, Poland. An examination of this program offers an in-depth look into one way in which Polish secondary teachers receive curricular support.

Jagiellonian University's Summer Holocaust Institute for Secondary Teachers

In 2006 the Jagiellonian University in Kraków, Poland, began offering a program for secondary teachers called the Summer Holocaust Institute for Secondary Teachers, which has been primarily funded by the Conference on Jewish Material Claims Against Germany and American sponsors such as the Illinois Holocaust Museum. The Institute is offered under the auspices of the Center for Holocaust Studies which is part of the School of International and Political Studies, inaugurated in 2008 as an outgrowth of the Research Group for Holocaust Studies which had been established in 1996 in the Centre for European Studies of the Jagiellonian University. The Center's mission is to conduct research about the Holocaust and to educate formally and informally about it. The Summer Holocaust Institute for Secondary Teachers' team includes professors from various disciplines as well as doctoral students at Jagiellonian University who have research and teaching interests related to the Holocaust. The purpose of this Institute is to give Polish secondary teachers up-to-date materials and strategies for teaching about the

Holocaust. Teachers who have attended the workshops and the Institute provide some anecdotal evidence of the state of these issues among Polish teachers.

During summer 2011, I was invited to conduct two workshops at the institute. Most of the 60 participants at the Institute were high school and middle school history teachers. However, one woman I talked to was an English teacher, one was a librarian, one a Polish teacher, and another woman was a friend of one of the presenters. I asked several of the participants why they were interested in attending the Institute. Most of them said that they wanted to broaden their knowledge about Jewish culture and about the Holocaust. Several also said that they wanted to learn techniques and strategies for teaching about the Holocaust.

Some of the teachers are especially interested in the Holocaust because they live in cities or towns that prior to World War II had Jewish populations. A couple of the teachers said that they were from Łódź, a large city in central Poland which had a large thriving Jewish population before the Holocaust. The first ghetto was established in Łódź and the Jewish population was quickly eliminated. One teacher who came from Kielce, the site of a massacre of Jews shortly after the end of World War II, said he wanted to understand Jewish history and culture better, as well as what happened in his city.

One of the teachers explained that one of her objectives is to try to examine and understand Polish attitudes toward the Holocaust, then and now. She thinks it is important to understand the social and political mechanisms that created the Holocaust. She said that developing a better understanding of anti–Semitism, in general, and becoming acquainted with individual experiences of the Holocaust will help her better understand these issues.

Another teacher lives in a small town in which a large percentage of the population was Jewish before the Holocaust. Because of her own personal interest in the subjects of the Holocaust and Jewish culture, she has already engaged in a project with her students called "Krzepice—two cultures-common memory" in which they studied the history of Jews of Krzepice, her town. She and her students have also taken on the project of caring for the Jewish cemetery there. Jewish cemeteries all over Poland are in disrepair, either through neglect, through deliberate destruction before and after the war, or both.

One teacher mentioned her desire to learn how to teach young people about these difficult issues. She is working on a tolerance project through the European Union and she hopes to integrate information about the Holocaust into her project.

Several teachers spoke about their interest in broadening their knowledge not only for themselves, but specifically so they could teach their students more effectively. Several said that they not only wanted to be able to teach their students the facts about these difficult topics, but to also to help them have respect and compassion for others. They expressed the need for strategies and methods of teaching students about stereotypes, prejudice, and anti–Semitism as issues that impact human relationships. One teacher felt that the philosophical question: How could people do this to other people? was key in helping her students develop this type of understanding. Another said that through such education her students could become more sensitive to the suffering of others.

Another teacher explained that if a teacher does not approach the topic carefully, the Holocaust can be construed as banal and superficial. She wants her students to realize the depth of human suffering by learning to respect individual experience. She also said that she is looking for "the thread which was broken." She wants to see Poland again become a multicultural country where everyone is welcome.

Robert Szuchta is a Polish secondary teacher who often presents at the Institute and helped develop the Holocaust curriculum for Polish schools. His article "Against silence and indifference: Why teach about the Holocaust: The reflections of a teacher" highlights the complexity of Poland's history and underlines the significance of Holocaust education for Polish teachers and students.

> I teach about the Holocaust in order to pass on knowledge about Polish history, not allowing myself to forget, that for several hundred years Jews lived among us, they built their own unique culture, enriching Polish culture. It is difficult to explain Polish history without talking about the place and role of her Jews. If I omit this part of Polish history, pupils receive knowledge that is fragmentary and incomplete, which means that the picture of the past will be false. Polish history is the state and social history of many ethnicities, the achievements of many nations settling on Polish soil, among them the Jews. This world ceased to exist over sixty years ago, when it was interrupted by the Holocaust. Therefore I teach about the Holocaust that took place on Polish soil against Polish will, but with their participation. It gives birth to questions about diverse attitudes towards extermination. How did the Poles behave towards the extermination of their Jewish fellow citizens—neighbors? How did other communities of Europe, and the world behave? What was known? What was done? Although this problem was and is repeatedly raised in literature on the subject, it is not always explicitly evaluated. That does not release me from reflecting and discussing with pupils these difficult, and for many, painful issues [Szuchta, 2005, p. 56].

However, he goes on to say that he is not interested in teaching about the Holocaust only as a Polish issue, but also as a broader issue affecting all of humanity.

> Finally, the most obvious reason for teaching about the Holocaust is that it is an element not only of Jewish history, but of universal history and Polish history ... I would like, when each pupil finishes school for them to have basic knowledge about the largest possible amount of concepts and for him/her to understand them, as he/she is entering adulthood with the baggage of general education.... Teaching about [the Holocaust], I try to make my pupils aware of the risks which accompany intolerance, nationalism, xenophobia and totalitarianism. It seems to me, that the best way is not only to provide pupils with basic facts about the Holocaust, but to make them aware of and analyze the mechanism which made it possible. I am convinced that to educate a person to be open, tolerant, sensitive to suffering, respectful of the life and dignity of the other person, we should give him/her fair knowledge of those times in which people are deprived of their dignity and life in an inhumane way. Even though teaching about the Holocaust is not an easy task, it is worth accepting this hardship with the hope, that we will at least change ourselves, others and the world a little, making it less cruel and more bearable. This is what I believe [Szuchta, 2005, p. 58].

Many others who organize and participate in these workshops, seminars, and institutes believe as Szuchta (2005) does that learning and teaching about the Holocaust and about Jewish life in Poland is an important undertaking. It is not by accident that the Summer Institute coincides with the Jewish Cultural Festival in Kraków. Attendees are encouraged to take part in the festival to add another dimension to their learning. This intertwining of formal learning and informal learning creates a breadth and depth to the experience that would not be accomplished otherwise. The participants of such programs are better prepared as teachers and as citizens of Poland to pass along their knowledge to their students and their communities. Although programs at universities serve an important function in providing academic exploration, research and scholarship in the fields of Jewish Studies and the Holocaust, what is going on at the secondary education level in Poland is important for the development of a citizenry which acknowledges a difficult past and moves to forward to understanding and adapting so that nothing like this happens again.

The next essay is written by a Polish academic who has been instrumental in bringing about Holocaust education for Polish students and teachers. Dr. Piotr Trojański, a historian, is affiliated with the Pedagogical University of Kraków, and serves as an academic advisor for the International Center for Education about Auschwitz and the Holocaust at the Auschwitz-Birkenau

State Museum in Oświęcim. His essay examines the creation of the background against his work has taken place and the development of the Holocaust Education curriculum for Polish secondary teachers and students.

The Legacy of the Holocaust in Poland and Its Educational Dimension
by Piotr Trojański

Dear Teachers:
I am a survivor of a concentration camp. My eyes saw what no person should witness. Gas chambers built by learned engineers. Children poisoned by educated physicians. Infants killed by trained nurses. Women and babies shot and burned by high school and college graduates.
So I am suspicious of education. My request is: Help your students become more human. Your efforts must never produce learned monsters, skilled psychopaths, or educated Eichmanns. Reading, writing, and arithmetic are important only if they serve to make our children more human [Ginott, 1972, p. 17].

This quotation by Chaim Ginott, a Holocaust survivor who wrote this letter to teachers at the school where he became principal after the war, became the motto of the first Polish school curriculum for teaching about the Holocaust. I decided to begin my essay with this quote because it shows the idea of how the Holocaust is taught in Poland, and how I believe it should be taught everywhere (Szuchta and Trojański, 2000).

Introduction

In my essay I am going to discuss the issue of the history of teaching about the Holocaust in Poland. In order to present it I will try to answer two general questions. First, what was the legacy of the past and how did it influence the perception of and the way of teaching the Holocaust in Polish schools? Second, how has the way of presenting the Holocaust in history curricula and textbooks changed over the last sixty years? Finally, I will show current trends in Holocaust education in Poland, its opportunities and obstacles.

Before I go to the heart of the matter I would like to make a few general remarks regarding the terminology used in teaching about the Holocaust in Poland, and its significance for Polish society. In Poland the terms: "teaching about the Holocaust" and "Holocaust education" are relatively new. They have been in use for about 15 years at this time, and I am afraid that there are still people who do not know yet what they mean exactly. Until the beginning of 1990s the word "Holocaust" was not used in Polish education at all. For many years, the most common term referring to what happened to the Jews during the war was "the extermination of the Jews." Although "teaching about the Holocaust" and "Holocaust education" are getting more and more common now, other terms such as Zagłada (the Polish word for annihilation) and Szoa (Shoah), which is popular in religious commentaries, are still in use.

The Holocaust is a very important event in Polish history. Its significance arises from the fact that it mostly happened in German-occupied Poland and that half of its victims where Polish Jews. In pre-war Poland Jews represented about 10 percent of the total population. Poland was the center of the European Jewry with one of world's largest Jewish communities (3.5 million people). Despite growing anti–Semitism, Poland was the country where Jewish cultural, religious, economic and political life thrived. Now there are only about 10,000 Jews living in Poland. The world in which there were local synagogues, where Yiddish could be heard, where rabbis and Jewish traders could be seen, is almost completely unknown to the younger generation. That world disappeared seventy years ago leaving only a few traces—mainly empty synagogues, museums, monuments, cemeteries and memorial sites.

During the Holocaust Poland lost nearly all of its Jewish citizens and involuntarily became a graveyard not only for Polish, but also for European, Jewry. As Prof. Feliks Tych (1999) noted, "This makes the Polish people moral and physical custodians of the sites of the Holocaust" (p. 97). In completing this mission education can and should play a very important role. Therefore teaching students about the Holocaust in Poland has particular importance. Holocaust education is not only limited to commemoration of those who perished but it is also an attempt to revive them in the memory and awareness of the Polish people.

Although it seems that it should be obvious, such a conviction was not always predominant. This situation started to alter along with the political changes that came in Poland after 1989. Consequently, it allowed for the Holocaust to take an appropriate place in school education and to raise the level of awareness of the Poles concerning this issue.

Destruction and Reconstruction of Holocaust Memory

Just after World War II, the Communist government marginalized the Holocaust, using it almost exclusively as a tool of their so-called "antifascist" propaganda. The state authorities instrumentalized the Holocaust in order to defame the anti–Communist underground, specifically accusing the Polish Home Army (Armia Krajowa) of collaboration with the German occupiers in the persecution of the Jews. In the following years, the scale of the extermination was suppressed or the number of victims manipulated. Due to ignoring the truth and manipulating the ethnicity of victims, the Communist authorities succeeded in underestimating the significance of the Holocaust in Polish society (Steinlauf, 1997; Szuchta, 2008).

The most visible example of such a policy was the case of Auschwitz Museum, where erasing the memory of the Holocaust began at the beginning of the 1950s. It should be emphasized that from the very beginning of its existence Auschwitz Museum became an arena of clashes of various visions and ideas for commemorating the victims. In the act passed by the Polish parliament instituting the Museum it was decreed, that "the grounds of the former Nazi concentration camp in Oświęcim together with all the buildings and equipment located there shall be preserved for all time as a Monument to the Martyrdom of the Polish Nation and Other Nations" (Lachendro, 2007, p. 71). Jews, who constituted the vast majority of the victims of this camp were pushed into the category of "other nations." This statement determined the character of the place and the ways of commemorating the victims of Auschwitz for many years. Emphasizing the martyrdom of the Poles and other nations, together with diminishing the significance of the majority of the victims, that is the Jews, became a standard followed for many years by the exhibitions and expositions that marginalized extermination of the Jews. It should be emphasized however, that neither the State Museum, nor the Polish government, ever explicitly denied that the vast majority of victims at Auschwitz were Jews. However, this fact was not emphasized; nor did it designate Auschwitz in any distinctive way. Simply put, "Jews were usually included among the so-called 'martyrs' of Auschwitz and regarded as citizens of Poland, the Netherlands, France, Hungary, Greece or one of the many other countries under Nazi occupation" (Huener, 2003, p. 29). This policy was a result of government directives that obliged the administration of the Museum to vigilance in order, as it was put,

> not to separate out ethnic issues and above all the Jewish issue; not to give an impression, that Auschwitz was a place of death almost exclusively of the

Jews, but contrary, to emphasize that the enemy of the Jews was at the same time the enemy of the Poles and others [Wóycicka, 2009, p. 325].

That is why in publications on Auschwitz Jewish themes were not frequent, whereas the Polish and international character of the camp was emphasized (Kucia, 2005; Świebocka, 2000; Trojański, 2012).

The actions undertaken at that time by the Polish government had an immediate connection with the political situation in the world, and especially with the policy of the Soviet Union directed against Zionism. "Zionism" was used as a code word in the Soviet Union to mean "Jews" who at that time began to be suspected of being "agents of Western imperialism." This policy reached its apex in the beginning of the 1950s when political trials against people of Jewish origin took place in the USSR and Czechoslovakia. After that time, depictions of Jewish motifs in the exhibitions at the Auschwitz museum were limited to a minimum; at the same time it was officially proclaimed that mostly Polish citizens perished in KL Auschwitz, which *implicitly* meant non–Jewish Poles (Zaremba, 2001).

The thaw that followed Stalin's death brought about fundamental changes in the Museum. In 1955 a new main exhibition was composed. Its form was determined not only by political changes but also by the activities of the International Auschwitz Committee established in 1952. Its members emphasized the international character of Auschwitz and suggested that the new exposition should reflect differences in remembrance of various categories of victims, citizens of various countries. This policy found its manifestation in the unveiling of the International Monument to Victims of Fascism at Birkenau in 1967 and in creating the so-called "national expositions" presenting the histories of inhabitants of various countries deported to Auschwitz. Among them there was a "Jewish pavilion" opened in April 1968, which was closed soon after, however, due to the anti–Semitic and anti–Israel policy of the Communist authorities (Kapralski, 2011). Later it was made accessible only occasionally and almost exclusively for foreign visitors. After being widely criticized the "Jewish pavilion" was renovated and reopened in 1978 (Young, 1993).

In this way a specific process of polonization and internationalization of Auschwitz victims took place, which exerted a negative influence on the awareness of Poles regarding the Holocaust. A similar process took place in relation to other death and concentration camps.

Only in 1990 could Polish historians publicly admit that about 1.1–1.5 million people perished in KL Auschwitz-Birkenau and 90 percent of them were Jewish. Before then the counts presented by the government were much bigger and were used to emphasize the number of non–Jewish, especially Polish, victims. That is why for many Poles at that time it was difficult to accept the true numbers, because they thought that it was the Polish people who were the major national group that had perished in Auschwitz.

The intentional and conscious manipulation of historical facts by the Communist authorities strongly influenced the way in which the Holocaust has been perceived by Polish society and, consequently, what role it played in the public memory and collective identity of Poles. After the war, the Holocaust, or rather its key symbol, Auschwitz, was used to build Polish national identity in relation to its most "significant others," mainly the Germans that were generally identified with the Nazis, who committed crimes against the Polish people (Mach, 2006). Due to those actions the image of the suffering Pole oppressed by the Germans became rooted very deeply in the Polish mentality. It became almost an archetype, one of the principle elements of Polish national identity. It was promoted from the top by the Communist authorities in the sixties in school curricula and in party propaganda, in symbolic representations (monuments) and in historical commentaries fashionable at the time, devoted to the war and occupation. It was to be the key factor of the integration of Polish society with the communist authority, presenting itself as a national movement liberating the Poles from the German occupation during the war (Zaremba, 2001). For the following twenty years, the memory of the Jewish tragedy, together with the entire Jewish-Polish history, was consequently erased from the public memory and historical awareness of Poles.

Such an image of the Holocaust was formed by an entirely centralized educational school system. The use of the past for political purposes made it very difficult to understand what had really happened during the war. Furthermore, the distinct instrumentalization of the Holocaust, which was being used in order to achieve short-term political goals, depreciated and undermined its significance. Two post-war generations of Poles grew up without receiving accurate knowledge about this event, as well as about the Jewish contribution to the Polish and European heritage, neither in school nor in the media.

Therefore, today, as Prof. Zdzisław Mach (2006) noted

> Thinking about the Holocaust, the Poles tend to ... think of themselves as victims of it, or perhaps rather victims of another Nazi crime—the genocide of Polish people, which eventually was to lead to the total destruction of the nation. But there is no place in this thinking for any element of Polish guilt.... This is also why Poles find it difficult to accept the uniqueness of

the Jewish Holocaust. The interpretation, common among the Jewish people, of the Holocaust as unique genocide, unparalleled in human history, would mean that the Polish suffering cannot be compared with it [p. 101].

It is worth mentioning that during the Communist period there was not only no place in education for the Holocaust, but also for dozens of other important events from contemporary Polish history which did not reflect the vision of the past promoted by the Communist authorities. We should remember, however, that Poland at that time was not a sovereign state and the Communists for many years sustained the notion of the homogeneity of Polish society. Consequently, studies of Jewish history and the dissemination of their results, as well as teaching in schools about these issues, were difficult or even sometimes impossible.

This situation began to change in the 1980s when the generation of "Solidarity" demanded the true picture of the past, including the history of Polish Jews. Gradually, thanks to the intellectuals who had kept this memory alive, through oftentimes clandestine means, the truth about the Holocaust began to enter into social discourse. The Communist authorities allowed an open debate about Polish-Jewish relations during the war. This is when public discussion on the issue of Polish shared responsibility for Jewish tragedy started. It was also the beginning of the debate on Polish anti–Semitism before, during, and after World War II.

In the long process of "restoring memory" by Polish society, two events played important roles. In 1985 Polish state television broadcast parts of the acclaimed documentary film, *Shoah,* by the French journalist, Claud Lanzman. It was received negatively by Poles in the country and abroad. Two years later, the well-known Catholic periodical, *Tygodnik Powszechny,* published an essay, "The Poor Poles Watch the Ghetto," by Jan Błoński (1987), a professor of literature at the Jagiellonian University. Those works began a heated public debate, lasting practically until today, on the subject of Polish attitudes towards the Holocaust. This was also the beginning of the discussion on contemporary Polish anti–Semitism.

The debate has provided many Polish people with an opportunity to learn the truth about Polish-Jewish relations during the war. Public awareness was heightened by the knowledge that, although the Poles were not the instigators of the Holocaust, they displayed a range of responses: some hid Jews at great personal risk; others turned them over to the Nazis; and many were indifferent. For many Polish people this information was a shock because earlier the prevailing view was that Poles helped Jews in the vast majority of cases. This reaction was also the result of the former Communist authorities not allowing an open public discussion on that issue.

The situation changed after 1989 along with the political transformation of Poland. For Polish society it meant a new opening of the debate on Polish-Jewish historical relations that consequently resulted in giving the Holocaust an appropriate place in the public consciousness and in discussions by Poles.

However, before that happened, another decade had to go by. The commemoration of the 50th anniversary of the liberation of the camp at Auschwitz in 1995 played a very important role in that process. Then, thanks to the media, accurate and true information about Auschwitz and the Holocaust began to penetrate the majority of Polish society. One year later, in 1996, there was another commemoration that also exerted an influence on the level of Polish awareness with regards to Polish-Jewish relations. That was the commemoration of the 50th anniversary of the Kielce pogrom which showed the public the level of moral devastation that the Holocaust had on Polish society after the war.

Those events prepared the ground for the last big debate on Polish-Jewish relations from the war which was provided by the publication of the book *Neighbors* by Jan Tomasz Gross in 2000. This book revealed the tragedy of the Jews in a small town in eastern Poland, Jedwabne, where an anti-Jewish pogrom led by the Polish inhabitants took place in 1941. On one hand the Jedwabne debate showed that the topic of Polish-Jewish relations is still not easy issue, full of emotions and controversies. On the other hand it proved that Polish society had grown up and was ready for such challenges which required them to face the past. The involvement in the debate of many intellectuals, journalists and politicians resulted in transmitting the discussion into the ordinary people what consequently heightened the level of awareness of Polish society with regards to the Holocaust.[1]

Keeping in mind the transformation of Polish society discussed above one can say that today the memory of the Holocaust exists in Poland, as Prof. Mach (2006) writes, in two different contexts:

1. In the context of open society, pluralism of memory and pluralistic interpretation of heritage. The memory of the tragedy of the Holocaust and the question of Polish responsibility in it belong to this aspect, together with the memory of Jewish-Polish heritage.

2. In the context of closed society, xenophobic and dogmatic, with Jewish heritage excluded from the memory of Poles. The memory of the Holocaust is connected with the symbol and the meaning of the Holocaust in order to fight against the Poles and blame them for the Holocaust or Nazi collaboration (p. 102).

Presentation of the Holocaust in History Curricula and Textbooks

The intentional and conscious manipulation of historical facts by the Communist authorities meant that for decades the subject of the Holocaust in Polish schools, in our contemporary meaning, practically did not exist. When it appeared, it was distorted and treated marginally, as an inconsequential episode in the history of the Second World War (Radziwił, 1989). Therefore, if we want to understand the development of Holocaust education in Poland we have to understand how the Holocaust was presented in history curricula and textbooks alike.

Since the end of World War II, history curricula and textbooks in all kinds of schools have been changed many times. Owing to the tradition of centralized control of public education, they have been susceptible to political trends. They often represented a distorted picture of the occupation years, leaving out the so-called "delicate" and "sensitive" issues, which did not fit the established pattern of perceiving the past. One such "unwanted" issue was the extermination of the Jews. Thus the Communist authorities had a great influence upon the approach to teaching about the Holocaust in all Polish schools at that time.

By the beginning of the 1990s curriculum topics concerning this issue were closely connected with general subjects referring to the German occupation in Poland. They were included in the two following subjects: "The Situation of Polish Citizens under the German [and since 1992 also] Soviet Occupation" ("Minimum programowe," 1992) and "The Polish Resistance Movement" (Wydawnictwa Szkolne i Pedagogiczne, 1990). Therefore, the most frequently recurring curriculum topics referring to the Holocaust were: "The Extermination of the Jews" and "The Warsaw Ghetto Uprising" (Wydawnictwa Szkolne i Pedagogiczne, 1990). In the 1970s, the curriculum was enriched with the issue of Jewish uprisings in other ghettos and the problem of rescuing Jews—"Żegota," the code name for the Council for Aid to Jews in occupied Poland (Wydawnictwa Szkolne i Pedagogiczne, 1990, p. 36). The year 1981, thanks to "Solidarity," brought the next changes. The above mentioned issues were enhanced with the following topics from the Wydawnictwa Szkolne i Pedagogiczne (1990): "The Extermination of Gypsies" and "ŻOB" (Żydowska Organizacja Bojowa or JFO, Jewish Fighting Organization).

In 1996 for the first time the term "Holocaust" appeared as a mandatory topic in the national school curriculum but it was not separated within curricula as a major subject. Finally, this happened in 1999, when with the reform of the entire school system, the Ministry of National Education introduced teaching about the Holocaust as mandatory in all Polish junior and senior high schools, i.e. for students aged 13–19 (Wydawnictwa Szkolne i Pedagogiczne, 1999). Since that date the Holocaust has been part of every history curriculum in post-primary school. The recent history curriculum reform that took place in 2008 moved the issue of the Holocaust together with all of twentieth century history from the third grade of junior high school (ninth grade in the United States) to the first grade of the senior high school (tenth grade in the United States).

Like the history curricula during the past 60 years, history textbooks also have been changed very often and their content determined by many political factors. An examination of the content of history books from the 1950s to the present shows these trends.

The textbooks of the 1950s provided quite a lot of data about the Holocaust, but the authorities often used them as an argument justifying their fight against the anti–Communist underground. For instance, they accused the Polish Home Army of collaboration with the German occupiers, participating in, among other things, persecution of the Jews (Missalowa and Schoenbrenner, 1952).

In the textbooks of the 1960s a very common tendency can be traced for describing the Warsaw Ghetto Uprising as a Polish-Jewish common action. The authors concealed the fact that Jews fought almost alone and that a considerable part of Polish society was indifferent to the Jewish tragedy.

In the 1970s information about "the final solution" became more extensive, but an anti–Semitic campaign sponsored by the Polish United Workers' Party (PZPR), which took place in 1968, strongly influenced this topic. The textbooks stressed the aid provided to Jews by the Polish people; they completely ignored Polish indifference and the fact that some Poles blackmailed Jews. The books described mostly kindness and solidarity shown by the Poles towards Jews. While writing about the concentration camp in Auschwitz-Birkenau nothing was mentioned about ethnicity of its victims (Wapiński, 1979). Moreover, its number was incorrectly estimated as 3–4 million people. In textbooks from the 1960s, this number went even as high as up to about five million (Sędziwy, 1963). At the same time, information about other camps was being gradually introduced into textbooks.

Crucial changes occurred in the 1980s when teaching history, especially of the modern period, became the subject of heated discussions and controversies. Negotiations between "Solidarity" and the Ministry of National Education in 1981 resulted in important changes. Then textbook authors, describing Polish-Jewish relations during the war, began to show both acts of solidarity with the Jews as well as acts which took advantage of their tragedy. Unfortunately, the problem of blackmailing the Jews was treated as an unimportant issue and was presented together with information about Jewish collaboration with the invader. Polish aid was still exaggerated (Siergiejczyk, 1986).

The restrictions on freedom of speech ended in 1989; thus the textbooks which were being used during the 1990s began to discuss the problem of the Holocaust much more thoroughly and honestly. Concentration camps and death camps, such as Auschwitz-Birkenau, Treblinka, Majdanek, Sobibór and Bełżec, started to be clearly identified with their Jewish victims, and also Polish reactions to the Warsaw Ghetto Uprising were being introduced in a much more balanced manner. Textbook authors wrote about the limited aid provided to Jewish fighters by the Polish underground as well as the indifference of some Poles towards the tragedy. They also drew attention to the Allies' passivity and lack of action in the face of the extermination of the Jews.

In 1995, the bilateral Polish-Israeli textbook commission completed its work. It published recommendations regarding the presentation of the history of Jews in Poland and the history of Poland in Israel. Three years later, a critical evaluation of the implementation of these recommendations was prepared by the Jewish Historical Institute in Warsaw. Although the proposed changes were not immediately adopted by the authors of textbooks, at present we can observe considerable progress in this area. Even though there are still some mistakes in the history textbooks published after 1999, the situation has changed greatly for the better. As Tych (2001), the initiator of the textbook evaluation remarked:

> There is more empathy in them and more respect for the victims. Less frequently often is the Holocaust in most textbooks perceived only as a fragment of German occupation policy towards Poland, which was almost the rule two years ago. It is mentioned correctly more and more often in the context of the birth of totalitarian systems and racist ideology [p. 3].

However, in spite of these significant changes, which were taking place in Poland at that time, some old tendencies could be still noticed. For instance, there was a lack of a clear distinction between the situation of Poles and Jews during the war, a lack of ultimate identification of extermination camps with their Jewish victims, and an attempt to prove who suffered more and also an exaggeration of Polish aid provided to the Jews (Szuchta, 2008; Trojański, 1998; ŻIH, 1997).

At the beginning of the 2000s, along with school system reform, new history textbooks were introduced in which the Holocaust became a mandatory and prominent topic. In the current history textbook the Holocaust picture is more diverse, more complete. The authors do not avoid discussing difficult issues such as the Jedwabne pogrom. Information about the Holocaust is covered in separate short chapters such as: "The Destruction of the European Jews—The Holocaust," "Shoah—The Holocaust," "Holocaust Means Annihilation," or simply "The Holocaust" (Szymanowski and Trojański, 2003). In those textbooks the origins and the course of the Holocaust are widely discussed. Usually, the description of the Holocaust is preceded by information about the history and culture of the Jews in Poland and in other European countries before the Second World War. References are made to anti–Semitism, racism and German Nazism as causes of the Holocaust which encourage students to reflect on links between them (Węgrzynek, 2006).

Current Trends in Holocaust Education: Opportunities and Obstacles

For more than two decades now one can notice in Poland a considerable and growing interest in Jewish culture and history. The history of the Jewish community and Polish-Jewish relations has become a matter of interest, not only for historians, but also for wide circles of society. This situation creates specific opportunities and obstacles for Holocaust education in Poland today that I am going to describe briefly next.

The fall of Communism in 1989 led to the situation in which the Holocaust, like many other suppressed issues, gradually began to penetrate the educational system. However, even in post-communist Poland, political circumstances from the past affected teaching about the Holocaust. Most of all, they caused the didactical reflection of this issue to appear relatively late in Poland in comparison with other countries. Furthermore, the introduction of necessary changes was complicated by an insufficient level of research in the field of contemporary history. Several years had to pass before historians obtained full access to all archives. It is worth adding, that in the case of the Holocaust a change of textbooks was difficult for yet another reason: the results of new research did not always meet the expectations of wide circles of Polish society. It turned out that the lack of social acceptance for new findings regarding the Holocaust also created an effective obstacle blocking the introduction of these issues into school education. Nevertheless, as a result of many actions undertaken by various people and institutions, the issue of the extermination of Jews gradually entered into school discourse.

The beginning of teaching the Holocaust in post–Communist Poland is closely connected with grassroots activities such as teachers' workshops and seminars on Holocaust education (Ambrosewicz-Jacobs, 1998). One of the first seminars was organized in Kraków in 1997 by the Pedagogical University of Kraków and the Kraków Jewish Cultural Centre. At that time those initiatives were mainly supported by foreign organizations and state institutional involvement was limited.

The situation changed at the end of the twentieth century when Poland joined the International Task Force for Holocaust Education, Remembrance, and Research. In 2000 Polish president Aleksander Kwaśniewski signed the Declaration of the Stockholm International Forum (2000) on the Holocaust which pledged the signatories to promoting Holocaust education in their respective countries. This action created a positive climate for incorporating Holocaust education into the state educational system.

Since 1999, when the educational reform in Poland was implemented, new possibilities to teach about the Holocaust have appeared. As the result of national debate on the shape and content of the curricula, which has lasted for several years, the Holocaust was finally mandated and introduced to the core curriculum for the Humanities in secondary schools (students aged 13–19).

In 2000 the Ministry of National Education approved a curriculum for teaching about the Holocaust developed by Robert Szuchta, a high school history teacher, and me (Szuchta and Trojański, 2000). It was distributed to all of Polish junior high schools for free. Three years later the first textbook for teaching about the Holocaust was published. The curriculum[2] was addressed to teachers of the humanities, principally history, but also Polish language and civic education. It is designed for junior high school (gymnasium) and senior high school (liceum). Its authors assume that teaching the Holocaust is not merely a historical problem, but also a general educational issue, providing an opportunity to discuss fundamental democratic values. Therefore, teaching about the Holocaust may be placed in the context of combating racism and anti–Semitism; it is essential to link it to instilling tolerance, and overcoming stereotypes and prejudices. Discussing the Holocaust enables students to consider certain issues which can determine their view of the world and form their moral and social attitudes. Therefore teaching about the Holocaust should focus on the following three fundamental questions:

Why was it possible?
How did it happen?
What can be done to prevent it from happening ever again?

Curriculum should help students, who will be inquiring together with their teachers in order to find answers to these questions, not only to gain reliable knowledge about the past, but also to strengthen their own compassion and civic attitudes.

Teachers should acquaint students with the basic facts concerning the Holocaust and the events leading up to it. Using Lanzman's (1993) schema, we suggest starting the discussion at the point when Jews were told: "You must not have another religion" (in the Middle Ages), going on through the period when Jews heard: "You must not live among us cultivating your own identity" (nineteenth century), up to the point when they were told: "You must not live at all; you are not human beings" (the period of the Holocaust). With such an arrangement of the material, students should learn about, and be able to understand the origins of the Holocaust, its development and consequences. The Holocaust should be taught about in such a way that students realize that it is still possible for the crime of genocide to recur.

Most of the topics included in the syllabus relate to history lessons, but many of them can also be discussed within different subjects, such as literature, civic education, ethics, religion, and geography. The syllabus contains methodological suggestions concerning possible ways of implementation. Nevertheless, teachers, in spite of our suggestions, should decide for themselves which topics, within what subjects, and how should they be implemented.

The authors of the curriculum are convinced that the Holocaust should not be taught in isolation from teaching about Jewish history and culture. That is why a set of topics concerning these issues that can be used by teachers of humanities, especially history and literature, is included at the end of the syllabus. These issues cover a period of over 2000 years and can be discussed as early as in the first grade of junior and senior high school. Teachers should include these issues in their own individual lesson schedules. Another variant is to organize, in cooperation with teachers of various subjects, special lessons on the Holocaust, which should last for a few hours each. In this way students would have an opportunity to do in-depth analysis of an issue.

In 2003 this curriculum was complemented with a textbook for teaching about the Holocaust.[3] The book discussed the process of the formation of anti-Judaism, its development in the Middle and Modern Ages, the origins and development of anti-Semitism—the ideology of the nineteenth and twentieth century, the direct and indirect causes of the "final solution." In the opinion of its authors, the year 1945 must not be the closing date of the textbook. Therefore, the aftermath of the Holocaust and its impact on contemporary human beings, their value systems and cultures have also been included. We have offered an interpretation of the Holocaust as a product of modern technical civilization and as a warning of the possibility of a recurrence of new "holocausts" in the future. Therefore, some similarities between the Holocaust and other acts of genocide in the contemporary world are discussed in the textbook as well.

This curriculum and textbook were published in response to an increasing interest in the Holocaust, and the growing awareness of teachers concerning the need of teaching about it in schools. Consequently other teaching materials were published devoted to the Holocaust.[4] Among those worth mentioning are the educational packs issued by the Institute of National Remembrance.[5] Additionally, a monumental work entitled "Selected sources for teaching about the extermination of the Jews in occupied Poland" was published which is an invaluable aid in teaching about the Holocaust at all levels of education (Skibińska and Szuchta, 2010). Also, numerous articles and lesson plans on the issue of teaching about the Holocaust were published between 2000 and 2010.

In addition to more materials being made available for educators, in 2005 the Polish minister of education announced National Holocaust Remembrance Day to be celebrated in schools on April 19. Many NGO's and state institutions began to organize seminars for teachers and educators and publish teaching materials to help organize the Day in schools.

Since the mid-1990s teacher training programs have been developed, including workshops, seminars and conferences on how to teach about the Holocaust. In 1998, the Pedagogical University of Kraków together with the Auschwitz-Birkenau State Museum launched a pioneering postgraduate studies program entitled "Totalitarianism—Nazism—Holocaust," which still attracts a number of teachers from all over Poland. For many years Polish teachers and educators have also been participating in courses and teacher training organized by the Jewish Historical Institute in Warsaw, the Auschwitz-Birkenau State Museum and Center for Education Development, and various foreign institutions, such as Yad Vashem, the Anne Frank House in Amsterdam, House of the Wannsee Conference in Berlin, Memorial de la Shoah in Paris, and Facing History and Ourselves. There is considerable interest in these seminars among Polish teachers and educators.

Today in Poland there are also university research and teaching centers that offer various courses on the Holocaust at both the BA and MA levels. Since 2005, the Center for Holocaust Studies at the Jagiellonian University in Kraków has organized the Summer Institute for Teaching about the Holocaust. Similar forms of training have also been launched in other Polish cities, mainly in Warsaw. The most active are the Jewish Historical Institute, the Centre for Education Development, and the Polish Center for Holocaust Research at the Institute of Philosophy and Sociology of the Polish Academy of Sciences, all in Warsaw.

In Poland, the subject of the Holocaust is also taught beyond the classroom. Such classes are usually organized in museums or memorial sites that are located mostly in the former concentration and death camps. Education in an authentic memorial site has a particular dimension and one cannot overestimate it in teaching about the Holocaust. This is why hundreds of thousand young students from all over the world come to such places like Auschwitz, Treblinka or Majdanek to learn about what happened there. The educational centers that were created at memorial sites developed special programs to help teachers in preparing their groups for the visits. They organize guided tours, workshops, and seminars for students, teachers and educators who are coming there.

Among the memorial sites, a special role is played by the Auschwitz-Bireknau State Museum which was visited in 2012 by a record 1,430,000 people, almost two thirds of them (more than 1 million) young people. Such large numbers of visitors pose questions about the reasons why they come to this memorial. According to recent research, the main reason for visiting Auschwitz is education (Berbeka, 2012/2013). Young people from all over the world come to that place foremost to get knowledge of the camp, then to remember the victims and to pay tribute to them. For youngsters Auschwitz is the most important symbol of the Holocaust and a symbol of genocide in general. A visit to this memorial makes the visitors more aware of the facts, gives them an understanding of them, and leaves an emotional impression, or even more, is an existential experience that strongly shapes them (Kucia, 2008). That is why it is of utmost importance for a visit to Auschwitz to be part of the process of Holocaust education.

With this in mind, in 2005 the State Museum Auschwitz-Birkenau created the International Center for Education about Auschwitz and Holocaust as a response to the requests of former prisoners. The center cooperates with many Polish and foreign institutions offering them assistance in preparing and organizing study visits to Auschwitz. One recent project was a publication of the "European pack for visiting Auschwitz-Birkenau Memorial and Museum. Guidelines for teachers and educators" (Białecka, Oleksy, Regard, Trojański, 2010). It is an English language publication for those who are planning a visit for young people to the Auschwitz Memorial Site. The publication is the result of several years of work between the Auschwitz-Birkenau State Museum, the Council of Europe, and the Polish Ministry of Education. The book contains, among other things, practical information about visiting the memorial site, historical materials and texts, lesson plans, as well as an array of information about the contemporary meaning of Auschwitz.

Apart from those institutions, there are many NGOs, which organize exhibitions, websites, student projects, and other forms of educational work. Programs of those institutions include, among other things, meetings with survivors, exhibitions, lectures, and movies on the Holocaust. Each year these events attract a large young audience.

It should be stressed that the aforementioned examples show the multitude of various educational initiatives for teaching about the Holocaust in Poland today. Nevertheless, compared with the huge needs of students and teachers, there are still too few. Therefore I can say that during the last 10 years Poland has achieved enormous progress which most countries with a long tradition of teaching the Holocaust would envy.

Apart from the opportunities that I described above there are also some obstacles that make Holocaust education in Poland difficult. As I already mentioned, in 2008, the Ministry of National Education reformed the core curricula by changing the way of teaching history. The most important change is that teaching twentieth century history was moved from junior to senior high school. Consequently, teaching about the Holocaust was also moved to that level of education. Many teachers and educators have criticized this decision and expressed their concern about the possible marginalization of teaching the twentieth century history, in general, and the Holocaust, in particular. The only response of the Ministry of National Education to this criticism so far was the preparation of a recommendation on how to teach about the Holocaust in schools after the reforms went into effect (Szuchta and Trojański, 2012). Over time, we will be able to see whether or not these concerns were justified.

Now I am going to focus on some sociological issues related to teaching about the Holocaust in Poland that, in my opinion, could be some kinds of obstacles. These relate to Polish perceptions of the Holocaust, stereotyping, and the passage of time since the events happened.

The first problem is the so-called "competition in suffering" between Poles and Jews. This issue is related to the social perception of the uniqueness or unprecedented nature of the Holocaust. The large scale of (non–Jewish) Polish victims tends to cause the relativization of suffering of other groups, especially Jews. In this situation, in Poland, it is difficult to speak about the uniqueness of the Holocaust. A result of this peculiar "competition in suffering," which has lasted for many years now, is the creation of an image of the Pole as a representative of a nation that experienced war the most. In the words of Polish historian, Andrzej Paczkowski (1999)

> Poland is seen by all Poles, as a victim not only innocent, but on account of the size of martyrdom and lack of collaboration like a saint.... Such an opin-

ion, with minor changes, is present until today. Poles are proud of their own participation in the war, convinced that they suffered the heaviest losses and do not like to speak of—nor to hear—that there may be some flaw in this holy image [p. D1].

How difficult it is even to speak about this issue today was evident during discussions on the pogrom in the town, Jedwabne. This debate revealed defensive reactions especially from the older generation of Poles. They fear that their suffering might be forgotten, obscured by the suffering of the Jews. It seems to me that these psychological defense mechanisms, which in extreme cases could lead to a complete rejection or at least partial denial of unworthy deeds perpetrated by the Poles, should be taken into consideration in teaching about the Holocaust.

Other issues of a sociological nature which make teaching about the Holocaust difficult are the different forms of reluctance and resistance of students, having their source in long-lasting stereotypes and anti–Jewish prejudice. In a part of Polish society, hopefully rather small, the word "Jew," like "Gypsy," is still used as a derogatory term or to label an enemy. For example, anti–Jewish graffiti have often referred to the "Jewish Communist system" (Żydo-komuna) or to insult the "others," such as the members of an opposing football (soccer) club. Sometimes, but fortunately less and less, the word "Jew" is used as a political tool to influence public opinion and to create a certain stereotyped vision of the world.

For most of Polish society Jews are an abstract concept, due to the small size of the Jewish population living in Poland today. This creates a strange situation in which the attitude to a Jew is more an attitude to a concept than to a person. Clearly, this makes overcoming stereotypes much more difficult, because it is very hard in everyday life to confront the myth with reality. Having only a little knowledge about Jews and lacking contact with them, the students have stereotyped ideas that confirm clichés. They seem to repeat opinions they have heard at home, from friends, and from the media. Although, those opinions might not be rooted deeply, and might lack consistency, they can be an obstacle in teaching about the Holocaust.

The low level of acceptance of the Jews among Polish students can explain a certain lack of empathy toward Jewish suffering, as Dr. Jolanta Ambrosewicz-Jacobs (2000) showed in her 1998–2000 research project. She found that young Poles do not acknowledge the uniqueness of the Holocaust. Only 24.5 percent agreed that the Jews suffered most in the war; 20 percent did not agree with the statement; and 55.5 percent chose "hard to say." Like adults they express certain feelings related to "competition in suffering." In her opinion this situation could be changed by an educational program allowing students to meet an individual and learn his or her individual fate. Unfortunately, in Poland very little effort has been made to invite survivors to schools so they can describe their own experiences and bring their message to younger generations as they do in other countries. In this situation, knowledge about individual Jewish fates has to be drawn almost exclusively from literature, film, witnesses' accounts, and other indirect sources. That is why, the school and teachers should play a very important role in this work.

Most of the Polish schools, however, do not explore the roots of intolerance, the nature of social prejudice and discrimination. Self-confrontation with the choices which are possible to make in everyday life remains absent. What is more, students are often unaware of the danger and consequences of bigotry and Holocaust denial. Therefore in teaching about the Holocaust it is crucial to address questions associated with contemporary manifestations of anti–Semitism and to analyze hatred in their environment which can eventually lead to discrimination or persecution of others because of their ethnicity, nationality, race, religion or convictions.

Other obstacles that affect teaching about the Holocaust are the passage of time and the fact of the passing away of the generation of survivors. The temporal perspective causes changes in the attitudes of young people towards the Holocaust. For several years, there has been a noticeable and growing pupil fatigue with the issue of the Holocaust. The history of the Second World War is slowly becoming no longer living history for them and more and more often it is perceived as a distant event of the last century. This change in the perception of the Holocaust results from the natural reluctance of new generations to reflect over a tragedy in the past and the lack of personal connections to the event.

> The passing away in a short time the perspective of generations of victims, perpetrators and witnesses of the Holocaust will undoubtedly deepen the already existing emotional distance of young generations to these events, placing new barriers in their social and individual reception.... This causes dilemmas and poses questions about the possibilities and borders of present education, its place and role in reaching the imagination and sensitivity of a person living at the decline of the twentieth century, for whom "a different world," such as Nazi concentration camps and Stalinist lagers becomes already only distant history [Wysok, 1998, p. 31].

Finding answers to the above questions will demand making significant changes in thinking and in the reconstruction of historic awareness, not only of the young generation, but also of teachers and educators. Therefore it seems necessary to walk away from the martyrological viewpoint of history which through its archaism no longer fits the reality nor present day problems.

Conclusions

This essay was based mainly on the analysis of curricula, textbooks and ministerial documents. It is therefore an assessment of state educational policy regarding Holocaust education rather than school practice. For a full picture of the situation it should be also considered what the real effects of the state activities were. How much information about the Holocaust was passed to students and to what extent was it absorbed by them? It would also be worth considering what teachers thought about it, how they interpreted and were implementing ministerial recommendations in practice. The answers to these questions would give us a comprehensive sociological study that is unfortunately still missing in Poland.[6]

In conclusion, I would like to underline that teaching about the Holocaust in Poland, which was manipulated and neglected during the Communist time finally took an appropriate place in education after the political transformations. Along with school system reform the Holocaust was included in a mandatory core curriculum for the humanities that allowed giving due importance to teaching about this event in schools. The new political situation created new opportunities but at the same time new challenges. Taking into account the achievements gained in this field during the last two decades one can hope that the foundations of Holocaust education are solid enough to overcome the difficulties and obstacles that teachers face nowadays. We must remember that in overcoming them the legacy of the past still plays a very important role.

(This essay is a revised and extended version of a paper presented at the conference on "Les Européens et la Shoah" in Marseilles, 11–13 July. See conference proceedings: Długoborski, W., and Trojański, P. (2008). Facing the Holocaust in Poland: the history and the present. In Dray-Bensousan, R. (Ed.), *Les Européens et la Shoah*, Cahiers d'A.R.E.S no 6/7 Marseille.)

Notes

1. The most important press articles from the Jedwabne debate were published in 2001 in the Catholic periodical *Więź* titled "Thou shalt not kill: Poles on Jedwabne." During the following years Jan Tomasz Gross published two other well-known books on the Polish-Jewish relations but they did not produce as big a debate as this one on the Jedwabne pogrom. The aforementioned books are: Gross, J.T. (2006). *Fear: Antisemitism in Poland after Auschwitz: An essay in historical interpretation*. New York: Random House; Gross, J.T. (2012). *Golden harvest*. Oxford: Oxford University Press.

2. For a comprehensive description of the syllabus see the article published in the *Bulletin of the Museum Auschwitz-Birkenau*: Szuchta, R & Trojański, P. (2002, January). Help the students to be human beings.... *Pro Memoria*, No. 16.

3. Szuchta, R. & Trojański, P. (2003). *Holocaust—zrozumieć dlaczego*. Warszawa: Wydawnictwo Bellona. A new and revised edition of this book was published thanks to the support of the Ministry of National Education and the Memorial Foundation for the Victims of Auschwitz-Birkenau under a new title: Szuchta, R. & Trojański, P. (2012). *Zrozumieć Holokaust. Książka pomocnicza do nauczania o zagładzie Żydów*. Warszawa: Państwowe Muzeum Auschwitz-Birkenau w Oświęcimiu & Ośrodek Rozwoju Edukacji w Warszawie.

4. See a few examples: Chrobaczyński, J. & Trojański, P. (Eds.). (2004) *Holokaust. Lekcja historii. Zagłada Żydów w edukacji szkolnej*, Kraków: Wydawnictwo Naukowe Akademii pedagogicznej w Krakówie; Ambrosewicz-Jacobs, J. & Hońdo, L. (Eds.) (2005). *Why Should We Teach About the Holocaust?* Kraków: Centre for Holocaust Studies, Jagiellonian University; Ambrosewicz-Jacobs, J. & Oleksy, K. & Trojański, P. (Eds.). (2007). *Jak uczyć o Auschwitz i Holokauście. Materiały dydaktyczne dla nauczycieli*, Oświęcim: Państwowe Muzeum Auschwitz-Birkenau w Oświęcimiu; Tych, F. (Ed.). (2008). *Pamięć. Historia Żydów polskich przed, w czasie i po Zagładzie*, Warszawa: Fundacja SHALOM; Trojański, P. (2008). *Auschwitz i Holokaust. Dylematy i wyzwania polskiej edukacji*, Oświęcim: Państwowe Muzeum Auschwitz-Birkenau w Oświęcimiu.

5. *Auschwitz—pamięć dla przyszłości*, (2003). Warszawa: Instytut Pamięci Narodowej; *Zagłada Żydów polskich w czasie II wojny światowej* (2005). Warszawa: Instytut Pamięci Narodowej; *Polacy ratujący Żydów w latach II wojny światowej* (2008). Warszawa: Instytut Pamięci Narodowej.

6. However some preliminary research has already been done by Prof. Marek Kucia and Dr. Jolanta Ambrosewicz-Jacobs from Jagiellonian University in Kraków: Kucia, M. (2001). KL Auschwitz in the social consciousness of Poles, A.D. 2000. In Maxwell, E. & Roth, J.K. (Ed) *Remembering for the Future: The Holocaust in an age of genocide*. Vol. 3, London: Palgrave; Kucia, M. (2005). *Auschwitz jako fakt społeczny. Historia, współczesność i świadomość społeczna KL Auschwitz w Polsce*. Kraków: UNIWERSITAS; Ambrosewicz Jacobs, J. (2011). Do We Want to Remember? Commemorating the Holocaust in Practice in Post-Communist Poland from European Comparative Perspective. In Misztal, M. & Trojański, P. (Eds.) *Poles and Jews: History—culture—education*. Kraków: Wydawnictwo Naukowe Uniwersytetu Pedagogicznego: Ambrosewicz-Jacobs, J. (2011). Świadomość Holokaustu wśród młodzieży polskiej po zmianach systemowych po 1989 roku. In Tych, F. & Adamczyk-Garbowska, M. (Eds.), *Następstwa zagłady Żydów. Polska 1944–2010*, Lublin: Wydawnictwo UMCS w Lublinie & Żydowski Instytut Historyczny w Warszawie.

References

Ambrosewicz-Jacobs, J. (1998, Fall). Teaching the Holocaust in post-Communist Poland. In: Y. Elliot and C.A. Zeltser (Eds.). *Jews in Eastern Europe*, 2 (36), 5–18.

Ambrosewicz-Jacobs J. (2000, Fall). Attitudes of young Poles towards Jews in post–1989 Poland. *East European Politics and Societies*, *14* (3), 565–596.

Ambrosewicz-Jacobs, J. (2006). Conflicts of Memory: Case Study of obstacles in teaching about the Holocaust in Poland. In D. Nałęcz and M. Edgaro (Eds). *Fact and Lies in the Common Knowledge on the Holocaust*, pp. 189–198. Warsaw-Kraków: Oficyna Wydawnicza ASPRA-JR.

Ambrosewicz-Jacobs, J. (2011). Do we want to remember? Commemorating the Holocaust in practice in post–Communist Poland from European comparative perspective. In M. Misztal and P. Trojański (Eds.). *Poles and Jews. History—Culture—Education*. Kraków: Wydawnictwo Naukowe Uniwersytetu Pedagogicznego.

Ambrosewicz-Jacobs, J. (2011). Świadomość Holokaustu wśród młodzieży polskiej po zmianach systemowych po 1989 roku. In Tych, F., and Adamczyk-Garbowska, M. (Eds.) *Następstwa zagłady Żydów. Polska 1944–2010*, Lublin: Wydawnictwo UMCS w Lublinie & Żydowski Instytut Historyczny.

Ambrosewicz-Jacobs, J., and Hońdo, L. (Eds.) (2005). *Why should we teach about the Holocaust?* Kraków: Centre for Holocaust Studies, Jagiellonian University

Ambrosewicz-Jacobs, J., Oleksy, K., and Trojański, P. (Eds.). (2007). *Jak uczyć o Auschwitz i Holokauście. Materiały dydaktyczne dla nauczycieli*, Oświęcim: Państwowe Muzeum Auschwitz-Birkenau.

Berbeka, J. (Ed.). (2012). *Turystyka martyrologiczna w Polsce na przykładzie Państwowego Muzeum Auschwitz-Birkenau*. Kraków: Proksenia.

Berbeka J. (Ed.) (2013). *Martyrology tourism: Polish perspective*. Kraków: Proksenia

Białecka, A., Oleksy, K., and Regard, F. Trojański, P. (Eds.). (2010). *European pack for visiting Auschwitz-Birkenau Memorial and Museum: Guidelines for teachers and educators*, Strasbourg: Council of Europe.

Błoński, J. (1987). Biedni Polacy patrzą na getto, *Tygodnik Powszechny*, (2). Retrieved from http://tygodnik.onet.pl/30,0,21303,7,artykul.html.

Blonski, J. (1990). The poor Poles look at the ghetto. In A. Polonsky (Ed.), *My brother's keeper? Recent Polish debates on the Holocaust* (pp. 34–52). London: Routledge.

Chrobaczyński, J. and Trojański, P. (Eds.). (2004) *Holokaust. Lekcja historii. Zagłada Żydów w edukacji szkolnej*, Kraków: Wydawnictwo Naukowe Akademii Pedagogicznej w Krakówie.

Dłuska, M., and Schoenbrenner, J. (1953). *Historia dla klasy IV*. Warszawa: Panstwowe Zaklady Wydawnictw Szkolnych.

Ginott, H. (1972). *Teacher and child*. New York: Macmillan.

Gross, J. T. (2001). *Neighbors: The destruction of the Jewish community in Jedwabne, Poland*. Princeton, NJ: Princeton University Press.

Gross, J. T. (2006). *Fear: Antisemitism in Poland after Auschwitz: An essay in historical interpretation*. New York: Random House.

Gross, J. T. (2012). *Golden harvest*. Oxford: Oxford University Press.

Huener, J. (2003). *Auschwitz, Poland and the politics of commemoration, 1945–1975*. Athens: Ohio State University Press.

Instytut Pamięci Narodowej. (2003). *Auschwitz—pamięć dla przyszłości*. Warszawa: Instytut Pamięci Narodowej.

Instytut Pamięci Narodowej. (2005). *Zagłada Żydów polskich w czasie II wojny światowej*. Warszawa: Instytut Pamięci Narodowej.

Instytut Pamięci Narodowej. (2008). *Polacy ratujący Żydów w latach II wojny światowej*. Warszawa: Instytut Pamięci Narodowej.

Kapralski, S. (2011). Od milczenia do "trudnej pamięci." Państwowe Muzeum Auschwitz-Birkenau i jego rola w dyskursie publicznym. In F. Tych and M. Adamczyk-Garbowska (Eds.), *Następstwa zagłady Żydów. Polska 1944–2010* (pp. 527–551). Lublin: Wydawnictwo UMCS w Lublinie & Żydowski Instytut Historyczny w Warszawie.

Kucia, M. (2001). KL Auschwitz in the social consciousness of Poles, AD 2000. In Maxwell, E., and Roth, J.K. (Ed). *Remembering for the Future: The Holocaust in an age of Genocide. Vol. 3.* (pp. 632–651). London: Palgrave.

Kucia, M. (2005). *Auschwitz jako fakt społeczny. Historia, współczesność i świadomość społeczna KL Auschwitz w Polsce.* Kraków: Uniwersitas.

Kucia, M. (2008). Optymistyczne dane—niepokojące pytania—radykalne wnioski. In P. Trojański (Ed.), *Auschwitz i Holokaust—dylematy i wyzwania polskiej edukacji* (pp. 35–44). Oświęcim: Państwowe Muzeum Auschwitz-Birkenau.

Lachendro, J. (2007). *Zburzyć i zaorać…? Idea założenia Państwowego Muzeum Auschwitz-Birkenau w świetle prasy polskiej w latach 1945–1948*, Oświęcim: Państwowe Muzeum Auschwitz-Birkenau.

Lanzman, C. (1993). *Shoah. (M. Bienczyk, Trans.).* Koszalin: Novex.

Mach, Z. (2006). The Holocaust in public memory and collective identity of Poles. D. Nałęcz and M. Edgaro (Eds). *Fact and Lies in the Common Knowledge on the Holocaust* (pp. 99–103). Warsaw-Kraków: Oficyna Wydawnicza ASPRA-JR.

Minimum programowe w zakresie historii (szkoła średnia). (1992). *Wiadomości Historyczne*, 5, 199 (XXXV).

Missalowa, G., Schoenbrenner, J. (1952). *Historia Polski.* Warszawa: Państwowe Zakłady Wydawnictw Szkolnych.

Paczkowski, A. (1999, 4–5 September). Nazizm i komunizm w pamięci i świadomości Polaków. Doświadczenie egzystencjalne. *Rzeczpospolita, 207* (349), p. D1.

Radziwił, A. (1989). The teaching of the history of the Jews in secondary schools in the Polish People's Republic, 1940–1988. *POLIN: Studies in Polish Jewry, 4,* 402–424.

Sędziwy, T. (1963). *Historia dla klasy VII.* Warszawa: Panstwowe Zakłady Wydawnictw Szkolnych.

Siergiejczyk, T. (1986). *Dzieje najnowsze 1939–1945. Historia dla szkół średnich (klasy: IV LO oraz III technikum i LZ).* Warszawa: Państwowe Zakłady Wydawnictw Szkolnych.

Skibińska, A., and Szuchta R. (Eds.). (2010). *Wybór źródeł do nauczania o zagładzie Żydów na okupowanych ziemiach Polskich.* Warszawa: Stowarzyszenie Centrum Badań nad Zagładą Żydów.

Steinlauf, M. (1997). *Bondage to the dead: Poland and the memory of the Holocaust.* Syracuse, NY: Syracuse University Press.

Stockholm International Forum on the Holocaust. (2000). Proceedings from *the Conference on Education, Remembrance and Research,* 2000, 26–28 January. Stockholm: Regeringskansliet.

Szuchta, R. (2008). Teaching about the Holocaust: Polish experiences on the threshold of the 21st Century. In S. Rejak (Ed.), *Thinking after the Holocaust: Voices from Poland* (pp. 35–60). Warszawa-Kraków: Wydawnictwo MUZA SA.

Szuchta, R. (2008). Zagłada Żydów w edukacji szkolnej lat 1945–2000 na przykładzie analizy programów i podręczników szkolnych do nauczania historii.

In P. Trojański (Ed.), *Auschwitz i Holokaust. Dylematy i wyzwania polskiej edukacji* (pp. 109–138). Oświęcim: Państwowe Muzeum Auschwitz-Birkenau.
Szuchta, R., and Trojański, P. (2000). *Holocaust. Program nauczania na lekcjach przedmiotów humanistycznych w szkole ponadpodstawowej*. Warszawa: Wydawnictwa Szkolne PWN.
Szuchta, R., and Trojański, P. (2002, January). Help the students to be human beings.... *Pro Memoria* (16), 31–36.
Szuchta, R., and Trojański, P. (2003). *Holocaust—zrozumieć dlaczego*. Warszawa: Wydawnictwo Bellona.
Szuchta, R., and Trojański, P. (2012). *Zrozumieć Holokaust. Książka pomocnicza do nauczania o zagładzie Żydów*. Warszawa: Państwowe Muzeum Auschwitz-Birkenau and Ośrodek Rozwoju Edukacji.
Szuchta, R., and Trojański, P. (2012). *Jak uczyć o Holokauście. Poradnik metodyczny do nauczania o Holokauście w ramach przedmiotów humanistycznych w zreformowanej szkole*. Warszawa: Ośrodek Rozwoju Edukacji.
Szymanowski, G., and Trojański, P. (2003). *Ludzie i epoki. Historia z Pegazem. Klasa 3*. Kraków: Wydawnictwo ZNAK dla Szkoły.
Świebocka, T. (2000). The Auschwitz-Birkenau Memorial and Museum: From Commemoration to Education. *POLIN: Studies in Polish Jewry, 13,* (290–299).
Trojański, P., (1998). Nazism and the Holocaust in primary school history education, *Pro Memoria*, (9), 67–70.
Trojański, P. (Ed.) (2008). *Auschwitz i Holokaust. Dylematy i wyzwania polskiej edukacji*, Oświęcim: Państwowe Muzeum Auschwitz-Birkenau.
Trojański, P. (2012). Upamiętnianie ofiar Auschwitz na terenie Państwowego Muzeum Oświęcim-Brzezinka w latach 1947–2000. Zarys problemu. *Krakówskie Studia Małopolskie, 17 (17/2012)*, 65–78.
Tych, F. (1999). *Długi cień Zagłady. Szkice historyczne*. Warszawa: Żydowski Instytut Historyczny IN-B.
Tych, F., (1999). *Problematyka Zagłady w polskich podręcznikach szkolnych do nauczania historii*. In F. Tych, *Długi cień Zagłady. Szkice historyczne* (pp. 97–117). Warszawa: Żydowski Instytut Historyczny IN-B.
Tych, F. (2001). *Holokaust w polskich podręcznikach szkolnych*. A manuscript of the paper presented at the conference for Polish-Lithuanian teachers on teaching about the Holocaust: "Between Myth and Reality," Kraków, 14–18 October, 2001.
Tych, F. (Ed.). (2008). *Pamięć. Historia Żydów polskich przed, w czasie i po Zagładzie*, Warszawa: Fundacja SHALOM.
Wapiński, R. (1979). *Historia dla klasy 4 LO oraz dla klasy 3 technikum, część druga*. Warszawa: Panstwowe Zakłady Wydawnictw Szkolnych.
Węgrzynek, H. (2006). The Holocaust and Jewish history as presented in current Polish Textbooks. In D. Nałęcz and M. Edgaro (Eds.). *Fact and lies in the common knowledge on the Holocaust* (pp. 147–161).Warsaw-Kraków: Oficyna Wydawnicza ASPRA-JR.
Wóycicka, Z. (2009). *Przerwana żałoba. Polskie spory wokół pamięci nazistowskich obozów koncentracyjnych i zagłady 1944–1950*, Warszawa: Wydawnictwo TRIO.
Wydawnictwa Szkolne i Pedagogiczne. (1970). *Program nauczania Liceum Ogólnokształcącego. Historia klasy I–IV.* Warszawa: Wydawnictwa Szkolne i Pedagogiczne.

Wydawnictwa Szkolne i Pedagogiczne. (1980). *Program nauczania Liceum Ogólnoksztalcącego. Historia klasy I–IV.* Warszawa: Wydawnictwa Szkolne i Pedagogiczne.
Wydawnictwa Szkolne i Pedagogiczne. (1990). *Program Liceum Ogólnokształcącego. Historia klasy I–IV.* Warszawa: Wydawnictwa Szkolne i Pedagogiczne.
Wydawnictwa Szkolne i Pedagogiczne. (1999). *Podstawa kształcenia ogólnego. Historia. Gimnazjum. Rozporządzenie Ministra Edukacji narodowej z dnia 15 lutego 1999 roku, 14* (129).
Wysok, W. (1998 Winter). Doświadczenie Auschwitz a pedagogika pamięci. *Scriptores Scholarum, 18* (1), 30–38
Young, J. E. (1993). *The texture of memory: Holocaust memorials and meaning,* New Haven: Yale University Press.
Zaremba, M. (2001). Urząd zapomnienia, *Polityka,* 41, 72–73.
ŻIH. (1997). Tematyka żydowska w podręcznikach szkolnych. *Biuletyn ŻIH IB-N, No. 3–4.*

Websites for Further Information

The Centre for Education Development (CED), Warsaw, http://www.ore.edu.pl/index.php?option=com_content&view=article&id=422&Itemid=1. A national teacher training institution to provide educational support to schools and professional development for teachers to help them stay up-to-date with educational reform.
Centre for European Studies, Jagiellonian University, Kraków, http://www.ces.uj.edu.pl/. Offers master's degrees in Polish and English; a branch of the Institute of European Studies.
Centrum Badań Holokaustu Uniwersytetu Jagiellońskiego Szkoła letnia (Centre for Holocaust Studies, Jagiellonian University Summer Institute), http://www.holocaust.uj.edu.pl/szkola-letnia. Displays information on the most recent Institute (website in Polish; however, there is a link at the bottom which brings up the information in English).
International Centre for Education on Auschwitz and the Holocaust, Oświęcim, http://en.auschwitz.org/e/. Offers conferences, seminars and lectures aimed at a broad audience including online courses.
Polish Institute of National Remembrance, Warsaw, http://www.ipn.gov.pl/portal/en/. Offers publications, exhibitions, seminars, lectures, and workshops; coordinates the work of eleven sites in cities across Poland.
Totalitarianism, Nazism, and the Holocaust, http://en.auschwitz.org/m/index.php?option=com_content&task=view&id=1093&Itemid=7. Post-graduate program offered jointly by Auschwitz-Birkenau State Museum and the Pedagogical University in Kraków.

NGOs and Their Role in Holocaust Education and Jewish Studies

> He who changes one person, changes the world entire.—from Life in a Jar website, 2008

Another important medium for learning about Jewish life and culture and about the Holocaust is through a variety of NGOs (non-governmental organizations) set up in Poland for those purposes. The programs and materials offered by the organizations vary and may fall more under the description of formal education, in which participants are systematically taught about the topic and may receive some kind of recognition upon completion, or they may fall more under the informal education in which less systematic teaching and learning take place.

What are NGOs?

NGOs are non-profit organizations that are not part of the official state (governmental) structure (Wygnanski, 2011). Such organizations may include charitable organizations, volunteer organizations, and certain civic organizations, and may be set up as foundations, clubs, and other types of associations and groups. Non-profit refers to NGOs' economic structure; any profit realized by the organization is not distributed as profits to shareholders or others, but is used for the operating the organization and/or to achieve its goals. An NGO generally has a board which makes decisions and it may have personnel in paid or volunteer positions. An NGO which is set up as a charitable organization engages in philanthropic activities such as helping people, who are disadvantaged in some way, such as the hungry, the homeless, the sick, often with money, goods, and/or services. Volunteer organizations rely on people giving their time to help with various projects, usually of a social nature and often related to the type of work that charitable organizations support. Civic organizations generally are formed with a public (or civic) goal in mind. They may be charitable organizations, but may also be professional organizations, advocacy groups, and even some religious organizations.

NGOs are often created to fill a niche that is not covered by private business or by the government sector. They have some specific characteristics that separate them from other types of groups. Besides their non-profit nature, they are formally registered organizations, with a defined organizational structure that outlines their autonomy from public authorities, their governance structure, and the voluntary nature of membership. In addition to the goals of the organizations themselves, NGOs can serve several economic and social purposes in a society (Herbst, 2011).

One economic function that an NGO can serve is to provide employment to individuals who work for the organization. Depending on the size and nature of the NGO, these positions can vary. Another economic function that they serve is to provide volunteers with skills that they may be able to transfer to future employment, either within the organization or in others. Besides employment functions, NGOs also often provide high-demand, low-return community services more efficiently and effectively than commercial enterprises. These services are especially important for communities which are economically weak or for addressing issues that have poor market return, such as environmental issues. By offering theses services, NGOs can also take some of the burden from governmental agencies so that public funds can be distributed differently. Finally, because NGOs are by nature more flexible than government entities, they can often develop, implement, and even experiment with, creative solutions to problems, solutions that may not be possible with "taxpayer" money.

NGOs also serve important social functions. One purpose of an NGO is to bring people together who have common interests, values, and/or views who want to do something as a group, often with a goal of community enrichment in mind. For some NGOs, the goal may go beyond enrichment to upholding the common good in some way, or to providing necessary goods and services. NGOs may offer members a way to participate in public life or a place in which their voice will be heard on public matters. Some organizations are formed to serve as advocacy groups to "speak on behalf of those who, for various reasons, are not able to effectively do that" (Herbst, 2011, sect. Social, para. 3). Their advocacy may focus on members of their own group or they may focus on groups that are marginalized in some way. Advocacy groups generally draw attention to the issues, and often take some kind of action to ameliorate it or exert political pressure to effect social change. Finally, in many ways NGOs serve to educate the public about issues and concerns that impact society at large. This education may take place implicitly through advocacy or explicitly through formal and informal educational initiatives.

NGOs in Poland: Holocaust Education and Jewish Studies

There are a number of NGOs in Poland whose mission is related to either Holocaust education or Jewish Studies. Some of these NGOs are related to non-profits in other countries such as the Taube Center for the Renewal of Jewish Culture which is sponsored by the Taube Foundation for Jewish Life and Culture, an American philanthropic organization, and the Lauder Foundation which operates a Jewish day school and summer camp in Poland. Others, such as the Centre for Citizenship Education, Jewish Association Czulent, ZOOM, a Jewish youth organization, the Institute of Tolerance in Łódź, the Shalom Foundation, and the Foundation for the Preservation of Jewish Heritage, began as preservation societies or as groups for people with similar interests to meet and have evolved so that they now provide various formal and informal educational functions. While there are numerous such NGOs in Poland, these were selected to provide a sample of the different types of groups which exist.

The Centre for Citizenship Education: The Centre for Citizenship Education was established in 1994 with the goal of promoting civic engagement. Its teacher-training institute develops various curricula to accomplish this goal and runs about 25 educational programs on different topics across Poland in elementary and secondary schools. They have developed various joint projects with other organizations to educate teachers and students not only about aspects of Jewish history in Poland but to help them understand the need for and how to create preservation projects (Ambrosewicz-Jacobs, 2011).

The Institute of Tolerance in Łódź: The Institute of Tolerance in Łódź began in Łódź, Poland in 2001. Before the Holocaust, Łódź was the home of a large Jewish population. They sponsor a number of projects aimed at tolerance/intolerance in general, such as the painting over of hateful graffiti. Several of their projects specifically deal with the Holocaust, Children of the Ghetto and Colors of Deportation, in particular.

The Shalom Foundation: The Shalom Foundation has its roots in Łódź, Poland, but is located in Warsaw. Begun in 1988 at the instigation of Golda, Tencer, an actress and director with the Kaminska State Yiddish Theatre in Warsaw, the organization looks to the past and to the future. The foundation sponsors art and other cultural exhibits, including the Festival, Warsaw of Singer, as well as lectures and discussions. In addition to its cultural activities, the foundation also supports the first Jewish preschool in Poland since the Holocaust and offers "Sunday school" for Jewish children to learn about their history, culture and language. Their Third Age University offers adults a wide range of classes and lectures related to Jewish topics, such as Jewish cuisine, Jewish history and culture, and Yiddish and Hebrew classes. Competitions and publications also make up part of their offerings. One of their current projects is to establish a Center of Yiddish Culture: Center of Tolerance in Warsaw. They invite people to be part of this project whose foundation is built on the past, but whose windows overlook the future.

The Foundation for the Preservation of Jewish Heritage in Poland: The Foundation for the Preservation of Jewish Heritage in Poland was established by the Union of Jewish Communities in Poland and the World Jewish Restitution Organization (WJRO). Although much of their work is related to actual preservation of Jewish cemeteries and historical Jewish sites, part of their mission is also education.

In 2005 they began the "To Bring Memory Back" project which is an educational program for Polish teachers and school children. In these programs, school children learn about the Jewish history of their town or region, engage in a project, such as cleaning up a Jewish cemetery, and then create brochures and activities to educate others about the Jewish heritage of their area.

The foundation created the multimedia website POLIN in 2006 which provides a variety of information about the heritage of Jews in Poland and of the Holocaust. The premise of the website is that, using Web 2.0 technology, a portal of resources will be provided by educators and students for educators, students, and the public at large.

Jewish Association Czulent: Begun in 2004 in Kraków, Jewish Association Czulent is centered around the idea of the importance of Jewish identity for young people, whether religious or secular. Among other activities, they have created a public Jewish library which is in the Kraków's Jewish Community Center and they conduct classes and workshops focusing on anti-discrimination and tolerance, and promoting dialog between Jews and Poles.

ZOOM: ZOOM, the Polish Jewish Youth Organization is another group that aimed primarily at young people. Founded in 2007, their goal is to create a sense of Jewish community among all Polish-Jewish youth. One of their projects, to create a documentary, was funded by an EU (European Union) grant. Their plans are to use this documentary as the foundations for a series of workshops with participants from local schools to teach about discrimination, anti–Semitism through civic engagement.

Summary of NGOs—Holocaust Education and Jewish Studies

As stated earlier, these NGOs are just a few of those that exist in Poland which are actively engaged in various aspects of Jewish history and culture, and/or the Holocaust. While some of the NGOs focus on a specific area in Poland, some of their activities overlap. Most of them are attempting to educate Jews and Poles about some aspects or aspects of the Jewish heritage of Poland and about the Holocaust Most of them also are not merely conveying information; they are attempting to actively engage participants in activities and projects which create a deeper understanding not just of people and events but of the underlying issues and causes.

In the next essay, Jolanta Ambrosewicz-Jacobs looks at some of these organizations from her perspective as a Polish scholar of Jewish Studies. She examines why and how such institutions are involved in Poland's engagement with its Jewish past as well as its present and future.

Memory, Non-Memory and Post-Memory of the Holocaust: Coming out of Amnesia in Post-Communist Poland?

by Jolanta Ambrosewicz-Jacobs

Human memory is a marvellous but fallacious instrument. (...) The memories which lie within us are not carved in stone; not only do they tend to become erased as the years go by, but often they change, or even grow, by incorporating extraneous features. (...) Some mechanisms are known which falsify memory under particular conditions: Traumas, not only cerebral ones; interference from other "competitive" memories, abnormal conditions of consciousness, repressions, blockages [Levi, 1989, p. 23].

One third of Poland, said Robert Traba (2006, p. 17), consists of the Polish-German borderland and in Central-Eastern Poland we can notice traces of the cultural landscape of Polish Jews. Jan Józef Lipski said in "Instead of postscriptum" written in 1990, as a supplement to his great moral testament "Two homelands, two patriotisms," that cultural monuments always belong to the pride and achievements of their culture of origin and the level of development of a civilization is judged by the fulfillment of duties carried out by those who have the heritage of another culture on their lands as all such heritage comprises European culture. Having a feature of foreign culture is not a smaller, but a bigger commitment. Redefining the idea of Jan Józef Lipski, Traba (2006) says that we Poles did not only get the heritage, but we are also the spiritual successors of those lands. In other words, this is not our heritage, but we are putting into this material and non-material space new sense and new life, at the same time not forgetting about the former creators of the culture. Not forgetting requires memory, individual and collective. Being a successor of Jewish culture in Poland requires particular attitudes, competences and skills. The stakeholders who are involved in reconstructing the memory of Jewish life and death have a difficult task. This text looks both at the attitudes of young Poles towards the memory of the Jewish past, including the Holocaust, the most traumatic fact in world history, and at selected initiatives of the grassroots' movement in Poland and their effort to commemorate what was once a vibrant Jewish culture in this part of Central-Eastern Europe (The data presented are the results of the author's study "Attitudes of Young Poles toward the Jews and the Holocaust" conducted in 2008–2009 with the support of the International Task Force for Holocaust Education, Research and Remembrance, La Fondation pour la Mémoire de la Shoah and the Jagiellonian University in Kraków.).

The process of upsurge of memory is visible all over Europe and elsewhere. Counter-memories often threaten national memories. Acknowledgment of the Vichy government as a part of the history of France started in the seventies but official political responsibility was only acknowledged by [Jacques] Chirac in 1995. It took as many years to deal with getting justice related to Swiss gold or compensation for forced labor in Germany. In 2000 the Prime Minister of Finland Lipponen apologized on behalf of the State for the deportation of 8 Jews in 1942. The Truth Commission in Finland was established to provide transparent data related to the traumatic events of the past. Past is important for the whole of Europe, particularly for Central-Eastern Europe, because in this past "is hidden our wounded identity—as Jacek Żakowski (2002, p. 45) calls it—hidden by two big projects of the XX century—Nazism and bolshevism. And only now can we reconstruct our past."

Robert Wuthnow, a sociologist of religion, has pointed out that the indicator of success for the XXI century will be the ability to create "communities of memory" (Signer, 2001). According to Charles S. Maier (1993; 2001), modern historical memory, however, cannot be universal because "memory does not come in a social or political vacuum" and communities of memory cannot empathize with members of other communities of memory. There is rivalry between groups as each of them demands public recognition of the damage done to them and support for their claims. In opposition to that statement, I argue that memorial sites, artists' representations, public rituals and extra-curricular educational projects in post–1989 Poland, not always, but more and more frequently, provide a space for inclusive remembrance.

"In the consciousness of my generation" writes Michał Witkowski (2009) in the Polish weekly *Polityka*

> there is a more or less visible hatred of Jews, as there is a hatred of Russians identified in the book *The Polish-Russian War* by Dorota Masłowska: there are graffiti on the walls, there is no subject. Hate and graffiti, Stars of David at bus stops, and on the other hand conferences and exhibitions—everything facing emptiness because there is no subject. Hallucination [p. 60].

This text will address the attitudes of young Poles towards Jews, toward anti-Jewish graffiti, the activities of selected Polish civil society institutions and an attempt to address emptiness by artists and film-makers trying to integrate and reconcile Polish collective memory.

The lack of the subject of the memory coupled with unwanted memories of being witness to mass murder, the grabbing or the witnessing of the grabbing of Jewish property, and knowledge that people are living in Jewish homes has distorted the memory and then, with new generations, erased it. Memory became a non-memory. A non-memory of absence and a non-memory of emptiness. Memory was transformed into non-memory because of trauma. Karl Jaspers has called the basic situation which reaches the foundations of human existence, a borderland situation. There are: death, suffering, guilt, fighting, turning points changing the optic by which we perceive our existence. If the content of memory is too difficult to be accepted, rejection is in some ways a natural reaction. Intergenerational transfer of memory, according to the philosopher, also refers to transmitting the memory of trauma (Kuniński, 2007, p. 14). For those generations who do not have a direct contact with the witnesses and only react to descriptions and representations, it is not a memory, but as Marianne Hirsch (1997) called this phenomenon, a post-memory.

In reflecting on the terminology of memory the term post-memory should be introduced, a term which can be extended beyond the circle of survivors and their children to include "a space for remembrance, more broadly available through cultural and public, and merely individual and personal, acts of remembrance, identification and projection.... It is a question of adopting experiences...." (Hirsch, 1997 as cited in Zeitlin, 1998). Post-memory relates to the experience of those who were born after the traumatic events which former generations witnessed and it has been incorporated since the eighties into the development of a posttraumatic culture, which, according to Tokarska-Bakir (2004, p.97), is a reaction to the earlier "culture of silence." Post-memory, accompanying the passing away of survivors, is polyphonic and may generate myths. That is why activities connected with the remembrance of the Holocaust should be carefully watched so that they do not again distort history.

Emptiness is hard to address. Perhaps the most significant attempt is the work of Elżbieta Janicka simulating an empty Agfa film presenting the former camps as exemplified in the photograph *Treblinka II*, 07.10.2004. Academics try to explore archives, municipal authorities sometimes, but not all that often, put up commemorative plates on the walls of buildings or organize events recalling Jewish culture and traditions, sometimes even commemorating culinary traditions as in Chmielnik. But it seems that the most difficult questions are not asked by academics, but by artists, often challenging or even repudiating commemorative practices. A good example is Agata Siwek's installation "The Auschwitz Shop" (2003) or Mirosław Bałka pointing out the danger of commercialism inherent in "death tourism." Very interesting public ceremonies, events and rituals come from artists rooted in the alternative theatre which took place in communist Poland and who, after 1989, got involved in building up the voluntary movement, facing the non-memory of the Holocaust and playing an enormous role in bringing this memory back to older generations and introducing it to younger generations of Poles.

At the Buchenwald museum it is not that easy to find the traces of a small zoo built just outside the camp fence to entertain the families of the SS guards. How hard it must have been for prisoners to look at falcons and cuddly bears also imprisoned in the zoo, but on the other side of the camp perimeter. In the future, the operators of the Buchenwald Memorial (Gedenkstätte Buchenwald) are planning to make the remnants of the zoo more visible to visitors, as reported during an interview on May 12–13, 2009, within the EU project "The role of commemoration sites, original sites and historical museums in Holocaust education and Human Rights education in the European Union" led by the Swedish Government agency the Living History Forum.

Located on the right side of the entrance, the remnants of the zoo are currently not well interpreted and most visitors march left towards the gates as they approach the former camp.

A renowned Polish sculptor, Mirosław Bałka, addressed the issue of the small zoo built for German and Ukrainian guards in Treblinka, in the installation that he built in 2007 named: *250 × 700 × 455, × 41 × 41/Zoo/T, steel, light, red wine and pomp*. The title of this work relates to its inspiration: a small menagerie or zoo that existed at Treblinka, a death camp built by the Nazis in 1942 which, although only active for one year, claimed the lives of approximately 800,000 to 920,000 Jews. The zoo was principally a cage for foxes, which were housed at ground level, and for doves that were housed in its roof. The original design, which Bałka discovered when looking at photographs of the camp, was clad with thatch and the branches of silver birch trees which gave it the appearance of something strangely tropical in feel. In his sculpture, Bałka has shrunk the height of the zoo to 250 cm and proportionally rescaled the building to relate to the scale of his own body; 250 cm being the height of the artist with his arms outstretched above his head.

People could admire and take care of animals at the same time as taking part in mass killings. Such facts and presentations in public space make a large public, not only a handful of scholars, aware that the Nazis and their helpers were not monsters but ordinary people who, in particular circumstances, ended up on the side of evil. It would be desirable if education policy makers could take this knowledge, brought to the surface by social psychologists such as Milgram and Zimbardo and also by artists, into account and include it in the content of the education syllabus to stop "education" mantras being endlessly repeated by numerous politicians on various occasions.

In Poland, special attention should definitely be paid to hate and to common indifference to racist and anti–Semitic graffiti on walls, the visualization of hate as indicated above by Michał Witkowski. The data from the survey *Attitudes of Young Poles toward Jews and the Holocaust* (Jolanta Ambrosewicz-Jacobs, 2009), a project implemented by the Center for Holocaust Studies of the Jagiellonian University, indicates that although more students (altogether 39 percent) agree than disagree (24 percent) with the statement that anti–Jewish graffiti shame and disturb them, as many as 37 percent remain indifferent which is a bad result, supporting general indifference toward the issue of hate speech (refer to Table 1). Although these graffiti can be seen as a sign of gang warfare, incorporating the code of behavior of rival local football [soccer] teams in Kraków in the interwar period; Wisła (which didn't accept Jews) and Cracovia (which did accept them); does not diminish the fact that this is an anti–Semitic language.

TABLE 1: ANTI-JEWISH GRAFFITI SHAME AND DISTURB ME

Anti-Jewish Graffiti Shame and Disturb Me	Ogółem	Ogółem (%)
Strongly agree	193	9.3%
Rather agree	200	20.0%
Neither agree or disagree	367	36.7%
Rather disagree	139	13.9%
Strongly disagree	96	9.6%
Lack of answer	5	0.5%
Total (N=1000)	1000	100.0%

Note: Nationwide survey 2008/2009, random sample of 1000 students 17–18 years old.

The working definition of anti–Semitism (developed by OSCE together with Jewish organizations, such as the American Jewish Committee, AJC), states that it is a certain perception of Jews, which may be expressed as hatred toward Jews, rhetorical/physical demonstrations directed at Jewish/non–Jewish individuals and/or their property, community institutions, religious facilities. It can also target the state of Israel, conceived as a Jewish collectivity and may charge Jews with conspiring to harm humanity and be used to blame Jews for "why things go wrong." It employs sinister stereotypes and negative character traits. According to this definition, both, Jewish and non–Jewish targets of hatred make such rhetoric anti–Semitic, a fact which is sometimes not understood even among academic teachers in contemporary Poland.

Education through individual and collective experience is more frequently found in the activities of NGOs such as institutions providing leisure time activities for youth than in classrooms. The scope of their campaigns is often geographically limited. A number of young Poles are put to painting over racist, fascist and anti–Semitic graffiti. The first such campaign was initiated by the Institute of Tolerance Association in Łódź and became an annual event with much publicity. The political action that took place in Łódź under the name "Colourful Tolerance" as a reaction against racist, fascist and anti–

Semitic graffiti was until recently limited in space (to one city) and time (to one day a year). The head of the Institute of Tolerance Association in Łódź since 2002, Joanna Podolska, also organizes a journalism workshop within the Jewish Studies Section at the University of Łódź entitled "In Search of Traces of History. The Łódź Ghetto 1940–44." There have already been four Polish-Israeli Forums, coorganized by the Warsaw School of Economics and Tel-Aviv University, taking the form of a student exchange with one week in Poland and one week in Israel. Students in Poland emphasize the need to be taught, but more than that, the need to meet, talk and learn from each other.

On September 11, 2002, Kraków City Council established the Cultural and Ecological Education Center (CEKIE). On June 2, 2004, more than 30 volunteers took part in a day painting over graffiti in Kraków (the Paint Kraków project—More on the campaign at: http://www.cekie.Kraków.pl/zamalowac/index.php?l=projekt). The Center's activities particularly focus on the Krzemionki area where there was a forced labor and concentration camp (Płaszów)—and which carries the memory of the tragic events of the Holocaust.

The City Space Association is a recent initiative intended to prevent graffiti which is directed at the municipal and regional level, but covers, through tools available on the Internet, the whole territory of Poland. The main objective of the "City Space" project is, as stated on the website:

> The development of a civic attitude among the young generations of Poles and preventing the exclusion of minorities from civil society. Using widely available tools: the Internet and a digital camera (even the simplest one—such as mobile phone cameras) we would like to create an opportunity to document these elements in our surroundings that in their nature threaten the dignity of people in terms of their ethnicity, race, religion, beliefs or sexual orientation. Anyone can join our campaign. It is enough to take a photo, go to the main page, point to the location of the graffiti or poster on the map and enter the photo in the project database. The entries will be moderated so that only those photos which meet the project rules appear in the database. Next, the entries will be periodically passed over to the national or municipal police who will compel the building administrators to remove such graffiti or posters.

The extensive quotation of the developers of an interactive portal given above shows the language used by those who are sensitive and aware of the problem of hate speech among young Poles. Their efforts are designed to prevent the exclusion of minorities and to defend their dignity. This is the language of human rights which, it is hoped, will stop municipal authorities, politicians, educators and the inhabitants of the buildings concerned downplaying the significance of the graffiti.

One international project initiated by students of the University of Warsaw School of Journalism is called "Europe According to Auschwitz." The project's objective is to prepare a *Death Camp Chronicle/Reportage*, focusing on important events in the history of the camp. This will be carried out by an international group formed through cooperation between university-level journalism schools from Germany, Hungary, the U.S., Israel, Russia and Poland. It chronicles a story of the good and evil dormant in human nature. Auschwitz interests the students in this project not only as a deviation of humanity but as a system, an institution. The idea of international journalism workshops is a worthwhile one. The project not only gives the students a chance to work on an important subject, search archives, and fully comprehend the nature of the events, but also provides an opportunity to speak with and collect materials from surviving eyewitnesses. The *Chronicle* also offers a very useful educational tool, speaking to the imagination of the young generation, particularly since it was mainly produced by young people. The first two-week on-site session took place in Oświęcim in September 1999, then it was repeated in 2000 and 2001. Several works have already been produced reflecting daily life in Auschwitz, among them *The longest roll call in the history of KL Auschwitz, Rudolf Hoess, commandant of KL Auschwitz*, and *The story of Mala Zimetbaum and Edward Galiński*, available on CD and at the website of the project, http://www.reporter.id.uw.edu.pl/article/archive/295/. Multimedia projects on DVDs became more and more popular in the Polish educational system.

The project "Listen and Remember," initiated by Bruno Vastmans who lives in Poland, consists of three films presenting "Jewish oral history, collected by youth from Kraków, Nowy Sącz and Oświęcim" and was co-financed by Małopolskie Towarzystwo Oświatowe, the Municipality of Nowy Sącz and the Joods Humanitair Fonds. Films present interviews conducted by youth with the survivors of Oświęcim, recalling many friendly interactions between Poles and Jews living in the same town before World War II, an interview with Bernard Offen, a survivor of the Kraków ghetto and many camps, and Tanya Segal, a rabbi from Beit Kraków.

Although the main goal of the Jewish NGOs in Poland such as the Jewish Forum Foundation established in 1994 is to stimulate Jewish life in Poland, preservation of the memory of the Holocaust is also to varying degrees a focus of theirs. The Children of the Holocaust Association was established in 1991 by people who survived the Holocaust as children. The

Association belongs to the Federation of Jewish Child Survivors of the Holocaust and was created to share the experience of the Holocaust and to help people understand its effect on the lives of survivors. Members of the association meet with Polish youth and educate them through their unique memories drawn from personal experience (the publication *The Last Eyewitnesses: Children of the Holocaust speak* published by Northwestern University Press in 1998, which is a translation from the Polish [*Dzieci Holocaustu mówią...*] by Fay and Julian Bussgang, has assembled 65 testimonies of its members, Jewish children who survived the war in Poland and remained in the country). A major goal of the Association is to publish the life stories of the survivors.

One thing that unites Jewish NGOs in Poland is a deep belief that young Israelis coming to visit the country should not only see Poland as a Jewish cemetery. There is a need to show them the past and current Jewish life in Poland, to show them that there is continuity. The annual Jewish Culture Festival in Kraków, established in 1988, is Europe's largest one. Although created by non–Jews and drawing mainly non–Jews, it shows that Jewish culture is attractive in this part of the world.

The nine days of activities, including religious ceremonies, concerts, workshops in calligraphy, paper-cutting, Jewish and Hasidic dances, Yiddish singing, Hasidic singing, cooking, Yiddish language, lectures, exhibitions, theatre performances, walking tours, and film shows, demonstrate that even "virtual" Jewish culture (Gruber, 2002) is a sign of nostalgia for a world that has disappeared. As Janusz Makuch, director of the Festival expressed it in the brochure for the seventeenth festival "[t]he Festival is a holiday of memory, a victory of life over death, a word written with humility in the Kraków Yizkor Book."

During the 2002 Festival an annual ceremony was established to award diplomas issued by the Embassy of Israel in Poland in cooperation with the Jewish Historical Institute to honor exceptional non–Jewish Poles engaged in projects preserving Jewish memory in Poland. This ceremony recognizes those people who work within their communities to bring back the memory of Jewish neighbors and their culture.

The Shalom Polish American Israeli Foundation for the Promotion of Jewish Culture, together with the Polish Ministry of Education, has been organizing competitions for high school students every two years since 1993 on the "History and Culture of Polish Jews." Thousands of students have taken part in the competition, submitting original works related to the presence of Jews in their regions. The Holocaust is one of the topic choices. In

2001/2002, for the first time, the competition "On common soil" was aimed at primary and middle school students, with the goal of making them acquainted with the rich heritage of the Jewish people in their area. In one of the schools, 130 students participated in the contest. The youngest entrant was 9 years old. In 2005 the Shalom Foundation published the important book *Memory. History of Polish Jews before, during and after the Destruction,* edited by Feliks Tych, co-authored by Barbara Engelking, Feliks Tych, Andrzej Żbikowski and Jolanta Żyndul, with the financial help of the Ministry of National Education and Sport and the ITF and in 2008 a multimedia educational presentation in DVD *The Holocaust through the Eyes of a Child*, supported by the Ministry of Education in Poland, containing scenarios of leading Polish educators: Wiesława Młynarczyk, Bogusław Jędruszczak and Robert Szuchta.

Exhibitions are vital components of the process of reconstructing collective memory. In 1996 the Shalom Foundation organized an exhibition of photographs of Polish Jews, "And I still see their faces," in the Zachęta Gallery. In response to a call put out by the Foundation in 1994, 7000 photos were sent in to them. This exhibition has travelled to many cities and revealed that Poles were not totally indifferent to the fact of the annihilation of their Jewish neighbors whose memory was preserved in countless households in silence. Poles kept their photos for half a century, and answered the Foundation's call for these pictures, which depict an absence louder than many words. Between 30 May 2008 and 30 June 2008 a photographic exhibition of 66 photographs documenting Jewish cultural heritage authored by Martin Cahn and entitled "Jewish Heritage of Euroregion Tatry" took place at the Municipal Cultural Centre in Józefów.

The Forum for Dialogue Among Nations Foundation was established in May 1998 in Gliwice (Moved its location to Warsaw in 2005) and has been involved over the past few years in setting up and conducting encounters between Polish youth and Jewish groups visiting Poland. Each year thousands of young Israelis and Jews from other countries visit Poland for the March of the Living or other educational programs designed to educate people about the tragedy of the Shoah. The groups used to visit the concentration camps and death camps with hardly any contact with modern Poland and modern Poles. Educational programs of this type sometimes tend to present Poland as a cemetery and the final destination of the Jewish people rather than the land of their ancestors. In addition, young Jews visiting Poland can often see anti–Semitic graffiti on the walls. They then leave Poland carrying home the same or even worse stereotypes. Using the experience gained during the organization of different programs over the past few years, the

Foundation staff has created a data base of Israeli schools and other Jewish organizations showing an interest in establishing dialogue through meetings with Polish youth. Recently the Foundation has received more frequently approaches from different Jewish groups with requests to assist in the organization of youth meetings.

The International Youth Meeting Center (IYMC) in Oświęcim was founded as an educational institution in 1986 thanks to the commitment of many who took part in the process of Polish-German reconciliation and Christian-Jewish dialogue. The German organization Actions Reconciliation/Service for Peace (ARSP) had the idea of setting up the IYMC in 1970 after the signing of the Warsaw Agreement between West Germany and Poland. The organization's director, the poet Volker von Törne, dreamed of the creation of a house where young people from different countries could find a place to confront the difficult heritage of Auschwitz and become acquainted with different ways of life and styles of thinking. The work of IYMC is based on the premise that the events that took place in Auschwitz were too painful an experience for its victims and for all mankind to be forgotten, that we should learn and draw conclusions from these events in order to build a better future, and that learning about other cultures and people, getting to know others, dealing with history, enables us to overcome fears, prejudices and hostility.

The IYMC's educational work is based on memory, imparting knowledge, openness and tolerance of everything new and foreign. The Centre cooperates with the German-Polish Youth Office (GPYO) established in 1991. From 2002 to April 19, 2004, this institution hosted 485 groups and conducted 81 seminars (I am grateful for the information which Anna Musioł, a PhD. student of the Institute of European Studies of the Jagiellonian University, shared with me). The many projects organized at the Centre include the Polish-German-Israeli project "Meeting with History—a Road for the Future." The seminar "Women in Auschwitz" on November 22–29, 2003, followed an investigative current opening new perspectives on historical events and their interpretation. The seminar addressed the patriarchal order of National Socialist society, the social and political role of women today and in the past, the historical background of the persecution of women in the Holocaust, and their traumatic camp experiences. Since 1987 the International Youth Meeting Centre in Oświęcim has hosted young people from Volkswagen schools, the Alliance of Technical and Trade Schools in Bielsko-Biała, and the Alliance of Vocational Schools in Bieruń at "Learning through meeting" seminars dedicated to the history of the Third Reich and KL

Auschwitz-Birkenau. In addition to presenting historical material, the project informs young people about current threats to democracy and human rights. Participants work for two weeks, at the Auschwitz-Birkenau Memorial.

The Borderland Foundation saved the synagogue in the town of Sejny. There, non–Jews perform Jewish drama and non–Jewish youth play klezmer music. The Borderland Foundation was created in May 1990 and in January 1991, the governor of Suwalki Province established the Borderland of Arts, Cultures and Nations Centre, located in Sejny. The Foundation is especially concerned about education, integrating it with cultural activity. The Documentation Center of Borderland Cultures publishes the periodical *Krasnogruda*, as well as books in a series called *Biblioteka Krasnogrudy* [*Krasnogruda Library*]. The Borderland Foundation organizes an educational program for high school youth, which is intended to deepen knowledge of the Suwalki region, with a particular focus on its religious and ethnic diversity. The publication of the Polish version of Jan Tomasz Gross's book *Neighbors* by the Borderland Foundation started a new area of discussion on the Holocaust in Europe.

The City Gate–Theatre NN Centre, founded in 1990, is a local government promoted cultural center in Lublin working to preserve cultural heritage and to promote education. In its programs the Centre invokes the symbolic and historical meaning of its location, the Grodzka Gate (the former gate between the Christian and Jewish quarters), and of the city of Lublin, a meeting place of cultures, traditions and religions. The Centre reconstructed its headquarters, the fourteenth-century Grodzka Gate and adjoining townhouses, reinvigorating this part of the Lublin's old and dilapidated city center. The program of activities at the center is connected with restoring the memory of Jewish life in Lublin. The Centre organizes and hosts arts activities, exhibitions, meetings, sessions, book and magazine promotions, films, concerts and public activities. In 1998, the Centre began a program entitled "The Great Book of the City" gathering archive materials connected with the Polish-Jewish history of Lublin (photographs, oral history and documents). One of the projects, "Oral History," which differs strikingly from the narratives still found in Polish history textbooks, presents the memories of older people as they recalled the multicultural diversity of pre-war Lublin, urban history seen through the eyes of individuals. Such projects, carried out by people hidden behind the initials NN (Nomen Nescio—name unknown), keep alive the memory that before the war one third of the inhabitants of Lublin were Jews, almost all of whom perished in the Bełżec camp. The project, "The Primer Exhibition. Children in the Majdanek Camp" showed the history of children who were forced to work, were taken away from their parents and were tortured to death in concentration camps.... Many of them were old enough to go to school with *The Primer* in their schoolbags.... A clear difference between the lives of Jewish children and Polish and Belarusian children is presented there. The Jewish children were to be murdered from the very beginning.

Another project, "Letters to the Ghetto," has been continued since 2001. Letters sent to Jewish people living in the non-existent Jewish quarter in Lublin, returned to the sender with the post office note "addressee unknown" raised awareness of the loss of the Jewish people, their homes, and their culture. The former Jewish quarter was totally destroyed and a high speed road is situated on the site of the former synagogue. This project is an example of educational activity performed outside the classroom setting, going beyond learning about historical facts from the textbooks, aimed at involving participants' emotions.

Some Polish organizations co-operate closely with foreign institutions. The Auschwitz Jewish Center Foundation was established in 1995 in New York. Its sister organization in Poland has been in existence since 1996. Through the collaborative efforts of the two organizations, the Auschwitz Jewish Center in Oświęcim was opened in 2000 in the town's only surviving synagogue—Chevra Lomdei Mishnayot—fully restored to its pre-war appearance. The Center's mission is to provide all visitors with an opportunity to memorialize the victims of the Shoah through the study of the life and culture of the former Jewish town—on the eve of World War II the town was inhabited by over 7,000 Jews who made up close to 60 percent of the entire population. The Center conducts guided tours that include a short film *Remembering Oświęcim*, showing testimonies of former residents of Oświęcim. There are interactive meetings with various Polish school groups, and meetings between Polish, German and Jewish youth. The Center organizes lectures and seminars for teachers (including open "Conversations about Tolerance" in co-operation with the International Youth Meeting Center and Never Again Association [*Nigdy Więcej*]) and a summer student fellowship program. Future military leaders from the U.S. Naval Academy, West Point Military Academy, and the U.S. Air Force Academy take part in an intensive three-week program dedicated to study of the Holocaust and the events leading up to it.

The Polish not-for-profit organization the Center for Citizenship Education initiated co-operation with the Polish-German Centre in Kraków and with Anne Frank House in Amsterdam, to use the "Anne Frank—History for Today" exhibition for teacher training within the "Traces of the past" project. The training stresses the importance of teaching about local history and its influence on the present, and how to learn from history to prevent racism and xenophobia. In a project carried out jointly with the National Centre for Culture and the Royal Castle in Warsaw, students explore their own town and surroundings in order to discover interesting, often neglected buildings and other traces of the past. Then the students, in co-operation with local governments and local cultural institutions, "adopt" their chosen building or place; in other words, they dedicate themselves to taking care of it. Between October 2004 and September 2005, the Center developed the "Righteous Among the Nations—Righteous Among Us" project in co-operation with the Association of Children of the Holocaust. The project targeted students and teachers from 60 primary and secondary schools. The authors of the project felt it essential to highlight the story of people who rescued Jews, because there is a danger that their life stories may be forgotten. On June 12 a ceremony presenting the students' projects took place in the Nożyk Synagogue in Warsaw with the participation of survivors and the Righteous. It was a moving encounter of generations united to face the legacy of the Holocaust, but with the focus on exceptional deeds, when people risked their lives to save other human lives. This educational project is the fruit of intergenerational understanding, and a lesson from the past for young Poles. Nowadays only about 2,000 "Righteous Among the Nations" live in Poland. Their life stories are still waiting to be discovered, honored and spread.

The Foundation for the Preservation of Jewish Heritage, established by the Union of Jewish Communities in Poland and the World Jewish Restitution Organization (WJRO) in Poland launched the educational project "To Bring Memory Back" (supported by the Netherlands Embassy MATRA/KAP Program) in 2005. This was directed at school children and their teachers. The project stimulates the hands-on experience of discovering the history and culture of past Jewish neighbors in the immediate surroundings of students. Often students bring their own discoveries to the larger public in their communities. An integral part of the project is the restoration of local Jewish cemeteries.

The small grant competition carried out by the Batory Foundation in 2005, "What is common/What is different," was designed to develop open, tolerant attitudes toward ethnic and religious differences and has revealed that local NGOs in Poland are interested in reminding, discovering, and promoting the multinational heritage of Poland, particularly of Polish Jews.

There were 137 submissions and 26 projects were chosen to go to the next phase of the contest. Projects relating to the past were not the only target of the Batory Foundation; the institution supports ongoing dialogue and identifies projects aimed at searching what unites Poles and Jews rather than what divides them. Ethnographic research, oral history and initiatives called "maps of memory" were among the projects submitted. An oral history project was submitted by the Białoruskie Zrzeszenie Studentów from Białystok aimed at teachers and students of the high school in Hajnówka, whose goal was to create multimedia "maps of memory" of inhabitants of the Podlasie region, where there was a Jewish community living before World War II. A joint project of the Białostocki Ośrodek Badań i Inicjatyw Społecznych and Koło Naukowe Socjologów of the University in Białystok from the same region focused on learning the historical narratives of other cultural groups, ethnoreligious minorities, as a step toward reconciliation. Another "map of my city," namely Sokołów Podlaski where Jews constituted 50 percent of population before World War II, was developed by Fundacja Civis Polonus in Warsaw to counteract not only Jewish absence, but also the absence of the memory of Jews as well. The project "Avar—Past. What has happened to the Jews of Tarnów?" of the Komitet Opieki nad Zabytkami in Tarnów prepared a contest for high school students designed to search for traces of Jewish presence.

Usually the "maps of memory" projects involved interviews with the oldest people in town, collecting photos, documents, reprinting old photos, making maps and models, workshops getting acquainting with Jewish culture, publishing books, special issues of journals, newsletters, guides, CDs, translating (e.g., Yizkor Book Zgierz, *Pinkas Krynki*) and developing databases and websites informing people about the Jewish presence and the Holocaust (Ośrodek Inicjatyw Twórczych Piekarnia in Kielce, Stowarzyszenie Nikt—Ruch Kulturotwórczy in Wrocław, Muzeum Pamięci zgierskich Żydów of the Towarzystwo Ochrony Kultury Zgierza, Myślenice Community Association, Ustrzyckie Stowarzyszenie Turystyczne, Akcja Katolicka Diecezji Kaliskiej, Parafialny Oddział Sokolniki in Łódź voivodship, Ekologiczny Klub UNESCO in Piaski Luterskie near Lublin, Teatr Kana in Szczecin, Stowarzyszenie Panorama Kultur in Wojsławice, Towarzystwo Przyjaciół Ziębic "Ducatus," Villa Socrates in Krynki, Stowarzyszenie Inicjatyw Społeczno-Ekologicznych Ruch na rzecz Ziemi in Siematycze—project "Obrazy Pamięci" [*Pictures of Memory*]). Many proposals included as an integral component of the project, care of the local kirkut (in Zgierz, Ustrzyki, Piaski Luterskie), and the synagogues (Towarzystwo Przyjaciół Ponidzia in Pińczów—

project "Odnowienie i Pamięć," Polskie Towarzystwo Ludoznawcze in Zamość). Many projects envisage work with local youth and school students, also targeting negative stereotypes and prejudices against Jews (Stowarzyszenie Społeczno-Kulturalne Leżak in Dęblin, Stowarzyszenie Słyszę Serce in Łódź, Stowarzyszenie Homo Faber in Lublin). (I am grateful to Olga Katarzyna Szostkowska of the Batory Foundation for information provided about the 2005 small grants contest.)

An important question is how various civil society initiatives are reflected in the opinions of their recipients? This question requires, however, a deeper study than a quantitative survey and such research was planned in Poland in Autumn 2009. So far we know from the survey conducted in 2008/2009 (Ambrosewicz- Jacobs, 2009) that, when asked, 38 percent of young Poles confirmed that the memory of the Holocaust is personally important to them (more for younger and lyceum students (46 percent) than for older and those attending vocational schools). The responses also show that 13 percent of the total disagreed with the above statement and 47 percent of respondents answered "hard to say" (refer to Table 2).

TABLE 2: IS THE MEMORY ABOUT THE HOLOCAUST IMPORTANT TO YOU PERSONALLY?

	Total	Gender		Age		School Type		
		Women	Men	16–17	18–19	Lyceum	Technical	Vocational
Important	37.6%	37.6%	37.8%	39.1%	27.6%	46.2%	33.4%	21.1%
Unimportant	12.8%	9.1%	17.3%	11.7%	21.6%	8.7%	14.7%	21.1%
Hard to say	46.7%	49.6%	43.1%	46.3%	49.1%	42.4%	48.1%	57.0%
No answer	2.9%	3.6%	1.8%	3.0%	1.7%	2.7%	3.8%	0.8%
Total N=1000)	1000	558	439	880	116	450	422	128

Note: Nationwide survey 2008/2009, random sample of 1000 students 17–18 years old

More than one third of Polish youth seems to understand that Poland lost its Jewish citizens and this fact affects some students. Regional civil society institutions, such as those described above and many more, are very committed and effective in their educational endeavors and are doing grassroots work helping Poles to understand the significance of the loss of Jews and Jewish culture and properly commemorate it. Increasing numbers of festivals, such as the Multicultural Week in Myślenice, organized by the local NGO Myślenice Community Association in June 2005, the Jewish Culture Days organized by the local high school in Michów (Lublin region, near Lubartów) or since 2002 the Meetings with Jewish Culture in Chmielnik (in 2008 the town was awarded the Father Musiał Prize given by the Christians and Jews Club "Przymierze" for their efforts on behalf of Christian-Jewish and Polish-Jewish reconciliation) indicate that in some places, but not everywhere, there is a genuine need to remember Jews in contemporary Poland. There is presence of memory like in Myślenice, in the form of a plaque on the town square, a database of Jews from Myślenice, Dobczyce, Sułkowice and Wiśniowa who were murdered in the Holocaust, and there is an absence of memory, as for example in Miechów and many other towns and villages.

Why are so many civil society institutions in contemporary Poland involved in projects dealing with memory, in particular with a memory of trauma in the sense developed by Karl Jaspers? Their effort is not only to give a description, to depict a nonexistent Jewish world, although such terms are always present in their rationale. It is ultimately, as Miłowit Kuniński (2007) rightly noticed, to create awareness about human beings' ability to do good and evil, to remember victims and to make past experience a part of our individual and collective identity. "The memories which lie within us are not carved in stone," wrote Primo Levi (1989, p. 23). Let us hope that the next generations of Poles will carry on, with compassion, their knowledge about the life of Polish Jews and the destruction of European Jewry on Polish territory.

(Reprinted with permission from I. Głuszyńska and Z. Mach [Eds.], [2011]. *Threats to multiculturalism*. Bielsko-Biała, pp. 182–197. Poland: Wyższa Szkoła Administracji.)

References

Ambrosewicz-Jacobs, J. (2009). *Attitudes of young Poles toward the Jews and the Holocaust. Report from the empirical research.* (Unpublished manuscript). Jagiellonian University, Kraków, Poland.
Gruber, E. R. (2002). *Virtually Jewish: Reinventing Jewish culture in Europe.* Berkeley: University of California Press.
Hirsch M. (1997). *Family frames. Photography, narrative, and postmemory.* Cambridge, MA: President and Fellows of Harvard College.
Kuniński, M. (2007). Tożsamość i sumienie. Moralny sens pamięci indywidualnej i zbiorowej o traumie. In L. Suchanka (Ed.), *Pamięć—Odpowiedzialność* (pp. 9–18), Oświęcim, Poland: Wydawnictwo Państwowej Wyższej Szkoły Zawodowej w Oświęcimiu 2007.
Primo, L. (1989). *The drowned and the saved.* New York: Vintage International.
Lipski J. J. (n. d.), Dwie ojczyzny, dwa patriotyzmy. Uwagi o megalomania narodowej

i ksenofobii Polaków, *Otwarta rzeczpospolita: Stowarzyszenie przeciw antysemityzmowi i ksenofobii*, 43.

Maier, C. S. (1993). A surfeit of memory? Reflections on history, melancholy and denial. History and Memory. *Studies in Representation of the Past*, 5 (2), 136–152.

Signer M. A. (2001). Introduction: Memory and history in the Jewish and Christian traditions. In M. Signer (Ed.) *Memory and History in Christianity and Judaism*. Notre Dame, IN: University of Notre Dame Press.

Tokarska-Bakir, J. (2004). *Rzeczy mgliste. Eseje i studia*. Sejny: Pogranicze.

Traba, R. (2006). *Historia—przestrzeń dialogu*. Warszawa: Instytut Studiów Politycznych Polskiej Akademii Nauk.

Witkowski, M. (2009, April 18). Przygoda przy dozowniku Algidy, *Polityka*, 16.

Zeitlin F. I. (1998). The vicarious witness: Belated memory and authorial presence in recent Holocaust literature. *Studies in Representation of the Past 10*, (2), 5–42.

Żakowski, J. (2002). *Rewanż pamięci*. Warszawa: Wydawnictwo Sic.

Websites for Further Information

Batory Foundation, http://www.batory.org.pl/en. Partners with other foundations in Poland and abroad to promote awareness of citizens' rights and responsibilities in a democratic society.

Borderland Foundation, Sejny, http://pogranicze.sejny.pl/foundation,129.html. Dedicated to bridge building between people of different religions, ethnicities, cultures.

The Centre for Citizenship Education, http://www.ceo.org.pl/pl/o-nas/english. Promotes civic engagement; develops curricula for teacher and students in Polish elementary and secondary schools.

Children of the Holocaust Association, Warsaw, http://www.dzieciholocaustu.org.pl/szab51.php?s=index3.php. Composed of Holocaust survivors who were 13 or younger at the start of World War II or were born during the war; provides support for members and education for the community about the Holocaust.

Forum for Dialogue Among Nations Foundation, Warsaw , http://www.dialog.org.pl/en/. Promotes dialog and cooperation between Jews and Poles; sponsors "School of Dialogue" an educational program for Polish middle school and high school students.

The Foundation for the Preservation of Jewish Heritage in Poland, http://fodz.pl/?d=1&l=en. Supports preservation of Jewish cemeteries and historical Jewish sites; part of mission is education.

> To Bring Memory Back, project of the Foundation for the Preservation of Jewish Heritage in Poland, www.pamiec.fodz.pl. Educational program for Polish teachers and school children with hand-on activities for educating others about the Jewish heritage of their area (click Union Jack for English version).
>
> POLIN, project of the Foundation for the Preservation of Jewish Heritage in Poland, www.polin.org.pl. Multimedia website; uses Web 2.0 technology to provide a variety of information about the heritage of Jews in Poland and of the Holocaust (website in Polish).

Fundacja Ronalda S. Laudera, www.lauder.lodz.pl. Official website of the foundation which offers a variety of programming, camps, and other educational activities in Poland (website in Polish).

Grodzka Gate, http://tnn.pl/k_77_m_77.html. A municipal cultural institution fostering awareness of Lublin's multicultural history and developing a sense of local identity and tolerance for other cultures.

The Institute of Tolerance, Łódź, http://www.instytuttolerancji.org/. Sponsors projects aimed at tolerance/intolerance in general (website in Polish).

Jewish Association Czulent, Kraków, http://www.czulent.pl/en. Organization for Jewish young people, religious and secular.

Judaica Foundation for Jewish Culture, Kraków, www.judaica.pl. Official website of the foundation which offers a variety of programming for the public.

Life in a Jar: The Irena Sendler Project, http://www.irenasendler.org/. Presents the story of the school project in the United States which has become an international educational project honoring the life of Irena Sendler, a Polish social worker.

Righteous Among the Nations, http://www.yadvashem.org/yv/en/righteous/index.asp. Sponsored by Yad Vasehm in Israel to honor non-Jews who risked their lives to save Jews during the Holocaust.

The Shalom Foundation, http://www.shalom.org.pl/eng/index.htm, Warsaw. Sponsors art and other cultural exhibits, including the Festival, Warsaw of Singer, as well as classes, lectures and discussions; supports the first Jewish preschool in Poland since the Holocaust and offers "Sunday school" for Jewish children.

Stowarzyszenie im. Jana Karskiego (the Jan Karski Association), Kielce, www.jankarski.org.pl. Official website of the organization; focuses on programs and publications which promote openness and respect (website in Polish)

ZOOM/The Polish Jewish Youth Organization, http://www.zoom.edu.pl/info-in-english/. Fosters a sense of Jewish community among all Polish-Jewish youth.

Museums: Their Role in Holocaust Education and Jewish Studies

> "[T]here is at least one dominant theme that can be noted when reviewing these Jewish museums, either in Kraków alone or more broadly across the country [Poland]: they are typically museums, exhibitions, or other cultural forms of engagement with a community that *was*."—Craddy, 2010, p. 145

According to the International Council of Museums (2012) the meaning of what a museum is has evolved with changes in society. In 2007, they adopted the following definition:

> A museum is a non-profit, permanent institution in the service of society and its development, open to the public, which acquires, conserves, researches, communicates and exhibits the tangible and intangible heritage of humanity and its environment for the purposes of education, study and enjoyment [ICOM, 2012, para. 2].

Despite being defined as non-profit by ICOM, there are some private museums which may be run for profit. Additionally, not all non-profit museums are NGOs. Some are established and/or run by governmental bodies, either at the national, state or local level.

For the purposes of this chapter, the museum's role as a place of education and study are the key elements. However, this general definition needs some specific details to understand how museums serve as entities which educate about Jewish history, life and culture and about the Holocaust.

Overview of Jewish Museums

Seldin (1991) points out that there are several characteristics that differentiate one museum from another. These include "the size and nature of their collections ... their housing and exhibition space ... financial resources and staffing ... [and] their program emphases" (p. 71). While there are museums that contain collections pertaining to a variety of groups, some museums are specifically dedicated to one group's history and culture. Jewish museums collect, preserve, and exhibit material related to Jewish history and culture and offer programming that stimulates interest in and provides knowledge about this group's history and culture to the public at large, not just to Jews. Jewish museums, which are located in many parts of the world, may have general programs which focus on art, history, and/or culture or they may be specialized, focusing on one aspect of Jewish life or history, such as Holocaust museums. However, even specialty museums, such as Holocaust museums, generally provide some context or background for the featured aspect. In the case of Holocaust museums, there are often artifacts which show specific relevant phases of Jewish history or ritual objects used in the synagogue and at home.

The Association of European Jewish Museums (AEJM) is a professional organization which promotes communication and networking among the various Jewish museums in Europe. According to their by-laws, an institution can be a full member of the organization only if they are a legal entity

> registered in Europe operating a museum or museum service focused on the Jewish culture and/or history and employ at least one paid full-time professional whose primary responsibility includes: the acquisition, the maintenance or the exhibition to the public of objects which are the property of or used by the museum or the museum service [AEJM, n.d., Art. 4.2].

Currently in Poland only four institutions are members of this organization: Galicia Jewish Museum in Kraków, Oświęcim (Auschwitz) Jewish Center, The Museum of the History of Polish Jews in Warsaw, and the Emanuel Ringelblum Jewish Historical Institute also in Warsaw.

However, this number of registered museum members does not reflect the number of institutions in Poland that could be considered Jewish museums by using a broader definition. Auschwitz-Birkenau, Majdanek in Lublin and Stutthof near Gdansk and other concentration camps are considered museums of the Holocaust. The Old Synagogue Museum in Kraków, as well as the other six synagogues in Kraków certainly function as Jewish museums, since they contain collections of material related to Jewish history and culture and are open to the public. Many other inactive synagogues across Poland, such as the ones in Łancut and Pinczów which display Judaica could also be considered museums. The White Stork Synagogue in Wrocław (formerly Breslau, Germany) has been restored and will house a museum which focuses on the history and culture of Silesian Jews through exhibitions, lectures, and workshops. The Old Jewish Cemetery in Wrocław is designated as a municipal museum of cemetery art. Grodzka Gate in Lublin houses extensive archives and features various projects with educational value for learning about Jewish life in Poland and the disruption of the Holocaust. While they are not Jewish museums, some of the major museums in Poland have Judaica collections and often have temporary exhibits featuring various aspects of Jewish life and history, such as a 2012 exhibit at the National Museum in Kraków of Bruno Schultz's *The Booke of Idolatry*.

Even though they do not fall under the definition of museums, one should also consider heritage sites, memorials, and monuments as places and sites where one can learn about Jewish history and culture. The Warsaw Ghetto and a memorial site such as the Umschlagplatz in Warsaw, the site from which Jews were deported to Treblinka, remind and educate visitors of the tragedy of the Holocaust and the human suffering in those places. There are numerous plaques and monuments which memorialize the Holocaust, but there is also some evidence of Jewish life in these places before that time. Jewish cemeteries throughout Poland, where many famous figures are buried, such as Ludwig Zamenhof, the creator of Esperanto, Clara Sachs, an impressionistic painter, and Rabbi Moses Isserles, also known as Rema, a prominent sixteenth century Talmudist who founded Remuh Synagogue in Kraków, serve to remind visitors of the role that Jews played in Polish life throughout the centuries. The many synagogues, most now inactive, illustrate the active religious life of many Jews in Poland. Even the holes in doorposts where *mezuzot* (a holder for a piece of parchment with verses from Deuteronomy) were once attached attest to the lives of those who lived there before the Holocaust. However, these are not the types of experiences that fit the ICOM's or the AEJM's definitions of a museum. Therefore, this chapter will limit itself to a discussion of the four which are members of AEJM, as well as Auschwitz-Birkenau, the Old Synagogue Museum in Kraków, and Grodzka Gate.

Old Synagogue Museum, Kraków

The Old Synagogue Museum housed in the synagogue building known as the Alte Shul is part of the Historical Museum of Kraków. It is located in the heart of Kazimierz, the former Jewish quarter of Kraków. The original building was first built in the fifteenth century then rebuilt in the sixteenth century. For centuries it was a religious center and held a place of authority in the Jewish community. During World War II "the day to day running of the synagogue was transferred from the local Jewish Council to the Kraków Historical Museum" (Jewish Kraków, 2011, para. 2).

The Old Synagogue Museum has a permanent collection which focuses on the Jews of Kraków. The exhibits, arranged in the main sanctuary, are designed not only to display items but also to inform visitors of how these items were used in religious ceremonies or for holidays and the customs and traditions surrounding each ceremony or holiday. Historical pictures and other works of art are also on display which illustrate Jewish life in Kraków and in other areas of Poland. Temporary exhibits are often on display in the women's prayer room, which is off to the side of the main sanctuary.

As part of the Historical Museum of Kraków, there are workshops and classes that the public can attend which relate to topics of Jewish interest at the Old Synagogue and other museum sites around the city. For example, in May 2013 an interactive course presented at the Old Synagogue focused on the synagogue and religious ceremonies as well as the house and family life. Comparisons were made between Jewish and Christian scriptures as well as between the function and form of the religious buildings of the two religions. The symbolic significance of Jewish male religious attire, such as the kippah (head covering), and elements of the home, such as the mezuzah were also covered.

Auschwitz-Birkenau Memorial and Museum, Oświęcim

The Auschwitz-Birkenau Memorial and Museum is a state-run museum which is not a member of AEJM. It was opened in 1947 under the auspices of the Polish Ministry of Culture and Art (Ministerstwo Kultury i Sztuki—MKiS) with the guidance and advice of Jewish survivors of the camp. Its primary goal when established was to commemorate the victims of the Holocaust and to present the extent of German atrocities. In 1979 it became a UNESCO world heritage site. In the 1990s the focus of the museum changed to include more educational programs and in 2005 the International Center for Education about Auschwitz and the Holocaust was officially founded there.

> The center educates about all facets of the tragedy of the Jewish Holocaust, Polish victims and Nazi terror during the occupation, the destruction of victims in the concentration camp system, the persecution and mass murder of the Roma, and about the systematic exclusion of entire national groups from society [ICEAH, 2013, para. 4].

The Center conducts programs at the Auschwitz-Birkenau Memorial and Museum as well as elsewhere around Poland and in other countries. International cooperation with organizations such as Yad Vashem and the United States Holocaust Museum is an important part of its mission, as is educating young people and their teachers. Its programs promote knowledge about the Holocaust to students, teachers, and youth study groups, and at various institutions and research centers in Poland and abroad. In addition to a variety of lectures, classes, workshops, conferences and symposia, the Center sponsors film screenings, multimedia presentations, as well as drawing and writing contests. Teaching modules, such as historical, culture studies, philosophical, theological, sociological medical, legal, and so on, which may be of interest to a diverse group of people, including clergy, military personnel, journalists, lawyers, museum staff, secondary and university students, and teachers were designed by the Center, and can be used in different combinations to meet the needs and interests of different groups. In order to enhance the education of teachers about the Holocaust, the Center offers some postgraduate courses in collaboration with several Polish universities. The Center also arranges study exchanges with Yad Vashem for museum staff and professionals as well as teachers from Poland and Israel.

One educational program that the Center runs is the International Summer Academy, a five-day program for educators at all levels, museum staff, researchers, and anyone else interested in Auschwitz and the Holocaust. Run in collaboration with the Department of Jewish Studies at the Jagiellonian University, the Academy features lectures and discussions focusing on Polish-Jewish and Polish-German relations as well as subjects related to Auschwitz as a concentration camp and as a memorial site.

In 2013 the Center initiated the Polish-German-Russian Educational Project. The purpose of this project is to bring together representatives of three memorial sites, Auschwitz in Poland, Bergen-Belsen in Germany, and Perm–36 in Russia, to develop an international training program, the Transnational Training Programme, to begin in 2014. The training program will focus "on how to teach about human rights in places where mass atrocities have been carried out" (ICEAH, 2013, para. 3).

Oświęcim (Auschwitz) Jewish Center, Oświęcim

The Oświęcim (Auschwitz) Jewish Center is not part of the Auschwitz-Birkenau Memorial and Museum. A member of the AEJM, it was established in 1995 and opened its doors in 2000. The Center consists of a Jewish museum, a synagogue, and an educational center and has two primary aims: to commemorate 500 years of Jewish life in Oświęcim and to educate about the Holocaust. The Center accomplishes these aims through exhibitions, lectures, and workshops aimed at Polish adults and students as well as from other countries around the world. The goal of the center is not just to educate about the Holocaust but to also provide visitors and program participants with tools to be able to educate others about the lessons of the Holocaust. Documentaries, survivor stories, and an app for an online project called *Oshpitzin* (the Yiddish word for Oświęcim) are a few of the materials available.

Additionally, the Center offers programs promoting in-depth study of pre-war Jewish life as well as the Holocaust which are geared towards specific audiences. These include the *Auschwitz Jewish Center Fellows Program: A Bridge to History* for American graduate students; the *American Services Academies Program* specifically designed for students in the various American military academies; and *The Auschwitz Jewish Center Program for Students Abroad*.

Programs for local residents as well as for students across Poland are also offered. *Cultural Program* is designed with the general public in mind and its educational seminars are held monthly. Guest speakers, including academics, writers, and performs, speak on specific topics related to the Holocaust, Jewish life, and relations between Poles and Jews. The aim of these seminars is not only to inform the public about these topics and issues, but also to promote tolerance and understanding among different groups of people. The Center also offers *My Former Neighbors, Intercultural Dialogs*, and *Why Do We Need Tolerance,* educational programs specifically for Polish young people.

In this small town of Oświęcim the visitor can go to these two museums whose focus is the history of the Jewish people but from different perspectives. The Jewish Center illustrates and educates about the life of Jews mostly before the Holocaust, while Auschwitz-Birkenau will always stand as a symbol of the Holocaust. Both of the museums exist in their present forms due the changes in Poland since 1989. Polish people and people from around the world want to try to understand to whom and how this genocide happened. The mission of the Auschwitz-Birkenau museum has evolved over time so that it is now an educational center about atrocities and the Holocaust in particular, not just a memorial to those who were killed. The Jewish Center celebrates the lives of the Jewish inhabitants of this little town whose name has become synonymous with murder and the Holocaust.

Galicia Jewish Museum, Kraków

Opened in 2004, the Galicia Jewish Museum in the Kazimierz quarter of Kraków is housed in a pre-war mill. Galicia Jewish Museum, a member of the AEJM, serves as exhibition space, and meeting center, and offers a wide variety of cultural and educational programs about the Holocaust and Jewish life in Poland, specifically in Galicia, the area of Poland where the museum is located. During the paritions, Galicia was part of the Austrian parition, and was an ethnically and religiously diverse region with Jews making up 10 percent to 12 percent of the population. West Galicia was the area of Poland now known as Małopolska (smaller Poland) and Kraków was its capital. East Galicia, whose capital city was Lviv (Lwow; Lemberg) is now in the Ukraine. The museum's name and purpose pay homage to this heritage.

Whereas the Old Synagogue Museum is a historical museum, this museum's centerpiece is its permanent exhibition, Traces of Memory, a contemporary view of the area's Jewish past. This photo exhibit contains images of abandoned synagogues as well as of restored synagogues, Auschwitz and other sites of destruction. Temporary exhibitions have ranged from depictions of Jewish life in Lwów (now in the Ukraine) before the war to art exhibits by living Jewish artists and those who perished in the Holocaust. It also has one of the largest Jewish bookshops in Poland selling a wide range of books in several languages, as well as some Judaica. The museum's Media Resource Centre includes films on Jewish and Holocaust-related subjects.

During the Kraków Festival of Jewish Culture, Galicia Jewish Museum plays an active role, hosting various exhibits, lectures, workshops, and demonstrations related to the Festival as well as concerts and plays. For several years it has been the site of the production of "Tajemnice mojej baci" (Secrets of My Grandmother) a production of Midrash Theatre, as well as a variety of concerts and other performances.

A large part of Galicia's mission is education, and they offer an extensive range of programs about Jewish history and culture and about the Holocaust. They offer programs in Polish, English, or French for children and families, high school students, international youth exchanges, as well as university and other adult programs.

The Emanuel Ringelblum Jewish Historical Institute, Warsaw

The Emanuel Ringelblum Jewish Historical Institute is located in Warsaw near the site of the Great Synagogue which was blown up by the Nazis in 1943. The JHI originally opened in 1947, and in 2009 it gained the status of a cultural institution, a national center for research and documentation. It is a member of the AEJM.

One of the Institute's main functions is as a library/archive for thousands of books and documents, for the Ringelblum Archive, the Warsaw Ghetto Underground Archive and for works of art. The JHI also serves as an important clearinghouse for people engaged in genealogical research. The Institute is also actively involved in educational and cultural activities about the history and culture of Jews in Poland for the general public, as well as research and educational cooperation with research institutions around the world.

In 1992, the JHI began offering courses for teachers which taught content and teaching strategies about Jewish history, life, and culture, Judaism, the history of Jews in Poland, as well as courses on stereotypes, prejudice and anti-Semitism. They also offer museum classes for school-aged children. A recent emphasis has been to raise awareness about the Holocaust in Poland through international conferences for teachers.

These various educational endeavors reflect the shift in the Polish perspective about Holocaust education and Jewish studies that came about after 1989. Even before the mandate to teach about these issues to Polish schoolchildren was passed, teachers were looking for opportunities to learn about this part of their past which had been hidden for so long. Museums like the JHI were able and willing to step in and fill part of that void.

The Museum of the History of Polish Jews, Warsaw

The Museum of the History of Polish Jews, which opened in 2013, is a joint project of the Jewish Historical Institute, The Polish Ministry of Culture, and the city of Warsaw. Located in the former Jewish quarter which became the Warsaw ghetto, the museum uses twenty-first century technology to create a multimedia exhibition leading the visitor through 1,000 years of Polish-Jewish history. To symbolize a connection between the past and future, the museum was built facing the Monument to the Ghetto Heroes, which was dedicated in 1948 to commemorate the Warsaw Ghetto Uprising of 1943. The building contains several ramps or bridges which are a metaphor for the museum's goal of providing bridges between the past and present as well as between the people of Poland.

Even before it opened the museum began operating as an educational institution. Projects such as the replica of the roof/ceiling of the seventeenth century Gwoździec synagogue, the Educational Center and Akademia Polin (Polish Academy) have already been in place for some time. New educational programs, such as The Polin Academy Summer Seminar (PASS), are being developed which will further enhance the Museum's educational role.

The Gwoździec Reconstruction project which restored and reconstructed the roof/ceiling of this exceptional example of Jewish religious architecture is the centerpiece of the Museum's Core Exhibition. From its inception the project took 10 years to complete involving about 400 people from around the world. A thorough search of archives created the foundation. Workshops conducted in historic synagogues around Poland included not only how to create this artifact, but also cultural and educational activities about Jewish and Polish culture. This hands-on approach is one way in which this museum fulfills its educational mission.

The Educational Center of the museum also has been carrying out educational programming for some time before the museum opened. It offers a wide range of programming for young people and adults who want to learn more about Jewish culture in Poland. They have also organized Polish-Israeli youth exchanges to promote knowledge and understanding between these two groups. After the museum opened the Educational Center was able to expand it educational activities to focus on the Core Exhibition of the museum.

Akademia Polin (Polish Academy) is a unique museum staff training program. The purpose of the Academy is to train museum staff as well as educators who want to use the museum facilities. Participants engage in a variety of lectures, workshops, discussion, and hands-on activities by scholars, educators, and museum staff to develop educational materials and to help plan visits to the museum.

The Polin Academy Summer Seminar (PASS) was designed for North American educators. Its purpose is to provide North American educators, from all types of educational institutions, not just Jewish educational institutions, with information on the Museum and help them to explore and understand its resources. Customized educational tours form part of the experience. The programs take place in collaboration with the Polin Academy so that each group can learn from, interact with, and form relationships with the other. These one-week sessions, offered twice in the summer, are covered under a travel grant and a free to participants.

As with the programs highlighted here, most of the educational programs offered by the Museum seek not only to educate but to give participants opportunities for collaboration with others and to share what they have learned with others in creative ways.

Grodzka Gate, Lublin

Grodzka Gate in Lublin is not technically a museum of Jewish history and culture. However, it plays an important role in the eastern Polish city of Lublin as an archive and an educational setting. The Grodzka Gate (Brama Grodzka) project was developed by the theatre group, NN Theatre, in the early 1990s. The group enlarged its activities from traditional theatre productions to becoming a vehicle for uncovering, preserving, and sharing the past. The gate which overlooks Lublin's castle was one of the main entries into the old city of Lublin and served as the main passage between the Christian and Jewish parts of the city. In the period before World War II, Lublin's population was about a third Jewish. Most of their houses, businesses, and places of worship and study were located in the area around the castle and the Brama Grodzka. After the destruction of World War II, the gate fell into disrepair.

Today the Grodzka Gate houses an extensive archive of recordings, photographs, documents, and other memorabilia that documents the pre–World War II history of Lublin. The group has recorded the testimonies of over 800 people, about 2,500 hours of oral history, which focus on what Lublin and the surrounding area were like in the pre-war period. Transcripts have been analyzed and catalogued thematically. Many audio and video excerpts are available online. Their websites comprise the sixth largest digital library in Poland. There are numerous online links that give access to a variety of material. The Memory Gate Project "takes visitors for a walk around the streets of vanished Jewish city in Lublin, shows the spatial arrangement of the Jewish district and presents the most important places related with the Lublin Jewish community" (TNN.PL, n.d., Memory Gate Portal sect).

The creation of a model of what Lublin looked like on the eve of World War II, before much of the city, including the Jewish Quarter, was destroyed is another project the group has undertaken. This model has been converted to Google Earth, and the overlay of the pre-war city onto the contemporary city is available online. This "multimedia guidebook" allows the viewer to make comparisons between modern day Lublin and the city as it was 70 years ago. There are also plans to create virtual models of the city at various stages from the thirteenth century on.

Another project they have developed is "Letters to Henio." Henio was a boy who was murdered in Majdanek Concentration Camp. Photos and other information about him were preserved, and the group has created a memorial project in which many school children in the region are involved. One original conception of the project was to use the social networking site, *Facebook*, to involve participants. One organizer set himself up as "Henio." However, Facebook closed it down as an inappropriate use of the medium. Before being shut down, the site got over 3,000 hits.

Grodzka Gate is not limited to Jewish history in Lublin. Instead, it provides an important link between life in Poland before World War II for Jews and Poles alike. It provides primary and secondary source materials which are invaluable authentic materials for teaching about the coexistence of Poles and Jews before the Holocaust.

Summary of Polish Museums as Educational Centers

In keeping with the IOCM definition of museums as places of education and study, one can see that the museums discussed here fall into that realm. Each plays a specific role in educating visitors from Poland and other countries about the breadth and depth of Jewish life in Poland before the Holocaust. Because the Holocaust is the pivotal moment in Polish-Jewish history which ruptured Jewish life in Poland, it is often seen as the central element by many people. Contextualizing the Holocaust within this rich past and the slowly emerging future of Jews in contemporary Poland educates visitors not only about the people, places, and events of the past 1,000 years, but also about how human history influences and shapes the present and future. This contextualization cannot take place only through static exhibits, and in the twenty-first century, it should not. Interactive, educationally sound presentations, workshops, lectures, etc. provide the connections that are necessary to see how the past, present, and future are linked together. Because of the variety and large amounts of materials that these museums possess, they offer many opportunities and possibilities for education about Jewish life and history in Poland.

Websites for Further Information

Association of European Jewish Museums, http://www.aejm.org/. Promotes cooperation and communication between Jewish Museums in Europe; provides assistance, training, and support to member organizations.

Auschwitz-Birkenau Memorial and Museum, Oświęcim, http://en.auschwitz.org/. Commemorates the victims of the Holocaust; includes educational programs for all ages.

Emanuel Ringelblum Jewish Historical Institute, Warsaw, http://www.jhi.pl/instytut. Serves as a national center for research and documentation; member of the AEJM.

Galicia Jewish Museum, Kraków, http://www.en.galiciajewishmuseum.org/. Located in Kazimierz, former Jewish quarter of Kraków; member of the AEJM; offers cultural and educational programs about Holocaust and Jewish life, specifically in Galicia.

Grodzka Gate, Lublin, http://tnn.pl/k_77_m_77.html. Fosters awareness of Lublin's multicultural history and tolerance for other cultures

    Memory Gate Project maintained by Grodzka Gate, Lublin, http://tnn.pl/The_Gate_of_Memory_-_English,3362.html. Provides an overview of the history and function the Grodzka gate.

    Multimedia Guidebook maintained by Grodzka Gate, Lublin, http://teatrnn.pl/przewodniki. Uses Google Earth to overlay the pre-war city onto the contemporary city (website in Polish).

    Letters to Henio maintained by Grodzka Gate, Lublin, http://tnn.pl/pamiej.php?kat=3385. A memorial project involving school children in the region.

The Museum of the History of Polish Jews, Warsaw, http://www.jewishmuseum.org.pl/en/cms/home-page/. Official website of The Museum of the History of Polish Jews; uses twenty-first century technology to create a multimedia exhibition and educational facility.

    Akademia Polin (Polin Academy) of the Museum of the History of Polish Jews, Warsaw, http://www.jewishmuseum.org.pl/en/cms/polin-academy/. Museum staff training program for museum staff and educators.

    Educational Center of The Museum of the History of Polish Jews, Warsaw, http://www.jewishmuseum.org.pl/en/cms/education/. Offers a wide range of programming for young people and adults about Jewish culture in Poland.

    Gwoździec Reconstruction of the Museum of the History of Polish Jews, http://www.jewishmuseum.org.pl/en/cms/news/2234,replica-roof-of-the-gwozdziec-synagogue-installed-at-the-museum-/. Reconstruction project of restored and reconstructed the roof/ceiling the synagogue at Gwoździec; the centerpiece of the Museum's Core Exhibition.

    The Polin Academy Summer Seminar (PASS) of the Museum of the History of Polish Jews, Warsaw, http://www.jewishmuseum.org.pl/en/cms/the-polin-academy-summer-seminar-pass-/. Provides North American educators with information on the Museum and how to explore and understand its resources.

Old Synagogue Museum, Kraków, http://www.mhk.pl/oddzialy/stara_synagoga, Located in Kazimierz, Kraków's former Jewish quarter; houses a permanent collection focusing on the Jews of Kraków.

Oświęcim (Auschwitz) Jewish Center, Oświęcim, http://ajcf.org/jewish-museum/. Member of AEJM; consists of a Jewish museum, a synagogue, and an educational center; focuses on commemorating Jewish life in Oświęcim and educating about the Holocaust.

The Role of the Arts in Holocaust Education and Jewish Studies

"Painting is the way to express perceptions of reality, and for me, it is a way to work the past out," she said, sipping an iced coffee. "Things like 'Who am I? How was I brought up? What kind of people have I met?' all these things are on my canvas in some way. Not all artists are showing this directly but you can find links to Jewish culture in their works."—Quote from Zuzanna Ziolkowska (Brownell, 2012, para. 5)

The Arts as Cultural Education

The arts, which include such broad categories as visual arts, musical arts, dramatic arts, and literary arts, are a reflection of culture, and as cultural markers reflect and shape a community's character and identity, serving as a form of socialization (Graham, 2009). "Experiencing the arts can ... create a stronger identification with our own cultural history.... This identification often emerges through a strong emotional reaction to the subject matter and the way it is portrayed" (Lawrence, 2008, p. 75). Because of the internal and personal nature of emotions, their expression and their comprehension varies from person to person. However, one's cultural identity also influences how one manages the affective (emotional) domain and how one views its role in artistic expression.

Although "the cognitive and affective domains of knowing are intertwined and inseparable" (Lawrence, 2008, p. 70), the arts play a different role in learning than do subjects such as math or reading, because the purpose of the arts is not to be thought about (cognitive learning), but to be felt (affective learning). The arts provide tangible ways to express and to experience intangible attributes such as emotions (Templeton, 1965). Whether the tangible expression is with words, visually or through sound, the creator must examine the emotion he or she wants to evince and create symbols to represent it, so that the creator and the audience feel and comprehend the emotion. Furthermore, Moore (2004) says that creative expression allows us to explore feelings and emotions deeply, providing opportunities for transformation of emotionally laden issues. According to Lawrence (2008), "it is art that has the power to provoke emotional responses that inspire us to take action" (p. 71). The arts also allow the audience to experience alternative perspectives, evoking positive or negative emotions, ranging from despair to hope, anger to joy.

However, as Greene (1995) points out, just being exposed to the arts is not enough to effect change. This comprehension and subsequent learning from the "experience requires one to be fully in the experience: mind, body, heart, and soul" (Lawrence, 2008, p. 69). Rather than being preoccupied with the end product or in trying to figure out what is happening, sensory imagery, the arts, allows us to become totally involved in what we are experiencing, whether as creator or as audience, and reaching the state that Csikszentmihalyi (1996) calls flow.

One example is protest art, which Lawrence (2008) asserts can be "used to disturb and provoke" (p. 74). The protest music of the 1960s in the United States, for instance, explains the horrors of war or the injustice of racial discrimination. However, the songs do not just inform; the lyrics create an emotional impact by creating an image in the listener's mind and the melodies that accompany these words evoke emotional responses. Another example of protest art is

> Picasso's *Guernica,* painted in 1937 as a political statement depicting the Nazi bombing during the Spanish Civil War, [and] shows the violence and brutality from the perspective of the victims. Educators today still use it to provoke inquiry into the nature of war and conflict [p. 74].

Another important aspect of art is who is presenting the art form, what their motivations are, what their knowledge of the culture is and what their relationship to the art form is. Each of these alone or together can influence the representation. One does not necessarily have to be a member of the cultural group to represent its art authentically. However, if the presenter does not have a comprehensive and intuitive understanding of the art and the culture, there is a tendency toward presenting both as something exotic, something "other," and perhaps as somehow inferior to the arts and, ultimately, the values of the dominant culture. For example, klezmer music, a type of traditional music among Ashkenazi Jews, may be presented as unsophisticated dance music which reflects the "soulful" quality of the Jewish people, whereas Polish (or other) folk music may be presented simply as happy dance music, without making a stereotyped connection between the people's nature and their music. In this way, value is attributed to certain genres of music, and other art forms, and this value is often the reflection of a stereotype, not a true reflection of the culture being represented. However, if presented authentically, the arts can provide a broader base for appreciation of a wider range of genres from a variety of cultures which can help reduce stereotyping by making what was once unknown familiar.

Judaica and Other Visual Art Forms

As mentioned in the previous chapter, a number of museums include Judaica in their collections. The collection the Old Synagogue in Kraków, for instance, includes many ritual objects used in the synagogue and in the Jewish home. The displays offer context for the objects and provide explanations of how and why they would be used. Context helps create an emotional impact so that the object becomes a piece of art to which the viewer can connect rather than just an object. In this way, this display provides authentic educational value for the viewer. However, a display of Judaica in the National Museum of Kraków is just that—a display of labeled objects. Without background knowledge or an informed guide, the viewer sees only objects offered in no context.

From time to time Jewish artists are featured in museums, such as the 2012 exhibit at the National Museum in Kraków of Bruno Schultz's *The Booke of Idolatry*. However, by and large the work of Jewish artists is not highlighted in any way except in Jewish museums, such as Galicia Jewish Museum which regularly has temporary exhibits of Jewish artists and themes, and venues such as the Izak Synagogue in Kraków which features such artwork from time to time.

When artwork is contextualized it has educational value and can help break down stereotypical images. A photo exhibit at Galicia Jewish Museum of Polish-Jewish young people taking part in sport and learning to farm as part of the Zionist movement gives a different picture of pre–War Jews than the bookish Talmud scholar who is often depicted. The viewer can connect on an emotional level with the hope for a better life in Israel that these images project. In 2007, the International Cultural Centre in Kraków used photos as the backdrop for an exhibit, A World Before a Catastrophe: Kraków's Jews Between the Wars, which portrayed Jewish life in pre–Holocaust Poland. The exhibit showed the Jewish community as multi-dimensional and as a vital part of life in inter-war Kraków. Such contextualization helps the viewer look beyond stereotypical images and see the "other" as less exotic and more a part of the society in which they lived. It also increases the emotional impact of the pictures, by portraying a vibrant community of real people with real lives, and their hopes, their joys, feelings that the viewers can identify with on an individual and human level.

Literature, Print Media, Film, and Theatre

Literature, the written word, is also an important cultural marker that has educational implications for people of all ages. From the beginning of the twenty-first century numerous volumes of fiction and non-fiction have been published in Poland related to Jewish studies and the Holocaust. Some of these are Polish translations of works published in other countries, such as Isaac Bashevis Singer's *The Magician of Lublin*, while others are written by Polish authors specifically for the Polish audience.

The works of Jewish authors such as Bruno Schulz and Isaac Bashevis Singer are popular with Polish readers. Schulz was born in Galicia, in an area which is now in the Ukraine, but which was within Poland's borders after World War I. Although Jewish, he is recognized as one of the great Polish-language authors of the twentieth century. Singer was born in Poland but immigrated to the United States in 1935 before the Second World War. This Nobel Prize winning author helped establish Yiddish writing as a literary genre. One reason these writers are so popular is that the imagery in their writings evokes an emotional reaction in the reader. The reader can experience the eagerness of the young boy or the fear of a young wife and learn about them and their lives at a deeper level which goes beyond just entertainment.

Magazines are another print medium which can educate and entertain. *Midrasz (midrash)*, a monthly magazine published under the auspices of the Ronald S. Lauder Foundation, covers a wide range of topics about Jewish life, culture, and history. Although generally published in Polish, there are occasional issues in English. The articles cover a wide range of topics from a cover story about young Polish people who are cleaning up neglected Jewish cemeteries to an article which examines Jewish law and abortion. Articles on current events, literature, opinion pieces, and biographical sketches of Jewish artists and writers are regular features. *Słowo Żydowskie* (Jewish words) is a bi-weekly magazine which is also part of the Jewish press in Poland and features articles in Yiddish and in Polish. Like *Midrasz*, this magazine runs articles on a variety of topics from film to history to Jewish life in contemporary Poland. A one or two page Yiddish lesson is often included.

Another print genre that is popular is guidebooks about "Jewish sites" in Poland. Some focus on a specific area such as Jewish Kraków while others follow the traces of Jewish life in pre-Holocaust Poland. For example, the volume, *Sztetl: Śladami żydowskich miastecyek, which* was published by Austeria in 2005, provides historical and contemporary information about five former sztetls in the Małopolska region, the area around Kraków. Some years during the Jewish Cultural Festival in Kraków, a tour of the 5 sztetls featured in this book is offered. This combination of the written word with the experience of actually being in the places described with a knowledgeable guide can create a broader and more in-depth perspective for the reader/viewer.

Austeria, a publishing house which focuses on publications related to Jewish matters, has a bookstore located in Kazimierz in Kraków. Their offerings range from commentaries on the Torah to biographies to Yiddish literature to guidebooks as well as music CDs and film DVDs. Poetry by Israeli authors and plays related to Jewish life in Poland as well as calendars and postcards round out their contributions to literature and the arts about Jewish life in Poland, then and now. During the Jewish Cultural Festival in Kraków, this bookstore features music by artists performing at the festival, books by authors who are appearing, and films related to festival presentations.

However, one area in which there is a noticeable absence is children's literature and young adult literature related to Jewish culture and to the Holocaust. The group, Czulent, is attempting to fill this gap by publishing books for children related to Jewish life and culture. They have put together a book of Yiddish poetry and rhyming stories, in Yiddish and Polish, whose purpose is to introduce children to this rich literary heritage and to teach them about Jewish culture and traditions. The group also has plans for other children's books on Jewish holidays and the Yiddish alphabet. Their intention is that these books be distributed free to at least 1,000 Jewish families in Poland.

However, most of the materials about the Holocaust which are being published in Poland are aimed at the adult audience. Although organizations such as the United States Holocaust Museum in Washington, DC, and Yad Vashem in Jerusalem, Israel caution against education about the Holocaust before about age 10, there are numerous books available for young children and young adults in the United States and other countries which introduce the issues in an age-appropriate manner. While it is possible to find Polish translations of the *Diary of Anne Frank*, there are few other books available in Polish that would be of interest to young people. Even the bookshop at Auschwitz-Birkenau which does have educational programs for young people has little to offer young adults who want to read more about the Holocaust, and nothing for younger children.

The same absence is true of media such as films. While there have been a few films made in Poland regarding the Holocaust, few reflect Jewish life in Poland before or after the Holocaust. There are a growing number of documentary-type films which could be used in more formal educational settings, but few which would be offer less formal educational opportunities. One of these is *Korczak*, a film made by the well-known Polish director Andzej Wajda in 1990, which focuses on the Polish-Jewish doctor/educator Janusz Korczak whose orphanage in the Warsaw Ghetto was liquidated in August 1942. He, most of his staff, and the more than 200 children in their care were sent to the death camp, Treblinka. Filmed in black and white, the director used chiaroscuro effects to heighten the emotional impact of some scenes. At one point a child is frightened by a storm and this effect is used to simulate the child's fright as well as a sense of the magical as the doctor proclaims himself a wizard who controls the lightning in order to calm the child's fears. This film also sparked some controversy because of its fairytale-like ending. Many viewers and critics thought that it contradicted the seriousness of the film, and trivialized the emotional impact of the events. However, Wajda defended it because he wanted the film to end less darkly and on a more hopeful note. Besides using this film to educate about Janusz Korczak and the Holocaust, this controversial ending could be used as a discussion point around issues of the role of the affective domain in artistic expression, or about authenticity and the artists' role in presentation and representation.

Theatre has traditionally played a large role in Jewish life and culture. Yiddish and Jewish theatre were very popular with Jews and non–Jews alike in pre–Holocaust Poland, particularly during the inter-war period. The Ester Rachel and Ida Kaminska Jewish Theatre in Warsaw is the most well-known and longest operational theatre of its kind in Poland. Established in 1950, the theatre produces classics of Jewish drama as well as a more modern repertoire. Shows are performed in Yiddish and in Polish and include programs for adults and for children. In addition to performance, they offer workshops, such as musical workshops for children to teach them about the traditions and customs of Rosh HaShanah, the Jewish New Year.

Theatre provides ample opportunities for portraying the many facets of a people's life and culture, but also can portray and perpetuate stereotypes. Teyve, the milkman, in *Fiddler on the Roof* is one example. This beloved character is often romanticized as the typical Eastern European Jew. However, Jews in Eastern Europe were as different and as varied as any group. There were rich and poor and in-between. There were city dwellers and country dwellers. Some spent all day with their books or in a shop while others spent all day in a factory or in the fields. They dressed in the most up-to-date finery or in the attire of peasants. Theatre does often perpetuate these stereotypes, but it also has the opportunity to dispel them by presenting a wide range of productions which show the rich and varied life of Jewish people in Poland and elsewhere. Productions such as those by Midrash Theatre in Kraków present a contemporary view of traditional Jewish values, tradition, and customs which present a contrast to the more traditional theatre portrayals.

Music and Dance

One of the most popular cultural markers used when portraying cultures is music. Oftentimes cultural festivals and other venues for presenting a culture rely on music to attract the crowd. In the summer, it is not uncommon to come across a stage set up on the main marketplace in Kraków and see children and adults dressed in folk costume dancing traditional Polish folk dances for a clapping, smiling audience. Concerts indoors or in the park are another venue in which certain types of music are often featured. Generally, types and genres of music are not mixed at such events.

The music and dance of a culture can range from more formal styles such as what is generally termed classical music forms to more informal styles of music such as folk music. Music, like other cultural markers, has the potential to infer value because the forms are generally related to social status in the community. Most formal styles such as orchestral music or ballet tend to be associated with wealthier and/or higher status people in a society; therefore this type of music is often seen as more sophisticated and "better" (has more value) than other forms. The emotional impact of such music is often described in lofty terms, such as sublime or ethereal. Folk music is often viewed as unsophisticated music which is enjoyed by the masses with less value. This music is often described as making the listeners feel happy or sad, basic emotional responses that do not take the listener to a higher plane.

Jewish music is no different. It ranges from classical music to folk music with liturgical music also having a large place in the Jewish music repertoire. Generally when Jewish music is featured it is either liturgical music or klezmer music, which had its roots as dance music for celebrations such as weddings. Klezmer music in the United Sates was also influenced by jazz, so that there are different types of klezmer music (Davidow, 2013). Although a number of classical composers were Jewish, it is rare that one hears a concert by "Jewish classical composers." However, klezmer concerts abound and Jewish dance is a popular workshop offering. There is also a body of music which is loosely called Yiddish music, popular songs sung in Yiddish, such as "Mein Idishe Momme" (My Yiddish Mother) and "Az der Rebbe Tanst" (As the Rabbi Dances). In a later section, there is a fuller treatment of the role of music and dance in the Jewish cultural festivals held in Poland.

The other form of Jewish music which is an important cultural marker is liturgical music. As with any religious music, the various songs and tunes perform various functions in religious services and celebrations. Religious texts and poetry contribute to the body of liturgical music (MyJewishLearning, 2013). Generally, the role of liturgical music to enhance the spiritual experience or draw attention to some aspect of it. Even some popular Jewish music has its roots in the Ashkenazic and Sephardic religious traditions.

In the next section, Izabella Goldstein, former musical director and conductor of Tslil Jewish Choir in Poland, presents a personal account which describes the choir's experiences with music from the Holocaust. Tslil Jewish Choir (Clil, in Polish) is an amateur choir founded in 2003 in Poland. Its members are Jews and non–Jews primarily from Łódź and Warsaw. "The repertoire of the choir includes songs in Hebrew, Aramaic, Yiddish (the language of the Ashkenazi Jews), and Ladino (the language of the Sephardic Jews)" (Tslil, n.d., para. 2). The choir's aims are to connect its singers and listeners to Jewish culture and traditions through music, and in this way to foster tolerance and openness. Goldstein's essay highlights the emotional impact that music can have and how that impact can be part of a person's learning experience.

Teaching About the Holocaust Through Music
by Izabella Goldstein

"[T]he partisans were resistance fighters, Jews and non–Jews, in different countries who fought the Nazis in the forests and lived by their wits.... 'Songs were one of their weapons...' (Belsky, 1979, p. 92), and Glik's song [Zog nit keyn mol (Never say that you are treading the final path)] became their official hymn. '... [with] almost magical speed it was caught up by all the concentration camps ... and by a score of other peoples as well' (Belsky, 1979, p. 92)."—Chartock, 2001, p. 294

I grew up in a Polish-Jewish home. My parents were married in a Catholic church but they never went to church nor to synagogue. I knew that we were a mixed family, and I knew that a large part of my father's family perished in the Holocaust. My father often talked about history, but my own understanding of twentieth century history was quite superficial. My grandmother was a Yiddish-Polish translator, so I was accustomed to having books in Hebrew script at home, but this was not of deep interest to me. I knew, however, that it was better for me not to tell people about my roots. Not that this was easy to hide. My skin being several tones darker than the Polish average, I was sometimes approached on the street and spoken to in English. Elderly ladies on the bus would ask, "Where did you get those beautiful dark eyes, little girl?" As soon as I started studying opera singing I was told that I was the ideal type for Carmen.

In high school I studied literature on the Holocaust, part of the core curriculum in Polish schools starting in the 1990s, together with my non–Jewish classmates. We read and analyzed novels by Hanna Krall, Gustaw Herling-Grudziński, Tadeusz Borowski, poems of Czesław Miłosz, Zbigniew Herbert, and many other pieces. These, often first-hand accounts of people who went through Auschwitz (Borowski), the ghetto (Marek Edelman in Krall's book-long interview) or witnessed the Holocaust from the "Polish side," were difficult for all of us to study. It was interesting for me to see that despite my school being a "music school" and most of my classmates were usually focused on their professional development rather than on subjects such as literature, these were the books and poems that everyone read and many were eager to discuss. My classmates wanted to know more about the Holocaust and found it much more important than, for instance, eighteenth century Polish literature.

For university I went to music academies, first in Warsaw, later in Łódź. Neither the choral conducting program in Warsaw nor the opera singing program in Łódź included the smallest hint of Jewish music. The Polish system of music education is focused mostly on the great composers of classical music, Bach, Mozart, etc., and any music other than that is studied little.

This might had been one of the reasons why my own Master's investigation on *Hazzanut* (Goldstein, 2010) was received with so much interest by the faculty of the department were I studied.

My interest in *Hazzanut* (a form of Jewish liturgical music) though did not appear out of nowhere. During my studies in Łódź, I started working with Tslil, a Jewish choir. The offer to take this post came to me through my "music contacts" as I was not at that time engaged in any form of Jewish community life. However, when my work began I was very excited at having the chance to learn about Jewish music, which I had never before had the chance to study, but which I always believed was something exciting. I was also hoping to learn more about Jewish history, traditions and culture.

As soon as I started working as the choral conductor of *Tslil* I understood that I had to learn about Jewish music fast to be able to choose the new repertoire and understand it well enough to prepare meaningful programs for upcoming concerts. It was even more important because audiences often inquired about songs, and the choristers and I were often faced with questions which we were not knowledgeable enough about to answer. That was why we decided to prepare introductory texts and explain each song—its words, history, related traditions, stories of the lyricists and composers, etc. These texts were well received by our audiences but were also important to the choir members. They were better able to understand the repertoire we were singing. Working on these introductory texts, researching for the background of songs, arranging translations and learning about the various contexts of our broad repertoire was also a pretext for many of the choristers to deepen their Jewish knowledge. After all, we sang not only Yiddish songs of pre-war Poland but also chants in Ladino (the Sephardic Jewish language), hymns in Hebrew, *niggunim* (wordless melodies), Israeli songs, and many other pieces known to very few in Poland.

Many of our concerts were very emotional. People would often approach the choristers or me to talk about their feelings and emotions. Some would describe their own family histories or share whatever they knew about Jewish issues (sometimes very distantly, or not at all, related to our singing). Naturally, once we started to include Holocaust songs in our repertoire everything became even more emotional.

Holocaust-period songs were present in Tslil's repertoire from its earliest days, around 2003. The choir sang, among other Hebrew hymns, "Ani m'amin" (I believe) based on Maimonides's (a twelfth century Sephardic Jewish philosopher) "Thirteen Articles of Faith." The choir sang it, not to a joyful melody, such as that composed by Shlomo Carlebach (a twentieth century rabbi and composer know for his lively melodies), but to the slow and sad tune from the Warsaw Ghetto, which was known simply as "Varshever Ghetto Lid" (Song of the Warsaw Ghetto) (cited in Gilbert, 2005). Also the "Partizaner Lid" (the Partisans' Song), also known as "Zog Nit Keyn Mol" (Never Say), was practiced by the choir and sung during various ceremonies. I remember when we sang it for TSKŻ (the Social-Cultural Association of Jews in Poland), one of the largest non-religious Jewish organizations in the country. As soon as we started to sing it, people stood up. All my choristers (Polish and Jewish) sang in a very emotional way. They knew what they were singing about and how important this song was for Jewish partisans during the Holocaust. The audience started to cry, and soon my choristers and I did as well. We hardly managed to finish our singing. This concert was one of those which I will never forget. We all felt like these partisans who wanted to fight till the end of their life with hope of better times and a better world.

However, it was only in 2005, when *Tslil* was asked to sing a concert during the sixty-first anniversary of the liquidation of the Łódź Ghetto, when the choir really started to build a "ghetto repertoire." It is important to understand that preparing a concert is not a fast process. For the choir members of *Tslil* it meant attending a two-hour rehearsal twice a week for at least two months. That is quite a lot of time spent with the "ghetto repertoire" considering that for most of the choristers *Tslil* rehearsals were supposed to be a "time to relax" after a full day of work or studying. The songs of the Łódź Ghetto, which we sang (most were acquired from the volume by Gila Flam, 1992) were far from relaxing. In fact, the process was so overwhelming that one of the choristers left the choir saying that she was not able emotionally to handle the new repertoire.

Nevertheless, many others decided to keep coming to the rehearsals and they gave their best efforts. As a choir conductor, I believe that people join an amateur choir out of the necessity to have something more in their life than a job and money. They are searching for new experiences, want to do something artistic, and to be part of a group. However, at the same time people have families, jobs, friends, problems. Here, in their spare time, my choristers were given Holocaust songs to sing and numerous concerts at which to present them. Some of the choristers were at first uncertain about the idea. Others were surprised that there was so much music from the ghettos. We all deepened our knowledge about the Holocaust, and, in fact, also about pre-war Jewish life in Poland while working with this repertoire. We spent a lot of time learning to sing songs, but also trying to understand them. Few of us knew Yiddish, but we were eager to know what we were singing about.

The choristers wanted to know who wrote each song and why. They kept sharing their emotions and feelings. Several became engaged in researching ghetto music, ghetto realities, or even the language. Thanks to this interest and engagement, when we decided to record the CD "Songs from the Łódź Ghetto," we were able to sing these songs in *Lodzher Yiddish*—Łódź's own Yiddish dialect. By singing, learning, researching and emotionally experiencing the songs, the choristers developed a new, deeper, understanding of the Holocaust, an understanding formed through full involvement: with bodies, minds and souls. During the concerts they were trying to pass this understanding on to other people. I believe they managed. Many of the people who listened to our concerts or to our CD approached us to say how strongly affected they were. One woman, who bought our CD, said that it was the first time in her life that after listening to a CD she "felt as though the silence after the last song was screaming" (personal communication).

What probably made the strongest impression on everyone were the songs in Polish (Jews were sent to ghettos even if they were completely linguistically assimilated). One such song was "Jadą dzieci" (The Children Are Going) (Flam, 1992). The song, written by Miriam Harel, who spent four years of her youth in the Łódź ghetto, is a modification of one of the best known Polish children's songs, written by Maria Konopnicka, a nineteenth century Polish author. In the original first stanza, which is also the refrain, "Children are going (in a vehicle), little sister and little brother, and they are astonished: what a beautiful world." Miriam Harel's verse is nearly identical, the only difference being that "beautiful" is substituted with "cruel." In the well-known version by Konopnicka, the lyrics which continue are banal and form an atmosphere of a blissful childhood:

> *Here is hidden a small house*
> *Under a straw roof,*
> *Next to the house is a wide-branched tree*
> *And a scarecrow stands in a potato field* [Flam, 1992, p. 118].

However, in the ghetto song, while the original Polish folk melody of a lullaby stays the same, the verse becomes very different... Harel (Flam, 1992) refers to a "yellow patch" the yellow star that Jews had to wear, a "barbed-wire fence" which they lived behind as well as the "worn-out clothes and wooden shoes" which the Jews were forced to wear. She then refers to the orphans and children who are sent away on trains, on trains that "keep going."

For the Polish listener the tragedy of the song is augmented by the fact that unlike the English word "going" which could mean "walking," the Polish word "jadą," repeated in the refrain, indicates that the children of the song are going in a vehicle, possibly a horse-drawn carriage in the original, but here, as one can guess, on the train, taking them to their death. Our choir's interpretation of the song (Harel, 2010) was very simple but at the same time very difficult. With a soloist singing the lyrics, the remaining choristers repeated throughout the song "jadą" in the rhythm imitating a train.

One of the concerts where we presented this and other Songs of the Łódź Ghetto (which we later recorded) was a concert which formed part of the commemoration of the 65th anniversary of the liquidation of the Łódź Ghetto in August 2009. The atmosphere was really special. We sang on Łódź's Old Market Square, directly in the Ghetto area. It was late evening and it was dark. Our shadows were projected on the light-tinned background screen behind us. We had just enough light to see the scores. The concert was open for everyone to come, and was announced in some of the most widely read newspapers. Many people came—Jews and non–Jews. We asked the audience not to clap. The choristers were deeply moved as was the audience. The silence which echoed between the songs was terrifying. At such moments we realize how important our efforts, our many months of work with this traumatic repertoire, are.

References

Flam, G. (1992). *Singing for survival: Songs of the Łódź ghetto, 1940–45*. Urbana: University of Illinois Press.
Gilbert, S. (2005). *Music in the Holocaust: Confronting life in the Nazi ghettos and camps*. Oxford: Clarendon.
Goldstein, I. (2010). *Chazanut—Śpiew Operowy w Żydowskiej Muzyce Liturgicznej [Hazzanut: Operatic chant in Jewish liturgical music]*. Unpublished master's thesis, Grażyna and Kiejstut Bacewicz Academy of Music of Łódź, Poland.
Harel, M. (2010). Jadą dzieci [recorded by Tslil Jewish Choir]. On *Piosenki z łódzkiego getta [Songs of the Łódź Ghetto]* [CD]. Warsaw: Tslil Jewish Choir.

Websites for Further Information

Chór Żydowski "Clil" (Tslil), Warsaw, http://www.clil.pl/about-the-choir.html. Amateur choir which sings various Jewish music, in Hebrew, Aramaic, Yiddish and Ladino (website in Polish and English).
The Ester Rachel and Ida Kaminska Jewish Theatre, Warsaw, www.teatr-zydowski.art.pl. Most well-known theatre of its kind in Poland; produces classics of Jewish

drama as well as a more modern repertoire in Yiddish and in Polish; includes programs for adults and children (website in Polish).

Midrasz (*Midrash*) magazine, http://www.midrasz.pl/en.php. Plays an educational role for Polish Jews and non–Jews alike who want to learn more about Jewish life and culture.

Słowo Żydowskie (*Jewish Words*) magazine, http://www.slowozydowskie.pl/. Polish and Yiddish language bi-weekly magazine on topics of Jewish interest (website in Polish).

Teatr Midraszowy (Midrash Theatre), Kraków, www.beitKraków.pl/midrash-theatre. Combines creative study of traditional Jewish texts (midrashim) with stage interpretations (website in Polish and English).

Wydawnictwo Austeria (Austeria Publishing), http://eng.austeria.pl/. Publishing house and bookshop; focuses on publications related to Jewish matters.

Jewish Cultural Festivals in Poland

"For me, Poland is above all a country where Jews were present for almost a thousand years. It is a country of Jewish religion, Jewish culture, and Jewish life. I cannot accept life in the shadow of death. This does not mean that I treat that death lightly, but that I live in the shadow of the seven hundred and fifty years of Jewish history of Kraków, and the almost one thousand years of the history of Jews in Poland. This is my space. This is my world" (Makuch, 2010, p. 132).—Organizer of the Jewish Culture Festival in Kraków, Poland

Cultural festivals of different types take place throughout the world. In general, they can be characterized as community events whose goal is to celebrate a specific culture, usually focusing on music, crafts, food, and other cultural markers. Who organizes the events, whose culture is portrayed, and which aspects of the culture are presented vary from event to event. These factors shape how the culture being represented is conceptualized by the creators and how the audience perceives what they are seeing, hearing and experiencing. When viewed not just as entertainment but as a sociological construct, these festivals can be characterized as presentations of identity and as educational events.

Cultural festivals in various cities around Poland use the arts to portray Jewish life and culture. The educational value of these festivals varies. Some are merely entertainment providing food and music which is labeled "Jewish" while others make a more focused attempt at educating the public about Jewish culture and Jewish life in Poland, past and present. What form this education takes, and what significance it has in creating and influencing perceptions about Jews in Poland, and elsewhere, is the focus of this essay. First, we look at cultural festivals in general as presentations of identity and as pedagogical constructs. Then the essay takes an in depth look at two festivals in Poland which are quite different, a small festival held in a former shtetl and a much larger one in Kraków. The contrast of these two festivals sheds some light on the connections between culture, representation, context, and formal and informal education about groups of people.

Cultural Festivals as Presentations of Identity

As stated earlier, identity is the result of a complex combination of factors, including social, cultural, legal, geographical, environmental, and psychological, which come together to create and maintain individual and group identity. When trying to represent a culture through a medium such as a cultural festival, decisions are made about which aspects of the culture are presented, which aspects of identity are represented. This chapter aims to examine this phenomenon of cultural festivals and how, on the one hand, these festivals may be reifying the stereotype of someone else's notion of another's identity based on a perceived historical model, and how, on the other hand, they are giving voice to a group that has been long ignored.

Bramadat (2001, 2005) situates his analysis of cultural festivals in Canada in the context of authentic presentations of identity. In his analysis of Winnipeg's Folkorama and Toronto's Caravan, Bramadat (2001) identifies four roles that such festivals play. First, he sees them as a place where the minority or the newcomer can have a place of higher status, at least for a short period of time. They are the "experts" and the ones who are knowledgeable about their culture. Next, he says, cultural festivals bring the notion of ethnic identity to the forefront. Rather than being subsumed in the larger culture, differences and similarities among cultures are high-lighted. Third, festivals give those being represented the opportunity to have a voice in how they are seen by others. They can decide which parts of their culture to highlight or how to represent themselves in a non-stereotypical fashion. Finally, these events are local endeavors not large-scale commercialized events. Therefore, they are about the community itself. Later, Bramadat (2005) argues that while there are those who "argue that these festivals perpetuate ethnic stereotypes and promote superficial, commercialized, and inauthentic versions of the cultures they are ostensibly intended to represent" (p.1) they also serve the purpose of giving voice to those who have been largely unheard and an opportunity to present themselves in the way they want to be represented.

Green's (2002) analysis of Carnival in Trinidad and Tobago supports Bramadat's (2005) assessment that cultural festivals can and do represent authentic cultural identity. He states that since culture serves two purposes, as a commodity to be used and exploited, and as a source of national pride, representations will be ambiguous, reflecting changes as they occur in a culture and society. In these ways, they also serve as educational events.

Cultural Festivals as a Pedagogical Construct

In order to examine the educational aspects of cultural festivals, Murillo (1997) analyzed a Latin Cultural celebration which took place in 1995 in a small town in North Carolina, a state which has a quickly growing Latino population, from the perspective of cultural festivals as a pedagogical construct. The festival weekend, which was organized by the local Latino population with input from other members of the community at large, attracted 13,000 people and included sports events, music and dancing, arts and crafts displays, and cultural exhibits. Murillo's (1997) conclusion was that such festivals serve to situate an immigrant population in a particular context. Besides educating the non–Latino community about their culture, Murillo (1997) also states that

> the festival acts as a "rite of passage" (Van Gennep, 1975) for the newcomer Latinos, sponsored by established middle-class Latinos, where an openness to the future is created, an imagined community is constructed, and the festival organizers ultimately assert their own metaphors and processual responses in their patterns and models of thinking and behaving [p. 277].

He asserted that the festival helped connect the Latino population to their historical roots, while showing where they fit into their new community. In this way, the festival also serves as an educational bridge between the old and the new for the newcomer, as well as educating the long-time residents about the newcomers in their midst.

Jewish Cultural Festivals in Poland

Jewish cultural festivals have gained popularity in Poland over the years since the end of the Soviet era. The Communist government of post-war Poland allowed little acknowledgement and almost no discussion about Jewish life in Poland prior to World War II and of the Holocaust. Since the end of the Soviet-Communist period in Poland, there has been a revival of interest in Jews and Jewish life, a population that was almost annihilated during the Holocaust. One way that this interest has manifested itself is through Jewish cultural festivals, generally organized by non–Jews. However, a number of Poles whom I have spoken to assume that these festivals are organized by Jews, so their perception is that they are witnessing "authentic" representations of Jewish culture. Therefore, an analysis of these festivals raises some of questions about presentations of identity. Whose identity is being presented? Whose perception of Jewish identity is being presented? However, based on their mission statements, the organizers of many of these festivals see them as serving a pedagogical function to help Poles learn about their past and about Jews in Poland. The festivals in the larger cities are visited by foreign visitors every year from all over the world, Jews and non–Jews alike. Therefore, other objectives of some of the festivals are to demonstrate Poland's acceptance of its past and the future of Jewish life in Poland. In this way, the festivals represent pedagogical constructs in the dialectical nature of the events.

There are regularly organized festivals in Warsaw, Wrocław, and Poznań, as well as in smaller cities across Poland. Although there are numerous Jewish festivals, large and small, that take place across Poland, this volume will focus on two festivals which are quite different in make-up and purpose. The small town of Chmielnik, a former shtetl, has organized a festival to recognize and celebrate their "shtetl history." The festival in Kraków is the oldest and largest in Poland. It started in 1988 as a Jewish film festival organized by some university students, which became a music and film festival and has now evolved into featuring many aspects of Jewish life and culture.

The significance of these festivals is that while they are serving to revive and educate about Jewish culture in Poland, they may also be serving to perpetuate stereotypes of Jews. Therefore, an analysis of them from an educational perspective is crucial in understanding not only the festivals but also the state of Jewish studies and Holocaust education in Poland.

To set the background for the festivals, it is important to look first at the history of Jews in Chmielnik and Kraków to establish the context since a place's history and its inhabitants' sense of their history shapes how they represent themselves. Since identity is not formed in a vacuum, we must ask: How is this world defined where the Jewish festivals take place? The history of these two places gives a sense of this.

Meeting with Jewish Culture: Chmielnik

Chmielnik is a microcosm of Polish remembrance of Jewish Poland. This small village, or shtetl, near Kraków was home to 10,275 Jews before the Holocaust (Sabor, 2005). Jews had lived there for at least 300 years according to available documents (Maciągowski and Krawczyk, 2007) and made up about 80 percent of the town's population in September 1939 at the outbreak of World War II. Like most Polish villages, after the war, Jewish inhabitants did not return, their property was taken over by others and their lives were forgotten by those who were trying to recover from the ravages of war and to deal with the Soviet takeover.

History: Although there are a few anecdotal references to Jews living in Chmielnik prior to the late 1600s, Maciągowski and Krawczyk (2007) point out that the first records of Jews living there are the tax records of 1674, with no Jews recorded in the 1673 tax rolls. They assert that the sudden appearance of Jews was a record keeping issue not a reflection of the reality of presence or absence of Jewish inhabitants. Discrepancies in numbers of inhabitants were common during that period due to inaccurate record keeping and can be difficult to trace due to destruction and loss of records at various times since then. The 1787 Chmielnik parish records show that there were 782 Jews living in Chmielnik while other data from 1764 show that there were 1445 Jews living there. Despite the discrepancies in the numbers, all the data agree that the majority of Jews living in Chmielnik worked in agriculture while the remainder made their living from trade of various kinds.

The Jewish community thrived enough during the period of the late 1600s to early 1700s to afford a rabbi and a synagogue. Although there is some reference to a synagogue being established in Chmielnik in 1683, Maciągowski and Krawczyk (2007) found no historical evidence for a permanent synagogue building until around 1730. Throughout the partitions, the Jewish community in Chmielnik thrived and flourished with a synagogue, two schools and a cemetery. As the home of several well-known rabbis, it also came to be recognized as a seat of Jewish learning.

During the 1800s Jewish Chmielnik came under the influence of Hasidism, the eighteenth century religious movement which began in the Ukraine, and was sweeping across Poland. Members of this movement were in conflict with the more traditional Orthodox members of the community, and struggles over who controlled the Jewish community ensued. In the meantime there were also disputes with the local administration over taxes, how much should be paid by whom, and how much could come back to help support the Jewish community. Maciągowski and Krawczyk (2007) point out that these issues were important for sustaining the growing Jewish population of Chmielnik, which by the end of the nineteenth century numbered more than 3,000 Jewish inhabitants, over half of the town's population. Most of the Jewish residents lived in the town while most of the Polish residents lived on the outskirts.

Maciągowski and Krawczyk (2007) identify Chmielnik with its majority Jewish population as a shtetl. They write that the term refers not just to the place identified as a small town or village, "but also to a specific social formation, characteristic of Jewish life in the province[s], isolated from new ideas, where two cultures, Jewish and peasants,' mixed and where Jews could live without any limitations cultivating their traditions" (p. 73).

During the mid–1800s, Chmielnik experienced a period of economic growth and a subsequent increase in population. During this period, laws were put in place which prohibited "Jews from settling on lands belonging to squires" (p. 85) and forced more Jews to leave rural areas for towns and cities. More Jews had to engage in trade, and in Chmielnik, more than 80 percent of the farms were owned by Poles. At the end of the nineteenth century, Chmielnik's economic growth slowed so that many Jewish businesses suffered, and the number of poor inhabitants increased. According to records found by Maciągowski and Krawczyk (2007), by 1897, there were 8,440 residents in Chmielnik of which 6,602 (78.2 percent) were Jews. First the economic problems of the early 1900s, then World War I, further reduced economic opportunities in Chmielnik and decreased its population. In 1921 the total population was 6,790 with 5,908 being Jews (Maciągowski and Krawczyk, 2007).

However, after the Armistice and subsequent Polish independence, there was a greater sense of freedom in Poland for all its inhabitants. Jews in Chmielnik began looking beyond their religious community for opportunities for political life, social life, and education. The control by Orthodox Jews of the Jewish community began to be challenged by non-religious Jews, especially Zionists, who wanted more say in the allocation of funds. The Zionists were mostly working class and young people who wanted support for cultural programs and physical education programs to prepare potential Jewish émigrés for the rigors of life in Palestine. Educational organizations, theatre, and the library flourished in the Jewish community. However, this increase of political and social life sometimes brought these groups into conflict with the Orthodox authorities.

In the years prior to World War II, small industries and trade were the mainstay of Jewish livelihood. Maciągowski and Krawczyk (2007) report that almost all trade in Chmielnik belonged to Jews by this time. The several hundred Jewish families who lived in Chmielnik in 1939 "were rich and poor, believers and non-believers, Orthodox Jews and communists. All of them, who felt they were Jews, paid their contribution to the religious Jewish community" (p. 139). However, this life ended during the Holocaust and Jewish life did not return to Chmielnik.

When World War II broke out on September 1, 1939, most of the more than 12,000 inhabitants (Sabor, 2005) of Chmielnik fled. Some of them returned in a few days, but "about 1,000 people, mostly of Jewish origin, went further east which saved their lives. Most of them never returned to Chmielnik" (Maciągowski and Krawczyk, 2007, p. 155). In 1941 a ghetto was created in Chmielnik and about 13,000 Jews were confined there, those from Chmielnik as well as surrounding areas. Some died or were killed in the ghetto, while others were sent to their death in other places, such as Treblinka. By March 1943, the ghetto was liquidated. As in every Polish village, town and city there were Poles who collaborated with the Nazis and Poles who tried to help their Jewish neighbors. There is also a report of one Jew from Chmielnik, who was tried and shot by the Polish underground for collaborating with the Nazis.

Remembrance: In 2005, a monument commemorating the Polish-Jewish heritage of Chmielnik was unveiled at the third *Meeting with Jewish Culture*. The monument's inscription says: "History does not walk on main streets, but most of all on side streets in quiet towns" (Maciągowski and Krawczyk, 2007, p. 256). This monument in this sleepy village just outside of Kraków symbolizes the hope for and commitment to remembering its past as a shtetl.

In the early years of the twenty-first century, at the urging of Chmielnik's mayor, Jarosław Zatorski, teachers and students at the local high school organized a contest. The purpose of this contest was for students to write down the memories of townspeople about the former Jewish inhabitants of Chmielnik. Even though 60 years had passed since the Holocaust, older people remembered the Jewish inhabitants who were so much of a part of their former lives. Maciągowski and Krawczyk (2007) point out how "the interviews create a unique and very vivid picture of former Chmielnik based on memories from people's childhoods and adult lives" (p. 176). These memories are based on "how Jews are remembered by Poles.... There are also descriptions of some funny situations and events as well as stereotypes so strongly rooted in the collective memory" (p. 176). When the same situation is mentioned by several people, the recollections take on historical value as authentic sources of events. However, each story has value as a personal narrative of a place and time that no longer exists.

In June 2001, Chmielnik celebrated its 450th anniversary of being granted civic rights. As part of the celebration, one day was set aside to celebrate the history of Jews in the town. The day was marked with food, exhibits and performances. Stalls sold Jewish cultural items as well as the ordinary everyday items that would have been sold in such stalls before the war. Teachers and students at the junior secondary school were instrumental in planning and preparing for that day. Painted sets lined the street leading to the synagogue representing pre-war Chmielnik. School children performed in plays that illustrated Jewish life before the war. These events were greeted with such enthusiasm and interest that the officials of Chmielnik decided to continue this celebration in the future.

Therefore in June 2003, *Meeting with Jewish Culture* started. The ambassador of Israel in Poland and visitors from Israel participated in discussions about Jewish life in Poland, and the war and its aftermath. Once again sets lined the streets to show what the town looked like before the war, and stalls and restaurants sold a variety of goods and food. Exhibits in the synagogue gave participants a chance to see the inside of the synagogue while illustrating some aspects of Jewish life and culture. Klezmer music and performances by local school children punctuated the festivities. In his final remarks the Israeli ambassador, Szewach Weiss, said: "We would have lived here together, we would have quarreled and made up, and together we would have built this town" (Maciągowski and Krawczyk, 2007, p. 247). These remarks highlight the possibility of normal relations between groups of people who live together in the same place.

Since 2004 the two-day festival has been organized jointly with the nearby town of Szydłów, where about 30 percent of the pre-war population was Jewish (Sabor, 2005). Like the previous events in Chmielnik, school children played a large role in the festivities, singing and performing in theatrical productions. The performances included a play based on a Jewish folk tale, a play about the Zionist movement, and a performance called "Purim," the Jewish holiday commemorating Queen Ester. The organizers point out that their purpose is to present as many aspects of Jewish life and culture as they can, not just religious aspects, but culture and history as well.

The Chmielnik mayor's vision in creating these meetings was to build a future that brought the two nations, Israel and Poland, together in brotherhood and friendship. He recognized that in order for this to happen, school children must be involved in the events. From the competition of interviewing their neighbors about Jewish life in Chmielnik to their active participation in all aspects of the meetings, school children were encouraged to learn and understand this culture that made up such a large part of their history.

Jewish Culture Festival in Kraków

There are numerous Jewish festivals, large and small, that take place across Poland, but the largest, longest running, most well-known is the

Jewish Culture Festival in Kraków. Since a place's history and its inhabitants' sense of their history shapes how they represent themselves, it is important to first look at the history of Jews in Kraków to identify the context and set the background for the festival. Kraków's history gives a sense of how this world is defined in which this Jewish cultural festival take place.

A Brief History of Jews in Kraków: When Jews first settled in Kraków in the thirteenth century, they lived in an area around what is today St. Ann's Street, on the western side of the main market square. However, during the fifteenth century several anti–Jewish demonstrations took place; officials of the Catholic Church in Poland and burghers were opposed to the Jewish population's growing market share of the local economy. In the late fifteenth century, most Jews left Kraków proper and settled in Kazimierz, which is on the southeast edge of the city. They maintained close economic ties with Kraków, despite the restrictions imposed on them by the burghers. The Jewish community in Kazimierz was large and prosperous, and its rabbis and elders were influential in many parts of Poland and Lithuania (Weiner, 2008).

In the sixteenth and seventeenth centuries, Jewish culture in Kazimierz thrived. Seven synagogues were functioning by 1644, including the Alte Schul (the Old Synagogue, a museum today) and the Remuh Synagogue (the only active synagogue in Kraków at present). Jewish schools and other centers of learning, publishing houses, and numerous businesses were located there. By the 1570's, the Jewish population of Kazimierz numbered about 2,060 (Weiner, 2008).

During the partition period (1772–1918), Kraków and Kazimierz were in the Austrian zone governed by the Austrian empire, and later, the Austro-Hungarian Empire. Kazimierz was incorporated into Kraków, and lost its independent government. Despite restrictions imposed by the Austrians, by 1833, the Jewish population of Kraków had grown to 10,820 (Weiner, 2008). The Austrians enacted laws so that Jews would have to assimilate in order to be citizens of the empire. The Jewish intelligentsia, in particular, fought against this compulsory assimilation and Jews finally re-won the right to free citizenship in the second half of the nineteenth century. Jewish cultural life continued to flourish and by 1900, Kraków had a Jewish population of 25,670, and reached 56,800, in 1931 (Weiner, 2008). Kraków was considered the center of Jewish political and social life in Poland.

However, despite the resistance to forced assimilation, many Jews in Kraków did assimilate to varying degrees especially after Poland regained its independence after World War I. The Jewish population was very diverse

(Gawron, 2012). As a result of changes in Jewish life that swept across Europe during the nineteenth century and the growth of the Reform or Progressive movement, the Orthodox was no longer the only group of Jews who lived in Kraków. There was also a growing number of secular Jews living in Kraków, as well as converts to Christianity. Among this diverse population acceptance for different manifestations of Jewishness developed, even among the Orthodox. Even among this group, the most traditional, there was a desire to modernize, even to the point of setting up special schools for the education of girls. Many girls from assimilated and less traditional families attended the local public schools.

While the Orthodox Jews continued to speak only Yiddish and Hebrew, more progressive Jews and the growing group of secular Jews spoke Polish rather than Yiddish as their first language. Many of the progressive Jews were also members of Zionist groups. These groups established sports clubs and teams as part of their mission. They believed that it was important that in order to live successfully in Israel and in order to present themselves as modern Jews, they needed to be fit and strong as opposed to bookish and prayerful which was the stereotypical view of Jews (Gawron, 2012). Jews also served in the Polish army, first fighting for Poland's independence and later in the Polish standing army. At the start of World War II, there were more than 60,000 Jews living in Kraków, one-fourth of the city's entire population (Weiner, 2008).

After the Germans invaded Poland, they selected Kraków as the capital of Nazi-occupied Poland. When the German occupation of Kraków began in September 1939, the Germans dismantled the Jewish community organization and appointed a Judenrat to administer Jewish affairs in the Jewish community and later in the ghetto which they established in March 1941. Jews were ordered to evacuate Kraków within four months of April 1940, resulting in 35,000 Jews leaving the city. The remaining Jews and about 6,000 from neighboring communities were enclosed in the ghetto when it was established south of the Vistula River in March 1941. This area, known as Podgórze, is across the river, just south of Kazimierz. Deportations began in June 1942 and several hundred Jews were put to death in the ghetto itself.

Of the more than 60,000 Jews who had inhabited Kraków before World War II, only about 2,000 survived the war and the Holocaust (Weiner, 2008). In the years immediately following the war, some other Jews who had lived in Russia during the war returned to Kraków. However, not many full Jewish families survived the war, so for many people this lack of family cohesion created a feeling of impermanence to their return. A fear of pogroms also prevented a Jewish community from becoming re-established. Between the lack of support and inability to make a living, as well as the limited opportunities for pursuing a Jewish life, many left after a short time, some to other parts of Poland, but most immigrated to Israel, the United States, and other places around the world. With the increase of incidents of anti–Semitism in the late 1960s and subsequent voluntary immigration and involuntary deportations of Jews of Poland in 1968 about 700 Jews remained in Kraków.

There has not been a strong presence of Jewish life in Kraków since World War II. The Orthodox Jews who remained wanted to re-establish their community, but it was too difficult. There was a lack of support and a lack of funding. There was no rabbi available so the community was led by the elders of the community (Gawron, 2012). Eventually there was a lack of Jewish people.

In the early 1980s as social and political change began in Poland, this change also affected the Jews who remained in Poland and in Kraków (Gawron, 2012). Young people started asking questions either about their own heritage or about the Jews who had been part of Polish history and culture for so long. For example, Daniela Malec (Easton, 2005) learned as a teenager, that her family is Jewish.

> "I found out from my mother when I was a young teenager. It was quite a shock really. It wasn't like bad or anything but it was quite strange. I just didn't know what to think about it or what it meant to me," she said. Later, she realised there were more people like herself. So she started up the support group Czulent. "We celebrate all the Jewish holidays together. We do a Sabbath dinner once a month. We actually koshered the kitchen of our friend so we now use it as a kosher kitchen" [para. 13].

In 2005, the Shavei Israel organization sent a rabbi to become Kraków's first full-time rabbi since the Holocaust (Easton, 2005). At that time, he reported that there were 157 registered members of the Jewish community in Kraków. Of the approximately 1,000 Jews who lived there in 2013, fewer than 300 identified themselves as members of the Jewish community, as members of the one active synagogue, the Remuh Synagogue, or as counted by the Jewish Community Center.

In 2008 a group of young people started Beit Kraków (House of Kraków). What began as a way for Polish young people to explore their Jewish roots has become more formalized. In 2009 Rabbi Tanya Segal arrived in Kraków to work with this group of young people. She is originally from Russia, where she majored in theatre, and trained as a Reform rabbi in Israel. She is also the first female rabbi ever in Poland. She combines traditional religious education and practice with less conventional methods such as drama, music, and photography to help teach her congregants, and anyone else who wishes to join them, about Judaism and Jewish life. Segal (personal communication, July 6, 2012) says that regardless of the medium, the purpose of such activities are to connect to God. The goals of Beit Kraków are to help rebuild Jewish life in Kraków, a Jewish life that Segal (personal communication, July 6, 2012) says will be like nothing Poland has seen before. This is Jewish life in Poland for the twenty-first century. She also reminds her congregants, however, that new social consciousness brings new challenges, and her role is to help prepare and educate them to meet these challenges.

One way in which the members of Beit Kraków educate themselves and the local community about Jewish life is through theatre and other art projects. Using a concept which they call Midrash Theatre, the members of this group and their rabbi select religious texts to study then create artistic pieces which reflect their perceptions and sense of how ancient texts, such as the book of Ruth, connect to their lives as Jews in Poland today. One example is the performance "Tajemnice mojej baci" (Secrets of My Grandmother). Young people created a midrash, an interpretation, based on the book of Lamentations in which young Polish-Jewish women are seeking and/or finding their heritage. This dramatic piece is based on true stories of members of the group, stories that are intertwined with a cry for knowledge and understanding of who they are. One young woman relates how at age 24 she learned she was Jewish from her aunt, a secret that slipped out. Her mother was frightened and fascinated by her daughter's exploration of her Jewish identity. Another tells of her boyfriend who was Jewish, but no one knew until one day in history class he stood up to confront the teacher's lies that there was no anti–Semitism in Poland in the 1960s. His family had fled to Sweden at that time because of the persecution. Another story interwoven with these is the story of a young girl whose family covertly observed Saturday as the Sabbath, but she never understood why. These stories create a theatre piece which interweaves the personal, the spiritual, and the social. By sharing this work with the community in performances several times a year, these young people share their journey, their learning, and their lives with those around them.

Since the 1990s, there has been renewed interest in learning about and preserving Kraków's Jewish past. Jagiellonian University has established a Department of Jewish Studies, which offers courses in Jewish history and culture, as well as Hebrew and Yiddish language study. The Rabbi Moses Isserles Remuh Jewish Library opened in 2005 to provide books in Yiddish,

Polish and English to the local Jewish community (Weiner, 2008). In 2008, under the sponsorship of Prince Charles of Great Britain, the Jewish Community Center opened which offers programs for adults and young people. Kraków is also the site of the most well-known Jewish cultural festival in Poland. Thanks in part to this festival, Kazimierz, the former Jewish quarter, is experiencing a revival as a Jewish center with a growing number of bookshops, restaurants, and museums, as well as cultural and social events which connect to Jewish history and life.

Background: The Jewish Culture Festival in Kraków is the oldest of the festivals in Poland. It began from modest roots and has become a 9 day spectacle visited by thousands of people from Poland and around the world. Because this festival was created by and is still run by Polish people who are not Jews there are detractors who claim that the festival is not an authentic representation of Jewish life and culture. On the other hand there are strong Jewish and non–Jewish supporters who believe that the festival is a worthwhile endeavor for teaching Poles and the world about Jewish culture in Poland. Some view it as a living museum experience, while others see it as a living reflection of Jewish life and culture.

The primary organizer, Janusz Makuch, has received several awards for his work with the festival. In 1998, he received an award from the Israeli Embassy in Poland during a ceremony at that year's festival recognizing his work in preserving Jewish culture and heritage in Poland (Mitchell, 1998). In 2008, Makuch received two awards for his work. He received the Poland Reborn Medal from the president of Poland (JTA, 2008). He was also the first person to receive the newly created Irena Sendler Memorial Award from the Taube Foundation for Jewish Life and Culture (JTA, 2008). In 2012, he was invited to present the Chris Schwarz Annual Memorial Lecture at the twenty-second Jewish Culture of Festival in Kraków. During that lecture, Makuch (2012) described his reason for starting and continuing the festival. An understanding of Makuch's motivation is germane to understanding the context of the festival.

Makuch (2012) was born in a small Polish town near Kraków, where he later came to study at the university. He grew up in the shadow of a palace of the Czartoryski family, a Polish aristocratic family, where he absorbed the history of the Polish people. He also learned about Jews during his studies, and about the friendship that the prince had with a Jew, Michal Strymski. Then as a teenager, Makuch developed a friendship with an Orthodox Jew who lived nearby. This man became a friend and a mentor, and helped set him on the path that eventually led to his being in this place at this time. He said that he believes it was his destiny to create this festival.

Living in Kazimierz, the former Jewish quarter, during the 1980s, Makuch along with many other young Poles at that time, was searching for the vestiges of Jewish life in Poland. In 1988, Makuch and a friend put together a Jewish film festival, a modest endeavor, the purpose of which was to shed some light on Polish and Jewish culture. He stated that it was logical and necessary that non–Jews start this education because they are obliged to cherish and remember the Jewish heritage which shaped their nation as greatly as did other influences. He sees the festival as a symbol of Jewish presence rather than Jewish absence.

Makuch (2012) went on to say that as the festival has continued and grown, it has changed and evolved. He points out that it reflects a wide range of cultural aspects, from traditional to avant-garde, as well as the range of Jewish religious life, from Orthodox to secular. He says that the festival aims to create awareness and to educate through providing a multi-layered experience.

During the 1990s, there were critics who claimed that the festival was building a virtual world, a world about Jews but without Jews. In an article in *The Jewish Daily Forward* Schaechter (2007) also addresses this issue:

> Indeed, the festival in Kazimierz, as the city's former Jewish quarter is known, has mushroomed into one of the largest events of its kind in the world, with one major difference: Hardly any of the participants were Jewish. To be precise, almost 85 percent of the Kraków festival's participants, and most of its organizers and activity leaders, were non–Jews [para. 1].

Makuch admits that there are those who willingly cash in on the popularity of the festival, but he thinks that the other benefits override this mercenary aspect. The festival serves as a bridge "between Poles and the Jewish culture that once thrived in their midst" (Schaechter, 2007, para. 12). In his lecture, Makuch (2012) stated that he believes that after 24 years of the festival, there is beginning to be a blurring of Poles and Jews as Jewish life reemerges in Kraków, and that people have the right to reach beyond their identity borders. He pointed out that Poles are the inheritors of their entire history, which includes the influence of Jews as well as anti–Semitism, a history which includes people who sold out their neighbors as well as the largest number of Righteous Among the Nations. He said that the festival demonstrates that being a Pole can mean being a Jew and being a Jew can mean being a Pole. He also thinks it is important that the 6 years of the Holocaust not be allowed to overshadow 1000 years of shared history. Makuch believes that the festival can and does have a positive impact on Polish-Jewish relations and that the festival is one way to overcome anti–Semitism (Schaechter, 2007).

The Festivals' Roles in Representations and Stereotypes

This volume examines one specific type of cultural festival in one specific country—Jewish cultural festivals in Poland. The two festivals that are examined here are two ends of a continuum. One is a large festival which displays multiple facets of Jewish life and culture and attracts participants and attendees from all over the world. The other is a small local festival whose aim is remembering local history.

In analyzing the impact of both of these festivals, an important issue to focus on is how they contribute to or break down stereotypes about Jews, and about Poles. According to *Webster's New Encyclopedic Dictionary* (1993) a stereotype is

> something conforming to a general pattern and lacking individual distinguishing marks or qualities; *esp*: a standardized mental picture that is held in common be members of a group and that represents an oversimplified opinion, emotional attitude, or uncritical judgment [p. 1013].

In this way a group's collective identity can be overgeneralized based on certain characteristics. When these generalizations are applied to an entire group by another or other groups, not only are individual differences being ignored, but so are other identity markers of the group.

As explained earlier, cultural festivals are one way that cultural identity markers are expressed. Some researchers (Bissoondath, 1994; Kates and Belk, 1991; Watts, 2002) assert that cultural festivals are consumer products which do not portray identity authentically and only serve to perpetuate stereotypes by focusing only on certain identity markers. Other researchers (Bramadat 2001, 2005; Green, 2002; Tye, 1994) assert that while these festivals may do that, they also provide some positive benefits for those being represented and those attending, by giving those being represented a voice and an opportunity to present themselves in the way they want to be represented.

One question to consider when examining such events is how important is the difference between presentation by self versus presentation by others, because as Schaechter (2007) points out, "almost 85 percent of the Kraków festival's participants, and most of its organizers and activity leaders, were non–Jews" (para. 3). In Chmielnik, a town without a Jewish population, the only Jews present are those who happen upon the festival or those who are invited, often from Israel.

One example of presentation is how music is presented. Many of the musicians who come to the festival in Kraków are not Jewish, so that one can say their relationship to the music is second or third hand, and the Jewish music they play is usually from the past. Generally, they do not play the Jewish music which has evolved over the past 70 or so years. Some of the presentation of music also relies on stereotypical representations, such as Rachel wearing a dark dress and a shawl over her head, and Tevye the Milkman with his cap and little tzitzit (ritual garment with fringes) from *Fiddler on the Roof*. The question these representations raise is, is this how Jews would represent themselves? In some cases, the answer would be "yes"; in others, "no."

While Bramadat (2001, 2005) is generally in favor of cultural festivals as a way for groups to identify themselves, he does raise the question: what if the community being represented is a community that no longer really exists? In many ways this is the big question when considering what and who is being represented at Jewish culture festivals in Poland.

What Stereotypes Are Being Perpetuated and How?

Stereotypes usually relate to physical attributes, such as appearance, clothing, and language. However, stereotypes can also relate to culture markers such as food, crafts, and rituals.

In several ways, physical appearance is often stereotyped in various representations of Jews in performances, pictures, and other representations that one sees at these festivals. The school children in Chmielnik perform plays that illustrate Jewish life before the war, so clothing such as that worn by Tevye the Milkman in *Fiddler on the Roof* or of Rachel with the long, dark dress and shawl are very commonly seen. While this clothing may be historically accurate for Jews in a shtetl, not all Jews lived in a shtetl, and of course, these are not accurate modern representations. However, they are the most commonly portrayed. In addition to clothing, most Jewish men are usually portrayed with beards, often with peyes (sidelocks), wearing skullcaps, having big noses, and bags under their eyes. Women are less often portrayed at all. When they are, they are often dancing. Men are often portrayed handling money.

Another stereotype which sets Jews apart from Poles is language. Although many Jews spoke Polish, at the festivals Hebrew and Yiddish are the languages that are presented as "Jewish" languages. Hebrew lessons and Yiddish lessons are offered. Singing in both languages is highlighted. There is little or no mention of Jews as Polish-speakers. Because a number of the Jewish guests at the Chmielnik festival are Israeli, Jews are represented as even one more step removed from the Polish neighbors.

Various arts, crafts, dance, music and food are presented as distinctly Jewish. For example, papercutting is often featured. While it is true this was a craft done by Jews in Poland, it is also done by Poles, Germans, and many other cultures. Sometimes the terms "Jewish food" and "kosher food" are used interchangeably, although there is a difference. The menu items referred to are often items like "borscht" (beet soup) which appears to be no different from the "barszcz" which is prepared in Polish households. Klezmer music is also heavily featured at these festivals. While it does reflect Jewish culture, it is not the only music composed and performed by Jews.

Oftentimes the Judaism presented at the festivals resembles Orthodox Judaism, and more specifically Chasidic Judaism. Historically, Jews in Poland were more commonly of these types. However, in the twentieth century Judaism worldwide has changed and evolved so that there are other ways of being Jewish. This evolution was not witnessed in Poland because there were so few Jews here and the ones that remained tended to cling to their old ways and traditions.

It seems fairly evident that many of these stereotypes are based in historical representations of Jews and Jewish culture. They are often rooted in a nostalgia for times past, for a time perceived as simpler, perhaps as better, in some way than the present. These images do not recognize how Jews and Judaism are part of the modern world. As Einhorn (Glass, 2002) pointed out, "All they have is the romance, and the memory, and none of the things that create problems."

What Stereotypes Are Being Broken and How?

However, there are attempts at these festivals to get away from the stereotypes. In Kraków, there are a number of tours offered which try to break some of the stereotypes of Jewish life in pre-war Poland. They often highlight how although Jews lived separately from the Polish population, they were part of Polish life. There are also exhibits and lectures about Jewish life in Poland before the Holocaust which portray life outside the shtetl. The organizers of the festival in Chmielnik point out that they want to present as many aspects of Jewish life and culture as they can, not just religious aspects, but culture and history as well.

Another way in which stereotypes are being broken is by including information about Israel. Part of Chmielnik mayor's expressed vision in creating the meetings there was to build a future that brought the two nations, Israel and Poland, together in brotherhood and friendship.

In Kraków during the year of Israel's 60th birthday the festival showcased various features of modern Israeli life, by showing Judaism and Jews as modern people in today's world. In 2008, there was also a group of Druze, a minority religious group related to Islam, who offered freshly baked pita as "a symbol of Israel's cuisine" showing yet another side of Israeli life.

In 2008 there was a focus on Sephardic Jews. Sephardic Jews, or Mediterranean Jews, have some cultural markers which are distinct from Ashkenazi Jews, the Jewish culture which developed in Germany and Eastern Europe. The vernacular that developed is called Ladino, which evolved differently from Yiddish. It was heavily influenced by the languages of the areas where Sephardic Jews lived, such as Spain, Turkey, and Greece. Likewise Sephardic cuisine has a more Mediterranean flavor than that of Ashkenazi Jews. Lectures and demonstrations gave a different perspective of what it means to be Jewish.

Lectures about similarities between Catholic and Jewish liturgy and other topics which compare the two religions also contribute to breaking down stereotypes. On both sides there are misconceptions about beliefs, rites, and rituals. For example, Polish Catholics prepare a basket of food to take to church for a special blessing the day before Easter. The items include a butter pressed into the shape of a lamb, to represent Christ; horseradish to represent bitterness; an egg which symbolizes the cycle of life and resurrection; salt which represents purification; ham to signify joy and abundance; and bread, the staff of life. If one compares these items to the seder plate, the ritual plate of symbolic foods which Jews prepare for Passover, the similarity is striking. The seder plate traditionally has a lamb shank to represent the meal the Jews ate before fleeing Egypt; horseradish to represent bitterness; an egg which symbolizes mourning; salt water which represents tears; another vegetable to represent pain of the slaves in Egypt; and chaorset, a mixture of honey and apples which represents the mortar used by the Hebrew slaves. Matzah, unleavened bread, while not on the seder plate, also plays a large role in the Passover meal and tradition. Lectures and workshops which highlight such traditions can help people understand the similarities and differences between the two religions and the two cultures, and create bridges by showing how people from both traditions have experienced joy and suffering.

One stereotype that I have heard some Poles express is that Jews think they are the only ones who suffered during World War II. In an attempt to break that stereotype, the festival in Kraków offers a ceremony for honoring Poles who helped Jews during the war. By making this an integral part of the festival, it pays homage to the shared history of Poles and Jews.

One final attempt at breaking down stereotypes is a series of open meetings which are a time for open dialogue between Christians and Jews. One can never judge immediately how effective such meetings are, but they do plant seeds that can take root and flourish. Open dialogue has the potential to be a strong weapon against prejudice and discrimination.

The Festivals as Pedagogical Constructs

From the perspective of education, these festivals are an interesting phenomenon. For Poles, Jews and non–Jews alike, these festivals may be the only exposure they have had to Jews and Jewish culture in post–War Poland. The festival in Kraków is even attributed by some to having helped revitalize Jewish life in Kazimierz, the former Jewish quarter. As Makuch told Ben Eliezer (2007), "[p]eople will be coming to Kraków to learn not just to be entertained" (para. 4). For the inhabitants of Chmielnik and Szydłow, the festivals are an opportunity to remember and commemorate.

As with literature related to Jewish life and culture and the Holocaust, most of the programming at the festival in Kraków is aimed at adults. However, there is some special programming for children. At the seventeenth festival in 2007, there was a series of workshops conducted in Polish for children which focused on Shavuot, one of the Jewish pilgrimage festivals which commemorates the giving of the Torah to the children of Israel. In 2012 during the 22nd festival, Galicia Jewish Museum offered workshops, tours, and games specifically designed for children and young people. One project involved a tour of places connected to Jewish history in Kraków riding in a pre-war tram.

While there is deliberate education going on at these festivals, direct teaching about the music, food, and customs of these cultures, there is also incidental learning going on that can have both positive and negative effects. In one way, the festivals help bring attention to, commemorate, and normalize a group that was almost wiped out. This recognition of the sudden rupture in the social fabric created a desire for remembrance on one hand but a tendency toward nostalgic and subsequent stereotyping on the other. The festivals by their nature tend to essentialize Jewish culture so that it is portrayed as one-dimensional. They can also trivialize what may be important parts of the culture, especially religious customs. In these and other ways, cultural festivals, in general, contribute to and help maintain stereotypes of these groups.

However, it is also worth noting that sometimes a group may choose to represent themselves in a stereotypical way. Such "strategic" essentialism (Bauman, 1999; Danius and Jonsson, 1993; Trinh, 1992) may serve to draw attention to various aspects of identity or to open doors to dialog beyond the stereotype. In his volume of essays, *Poland and the Jews: Reflections of a Polish Polish Jew*, Prof. Stanisław Krajewski (2005), talks about cultural workshops, lectures and exhibitions. Then he addresses the Jewish culture festivals:

> [These exhibitions and so on are] educational, not dialogue proper. By far the most important cultural happening of this category, and the only one that can be called a genuine dialogue event, is the annual Festival of Jewish Culture in Kraków. The high quality concerts, exhibitions, lectures, workshops, excursions attract crowds, including tourists from many countries. The musical performances are of top quality, presented by genuine creators of contemporary Jewish music, mostly from America. Unlike most other Jewish festivals, in Poland, and elsewhere, that easily fall into kitsch, for example presenting actors acting as Jews, the Kraków Festival, under the charismatic leadership of Janusz Makuch, is always genuine: the performers show what they do in their real lives, teachers present themes they really care about. The unique atmosphere created then enables contacts and the background for dialogue as almost nothing else in contemporary Poland [p. 233].

Therefore, according to Krajewski's view, the festival in Kraków, in particular, helps to de-essentialize Jewish culture and Judaism by offering a wide spectrum of views and perspectives.

As educational constructs which consistently present the breadth and depth of Jewish life, history and culture, the festivals are flawed. In their various iterations, they often over-represent some aspects of Jewish life and culture, and underrepresent other aspects. However, the festivals serve an important purpose as starting points for learning, for teaching, for dialogue, for critique of society, for building relationships. They provide a bridge to the Jewish heritage of Poland, changing to reflect the mutability of the reality of Polish society. From the educational perspective they present a microcosm of what is going on educationally in Poland around topics related to Jewish studies and Holocaust education, informally and formally, at all levels. In remarks at the 2013 festival, Jonathan Ornstein, director of the JCC in Kraków, even credited the Jewish Cultural Festival as being a cornerstone of the renaissance of Jewish life in Kraków. Evolution in the Jewish Culture Festival in Kraków reflects these changes as it has moved from an almost completely entertainment-based festival to including more lectures and presentations by scholars in the field of Jewish Studies, and representatives of Jewish organizations throughout Poland.

Websites for Further Information

Beit Kraków (House of Kraków), Kraków, www.beitKrakow.pl . Reform congregation in Kraków.

Festiwal Kultury Żydowskiej Simcha, Wrocław, http://www.simcha.art.pl/. Official website of the festival; has current information as well as the history of the festival (in Polish).

Festiwal Kultury Żydowskiej w Krakowie (Jewish Cultural Festival of Kraków), Kraków, www.jewishfestival.pl. Official website of the festival; has current information as well as archives of previous festivals.

Festiwal Kultury Żydowskiej Warszawa Singera (The Warsaw Singer Festival), Warsaw, www.festiwalsingera.pll. Sponsored by the Shalom Foundation (parts of the website are in English—click English).

Shalom Foundation, http://www.shalom.org.pl/. Official website of the American-Polish-Israeli Shalom Foundation. (Click the Union Jack icon for the English version.)

Conclusion

> The dispute about Polish anti–Semitism, the discussion on the subject of Polish-Jewish relations, is a matter which is much larger. It is a dispute ... over the choice of a model for Polish culture, what kind of culture it is, changing, as does any culture over the ages, and what form it ought to have [from "Ethical Problems of the Holocaust," Jerzy Turowicz]—Polonsky, 1990, p. 219

Education in its broadest sense is gaining information and strategies for being part of human society and culture. Education as a social construct tends to focus on how to be part of a particular society or culture. Formal education helps create social and cultural identity so that members of a particular social and/or cultural group understand how to be members of that group. Informal education can also play a role in this socialization. Education not only teaches individuals how to be functioning members of their group, but it also helps them identify who is not part of their group.

In human society, there are often groups which are different in various ways that must live together and function together in order to create a community, a functioning society. Martin Buber (1965) said that people do not have to agree and be completely like-minded in order to be part of a community. However, they must be open to one another, must carefully consider the opinions of others. He does not say people have to accept the opinions of others, necessarily, but must be open to finding the best solution to differences, which is where formal and informal education come in.

In analyzing the issues related to Jewish Studies and Holocaust Education in Poland, questions arise because there are a number of elements that need to be considered whether examining the formal education of the university and secondary school systems or the informal education of cultural festivals or programs offered by NGOs. There are emotional issues, as well as cultural, intellectual, financial, political, and religious issues which come in to play.

The context of Poland itself has to be considered. As is demonstrated by the absence of education about Jews and the Holocaust during the time of Soviet domination, the festivals and the formal educational efforts that have come about in the past 25 years reflect the more open political and social climate currently in Poland. As Trojański pointed out in his essay, this openness has provided opportunities for public awareness as well as public debate, open discussion that was not possible before 1989.

Context also determines how success is measured. Is success for the festivals measured in the amount of money that is brought in or in the number of cross-cultural contacts that are made as a result of the festivals? Is success for the educational initiatives measured by the number of graduates or by the decrease in anti–Semitic slogans at soccer matches? In 2013 the Auschwitz Jewish Center released the results of a research project on the effectiveness of their programs which showed that their programs do make a difference. The Center for Research on Prejudice affiliated with Warsaw University conducted a study with 2,000 Polish high school students who participated in a one-day program called Oświęcim: A Different Perspective. The results showed that not only did negative stereotypes and feelings against Jews and Romas decrease, but students also reported more positive feelings toward these two groups (AJCF, 2013).

It is also important to consider the people who are involved in the various activities and undertakings. There are Poles, and there are Jews and non–Jews from inside and outside Poland. There are people who are curious; there are philosemites; there are anti–Semites, and there are people who are just looking for entertainment. Who these people are and how they interact with others shapes what is presented in the various venues and how. Someone looking for entertainment may be easily satisfied with a stereotypical presentation of another culture. The person who suddenly discovers they have Jewish roots may have a completely different set of needs and desires as they try to figure out who they are, how they fit into Polish society, and, perhaps, how to be a Jew. On the other hand, an educator who is trying to teach his/her students about difficult issues in history, such as the Holocaust, needs a more serious and in depth look at cultural and identity issues, their own and others.'

It seems that all of these efforts are an attempt and an opportunity for Poles, Polish Jews, Jews, and Poland as a nation to come to terms with a difficult part of their history. Formal or informal education in isolation is not enough. A blending of formal and informal education provides opportunities for addressing the emotional issues, as well as the cultural, social, intellectual, political, and religious issues which are part of the equation. In writing about teaching about the Holocaust Zdzisław Mach (2005) reflected on the importance of molding "a uniform group consciousness and identity for the Poles" (p. 24) which demonstrates a respect for cultural pluralism, tolerance, "and to forge attitudes that encourage the building of a new, shared, pluralistic, open and tolerant Europe, and within it a Poland capable of dealing with its legacy" (p. 25).

The implications of the influence of formal and informal education in addressing cultural pluralism and for healing historical wounds go beyond Poland and Europe. Globalization makes these issues immediate and relevant for the entire world. The lessons learned from the Polish experience demonstrate the need for creating a context in which the conception of a collective consciousness which is inclusive rather than exclusionary is possible. The Polish experience also provides evidence that formal and informal educational experiences for children and adults alike can provide a means through which change can be realized, on the individual and on at societal levels. The change may be slow and there may be false starts, but as Lao-Tzu, an ancient Chinese philosopher, reminds us: A journey of a thousand miles begins with a single step.

Epilogue

Even though this book is finished, the changes happening in Poland related to the Holocaust are not. The Jewish population there is growing and changing. Ethnic Poles are questioning and exploring the Jewish heritage of the country. Kazimierz is developing less of a museum-like atmosphere and becoming sort of a Jewish center again with the Jewish Community Center, Galicia Museum, the Jagiellonian University's center and other centers of Jewish culture and learning located there. The opening of the Jewish museum in Warsaw is casting a new light on Jewish life in Warsaw and in Poland. Festivals, commemorations, celebrations are happening all across Poland to recognize and to eulogize the past and to look toward the future.

What began for me as curiosity about a particular event, the Jewish Cultural Festival in Kraków, sent me on a journey I did not anticipate. I have talked to people, Jews and non–Jews alike. I have participated in a wide variety of events and given presentations on what I have learned. I have read scholarly and non-scholarly books and articles, and now, have written my own. All of these have been part of my own learning experience and the more I have learned the more I want to know. For me the journey has not ended with the completion of this book. I want to see what happens next.

In closing, I want to thank everyone who encouraged me and supported me on this journey. Most especially I would like to thank those who contributed essays to lend their authentic voices to mine, the voice of an outsider whose knowledge is based on research, analysis, reflection, and musing, not lived experiences such as theirs.

Appendix: Further Reading

Ackerman, D. (2007). *The zookeeper's wife: A war story.* New York: W.W. Norton.
Ambrosewicz-Jacobs, J. and Hońdo, L. (Eds.). (2005). *Why should we teach about the Holocaust?* Kraków: Jagiellonian Institute of European Studies.
Ambrosewicz-Jacobs, J. (2009). *The Holocaust: Voices of scholars.* Kraków: Austeria.
Armstrong, D. (2002). *Mosaic: A chronicle of five generations.* New York: St. Martin's.
Bau, J. (2000). *Dear God, have you ever gone hungry?* New York: Arcade.
Bender, S. (2008). *The Jews of Bialystok during World War II and the Holocaust.* Lebanon, NH: Brandeis University Press.
Bergen, D. (2003). *War and genocide: A concise history of the Holocaust.* Lanham, MD: Rowman and Littlefield.
Bock, J., Stein, J., Aleichem, S., and Hamick, S. (1965). *Fiddler on the roof.* New York: Crown.
Crowe, D. (2004). *Oscar Schindler: The untold account of his life, wartime activities, and the true story behind the list.* Boulder, CO: Westview.
Czerniakow, A. (1999). *The Warsaw diary of Adam Czerniakow: prelude to doom.* Chicago: Ivan R. Dee
Dawidowicz, L. (1975). *The war against the Jews, 1933–1945.* New York: Holt, Reinhart, and Winston.
Davies, N. (1980). *God's playground,* vol. 1 and 2. Oxford: Oxford University Press.
Davies, N. (1984). *Heart of Europe: A short history of Poland.* Oxford: Oxford University Press.
Dobroszycki, L., and Kirshenblatt-Gimblett, B. (1994). *Image before my eyes: A photographic history of Jewish life in Poland before the Holocaust.* New York: Schocken.
Down, S. (2012). *Irena Sendler: Bringing life to children of the Holocaust.* St. Catherines, ON: Crabtree.
Gold, B. (2007). *The life of Jews in Poland before the Holocaust.* Lincoln: University of Nebraska Press.
Głuszyńska, I., and Mach, Z. (Eds.). (2011). *Threats to Multiculturalism.* Bielsko-Biala, Poland: Wyższa Szkoła Administracji.
Grollmus, D. (2012). Poland's real Jewish revival. *Tablet: A New Read on Jewish Life.* Retrieved from http://www.tabletmag.com/jewish-life-and-religion/116890/polands-real-jewish-revival.

Gross, J. (2001). *Neighbors: The destruction of the Jewish community in Jedwabne, Poland*. Princeton, NJ: Princeton University Press.
Gruber, R. (2007). *National Geographic Jewish heritage travel: A guide to Eastern Europe*. Washington, DC: National Geographic.
Gruber, R. (2002). *Virtually Jewish: Reinventing Jewish culture in Europe*. Berkeley: University of California Press.
Hoffman, E. (1990). *Lost in translation: A life in a new language*. New York: Penguin.
Hoffman, E. (1997). *Shtetl: The life and death of a small town and the world of Polish Jews*. Boston: Houghton Mifflin.
Kaufmann, J. (1997). *A hole in the heart of the world: Being Jewish in Eastern Europe*. New York: Viking.
Keneally, T. (1993). *Schindler's list*. New York: Scribner.
Korczak, J. (2003). *Ghetto diary*. New Haven, CT: Yale University Press.
Krajewski, S. (2005). *Poland and the Jews: Reflections of a Polish Polish Jew*. Kraków: Austeria.
Langer, L. (Ed.). (1995). *Art from the Ashes: A Holocaust Anthology*. New York: Oxford University Press.
Maciągowski, M., and Krawczyk, P. (2007). *The story of Jewish Chmielnik*. Kielce, Poland: XYZ.
Opdyke, I. (2004). *In my hands: Memories of a Holocaust rescuer*. New York: Laurel Leaf.
Redlich, S. (2002). *Together and apart in Brzezany: Poles, Jews and Ukrainians 1919–1945*. Bloomington: Indiana University Press.
Ringelblum, E., and Sloan, J. (2006). *Notes from the Warsaw ghetto*. New York: iBooks.
Sabor, A. (2005). *Sztetl: śladami żydowskich miastecyek*. Kraków: Wydawnictwo Austeria.
Santorski, J. (2006). *Difficult questions in Polish-Jewish dialogue*. Warsaw: Agencja Wydawnicza.
Shandler, J. (2002). *Awakening lives: Autobiographies of Jewish youth in Poland before the Holocaust*. New Haven, CT: Yale University Press.
Steinlauf, M. (1997). *Bondage to the dead: Poland and the memory of the Holocaust*. Syracuse, NY: Syracuse University Press.
Teichman, M., and Leder, S. (Eds.). (1994). *Truth and lamentation: Stories and poems on the Holocaust*. Urbana: University of Illinois Press.
Tomaszewski, I., and Werbowski, T. (2010). *Code name: Zegota: Rescuing Jews in occupied Poland, 1942–1945: The most dangerous conspiracy in wartime Europe*. Santa Barbara, CA: Praeger.
Walker, F., Neile, C., and Rosen, L. (2002). *Hidden: A sister and brother in Nazi Poland*. Madison: University of Wisconsin Press.
Wood, E., and Jankowski, S. (1996). *Karksi: How one man tried to stop the Holocaust*. New York: Wiley.
Zimmerer, K. (2004). Zamardowany Świat: Losy Zydow w Krakówie 1939–1945 [*The Murdered World: The History of Kraków's Jews 1939–1945*]. Kraków: Kraków Wydawnictwo Literackie. [Published in Polish only.]

References

Ambrosewicz-Jacobs, J. (2011). Memory, non-memory and/or post-memory of the Holocaust. Coming out of amnesia in post–Communist Poland? In I. Głuszyńska and Z. Mach (Eds.), *Threats to Multiculturalism* (pp. 182–197). Bielsko-Biala, Poland: Wyższa Szkoła Administracji.

Anti-Defamation League. (2001). *Stop hate: Anti-Semitism.* Retrieved from http://archive.adl.org/hate-patrol/antisemitism.asp.

Anti-Defamation League. (2012). Attitudes toward Jews in ten European countries, March 2012. Retrieved from http://archive.adl.org/Anti_semitism/adl_anti-semitism_presentation_february_2012.pdf.

Arce, C. (1981). A reconsideration of Chicano culture and identity. *Daedalus, 110* (2), 177–192.

Aries, E., and Moorehead, K. (1989). The importance of ethnicity in the development of identity in black adolescents. *Psychological Reports, 65* (1), 75–82.

Association of European Jewish Museums. (n.d.). Bylaws. Retrieved from http://www.aejm.org/mission.

Auschwitz Jewish Center Foundation. (2013). Data shows AJC program proven to fight hate and prejudice. Retrieved from http://ajcf.org/2013/02/11/data-just-released-shows-ajc-program-proven-to-fight-hate-and-prejudice.

Bar-Tal, D. (1997). Formation and change of ethnic and national stereotypes: An integrative model. *International Journal of Intercultural Relations, 21* (4), 491–523.

Bauer, Y. (1999). Academic research on the Holocaust. Retrieved May 1, 2006, from http://www.chgs.umn.edu/Educational_Resources/Curriculum/Stockholm_International_Forum/Task_Force_Report/2g/2g.html.

Bauman, Z. (1991). *Modernity and ambivalence.* New York: Cornell University Press.

Bauman, Z. (2001). *Community: Seeking safety in an insecure world.* London: Polity.

Bergman, E. (2009). Questions in the Polish landscape. In J. Ambrosewicz-Jacobs, J. (Ed.), *The Holocaust: Voices of scholars* (pp. 281–283). Kraków: Austeria.

Bissoondath, N. (1994). *Selling illusions: The cult of multiculturalism in Canada.* Toronto: Penguin.

Bramadat, P. (2001). Shows, selves, and solidarity: Ethnic identity and cultural spectacles in Canada. *Canadian Ethnic Studies, 33* (3), 78–98.

Bramadat, P. (2005). Toward a new politics of authenticity: Ethno-cultural representation in theory and practice. *Canadian Ethnic Studies, 37* (1), 1–20.

Brownell, G. (2011, June 5). Reasserting and redefining Jewish culture in Poland.

The New York Times. Retrieved from http://www.nytimes.com/2012/06/06/arts/06iht-poleculture06.html?_r=0.

Bruchfeld, S. (2000, January). Facing denial in society and education. Paper presented at the *Stockholm International Forum on the Holocaust*, Stockholm, Sweden.

Buber, M. (1965). *Between man and man.* New York: Macmillan.

Casey, K. (1996). The new narrative research in education. *Review of Research in Education, 21,* 211–253.

Chartock, R. (2001). Including music in a study of the Holocaust. In S. Totten and S. Feinberg (Eds.), *Teaching and studying the Holocaust.* (pp. 280–303). Boston: Allyn and Bacon.

Craddy, K. (2010). Jewish museums. In In K. Craddy, M. Levy, and J. Nowakowski (Eds.), *Poland: A Jewish Matter* (pp. 143–152). Warsaw: Adam Mickiewicz Institute.

Csikszentmihalyi, M. (1996). *Creativity: Flow and the psychology of discovery and invention.* New York: HarperCollins.

Davidow, A. (2013). Klezmer Shack: 10 years of Jewish music. Retrieved from http://www.klezmershack.com

Davies, N. (1984). *Heart of Europe: A short history of Poland.* Oxford: Oxford University Press.

De Laine, M. (1997, July 4). Third of teenagers deny Holocaust. *Times Educational Supplement.* Retrieved from http://www.tes.co.uk/teaching-resource/Third-of-teenagers-deny-Holocaust-69055/.

Drew, M. (1991). Merging history and literature in teaching about genocide. *Social Education, 55* (2): 128–129.

Dwork, D. (2009). The challenges of Holocaust scholarship: A personal statement. In J. Ambrosewicz-Jacobs, J. (Ed.), *The Holocaust: Voices of scholars.* (pp. 189–203). Kraków: Austeria.

Easton, A. (2005). Kraków rabbi spurs Jewish revival. BBC News. Retrieved November 10, 2008 from http://news.bbc.co.uk/2/hi/europe/4465954.stm.

Erikson, E. (1963). *Childhood and society,* 2d ed. New York: Norton.

Erikson, E. (1968). *Identity: Youth and crisis.* New York: Norton.

European Jewish Press (2009). Conflict over Kraków Jewish Festival. *EJ Press.* Retrieved from http://www.ejpress.org/article/culture/1537.

Fazel, R. (n.d.). Oratorio Terezin. Retrieved from http://www.ruthfazal.com/oldwebsite/Oratorio%20Terezin%20Website/OT%20Text.htm.

FRA. (2010). *Discover the past for the future: The role of historical sites and museums in the Holocaust education and human rights education in the EU.* Luxembourg: European Union.

Frankl, M. (2003). Holocaust education in the Czech Republic, 1989–2002. *Intercultural Education, 14* (2), 177–189.

Galas, M. (2012, July). A revival of Jewish Studies in Poland—Achievements and challenges. Lecture at 22nd Jewish Cultural Festival, Kraków, Poland.

Gawron, E. (2012, July). History of Jews in Kraków in the 20th century. Lecture at 22nd Jewish Cultural Festival, Kraków, Poland.

Glass, I. (2002, Sept. 20). Fake ID transcript. *This American Life.* Retrieved from http://www.thisamericanlife.org/radio-archives/episode/221/transcript.

Gold, B. (2007). *The life of Jews in Poland before the Holocaust*. Lincoln: University of Nebraska Press.
Graham, R. (2009). The function of music education in the growth of cultural openness in the USA. *Music Education Research, 11* (3), 283–302.
Green, G. (2002). Marketing the nation: Carnival and tourism in Trinidad and Tobago. *Critique of Anthropology, 22* (3), 283–305.
Greenhill, P. (1999). Backyard world/Canadian culture: Looking at festival agendas. *Canadian University Music Review, 19* (2), 37–46.
Gudykunst, W.B., and Kim, Y.Y. (2003). *Communicating with strangers: An approach to intercultural communication*. 4th ed. Boston: McGraw-Hill.
Hargraves, D. (n.d.). *Life as Prisoner Number 119 198*. Retrieved from http://hunza1.tripod.com/borowski/dachau.html.
Herbst, J. (2011). Po co są organizacje? Retrieved from http://osektorze.ngo.pl/x/631719.
Hewstone, M., and Brown, R. (Eds.). (1986). *Contact and conflict in intergroup encounters*. Oxford, UK: Basil Blackwell.
Hoffman, E. (1990). *Lost in translation: A life in a new language*. New York: Penguin.
Hoffman, E. (1997). *Shtetl: The life and death of a small town and the world of Polish Jews*. Boston: Houghton Mifflin.
Houwinkten Cate, J. (2010). The future of Holocaust studies. *Jewish Political Studies Review, 22*, 1–2.
ICEAH. (2013). *The International Center for Education about Auschwitz and the Holocaust*. Retrieved from http://en.auschwitz.org/e/index.php?option=com_contentandtask=viewandid=1andItemid=1.
ICEAH. (2013). Polish-German-Russian educational project. Retrieved from http://en.auschwitz.org/m/index.php?option=com_contentandtask=viewandid=1088andItemid=7.
International Council of Museums. (2012). Museum definition. *ICOM: The World Museum Community*. Retrieved from http://icom.museum/the-vision/museum-definition/.
Jewish Kraków. (2011). The Old Synagogue. *Jewish Kraków: A Visual and Virtual Tour*. Retrieved from http://www.jewishKraków.net/en/see/old-synagogue/.
JTA. (2008). Polish award named for righteous gentile. *JTA*. Retrieved April 2, 2008, from http://jta.org/news/article/2008/06/01/108857/Sendlerowapoland.
JTA. (2008). Poland cites Jewish festival chief. *JTA*. Retrieved April 2, 2009, from http://jta.org/news/article/2008/04/16/108128/makuchwarsaw.
Kaluzna, A. (2012, July). Jewish theatre at Lower Silesia, 1945–1968. Lecture at 22nd Jewish Cultural Festival, Kraków, Poland.
Kates, S., and Belk, R. (2001). The meanings of lesbian and gay pride day: Resistance through consumption and resistance to consumption. *Journal of Contemporary Ethnography, 20* (4), 392–430.
Kobayashi, A. (1993). Multiculturalism: Representing a Canadian institution. In J. Duncan and D. Ley (Eds.), *Place/Culture/Rrepresentation* (pp. 205–31). New York: Routledge.

Krajewski, S. (2005). *Poland and the Jews: Reflections of a Polish Polish Jew*. Kraków: Austeria.

Kubiszyn, M. (2012, July). From the treasury of Jewish memorial books. Lecture at 22nd Jewish Cultural Festival, Kraków, Poland.

Lawrence, R. (2008). Powerful feelings: Exploring the affective domain of informal and arts-based learning. *New Directions for Adult and Continuing Education* (120), 65–77.

Leigh, A. (1997, July 4). Extremists manipulate teaching of history. *Times Educational Supplement*. Retrieved from http://www.tes.co.uk/article.aspx?storycode=69056.

Mach, Z. (2005). The memory of the Holocaust and education for Europe. In J. Ambrosewicz-Jacobs and L. Hońdo (Eds.) *Why Should We Teach About the Holocaust* (pp. 22–25). Kraków: The Jagiellonian Institute of European Studies.

Maciągowski, M., and Krawczyk, P. (2007). *The story of Jewish Chmielnik*. Kielce, Poland: XYZ.

Makuch, J. (2010). The Jewish Culture Festival, Kraków. In K. Craddy, M. Levy, and J. Nowakowski (Eds.), *Poland: A Jewish Matter* (pp. 131–136). Warsaw: Adam Mickiewicz Institute.

Matar, J. (2001, April 23). In Denial. *The Jerusalem Report*, pp. 22–27.

Maslow, A.H. (1943). A theory of human motivation. *Psychological Review, 50* (4), 370–96.

Mickiewicz, A. (1992). *Pan Tadeusz: English and Polish text*. New York: Hippocrene.

Miles, W. (2000). Post-Communist Holocaust commemoration in Poland and Germany. *The Journal of Holocaust Education, 9* (1), 33–50.

Mitchell, S. *(1998). Israel honors Poles for work on preserving Jewish heritage.* JTA. Retrieved April 2, 2009 from http://jta.org/news/article/1998/07/09/3180/IsraelhonorsPoles.

Moore, T. (2004). *Dark nights of the soul*. New York: Gotham.

Murillo, E. (1997). Pedagogy of a Latin American festival. *Urban Review, 29* (4), 263–281.

MyJewishLearning (2013). Synagogue and religious music. Retrieved from http://www.myjewishlearning.com/culture/2/music/synagogue_and_religious-music.shtml.

Novick, P. (1999). *The Holocaust in American life*. New York: Houghton Mifflin.

Phinney, J. (1991). Ethnic identity and self-esteem: A review and integration. *Hispanic Journal of Behavioral Sciences, 13* (2), 193–208.

Phinney, J. (1992). The Multigroup Ethnic Identity Measure: A new scale for use with diverse groups. *Journal of Adolescent Research, 7* (2), 156–176.

Phinney, J. (1993). A three-stage model of ethnic identity development in adolescence. In M.E. Bernal and G.P. Knight (Eds.), *Ethnic Identity: Formation and transmission among Hispanics and other minorities* (pp. 61–79). Albany: State University of New York Press.

Phinney, J. and Tarver, S. (1988). Ethnic identity search and commitment in black and white eighth-graders. *Journal of Early Adolescence, 8* (3), *265–277.*

Pinchuk, B. (1986). Cultural sovietization in a multi-ethnic environment: Jewish culture in Soviet Poland, 1939–1941. *Jewish Social Studies, 48* (2), *163–174.*

Polonsky, A. (Ed.). (1990). *My brother's keeper? Recent Polish debates on the Holocaust*. London: Routledge.

Rosenblatt, P.C. (1964) Origins and effects of group ethnocentrism and nationalism. *Journal of Conflict Resolution, 8* (2), 131–46.

Rovit, R. (2005). Cultural ghettoization and theater during the Holocaust: Performance as a link to community. *Holocaust Genocide Studies, 19,* 459–486.

Sabor, A. (2005). *Sztetl: śladami żydowskich miastecyek*. Kraków: Wydawnictwo Austeria.

St. Louis, G.R., and Liem, J.H. (2005). Ego identity, ethnic identity, and the psychological well-being of ethnic minority and majority college students. *Identity: An International Journal of Theory and Research, 5* (3), 227–246.

Schaechter, R. (2007, July). Kraków Jewish fest features notable absence: Jews. *The Jewish Daily Forward*. Retrieved from http://www.forward.com/articles/111 42/.

Seldin, R. (1991). American Jewish museums: Trends and issues. *American Jewish Yearbook, 1991,* pp. 71–117. Retrieved from http://www.policyarchive.org/handle/10207/bitstreams/17744.pdf.

Short, G., and Reed, C. (2004). *Issues in Holocaust Education*. Bodmin, Cornwall: Ashgate.

Shtern, Y. (n.d.) Torah consumed by fire, 1938. M. Leberstein (Trans.). Retrieved from http://www.yisroelshtern.org/images/eng/poems/torah_by_fire.pdf.

Spencer, M., and Markstrom-Adams, C. (1990). Identity processes among racial and ethnic minority children in America. *Child Development, 61* (2), 290–310.

Steiner, J. (1995). *European democracies,* 3d ed. New York: Longman USA.

Streitmatter, J.L. (1988). Ethnicity as a mediating variable of early adolescent identity development. *Journal of Adolescence, 11* (4), 335–346.

Szuchta, R. (2005). Why teach about the Holocaust: The reflections of a teacher. In J. Ambrosewicz-Jacobs and L. Hońdo (Eds.), *Why Should We Teach About the Holocaust* (pp. 55–59). Kraków: The Jagiellonian Institute of European Studies.

Szymborska, W. (n.d.). Dzieci epoki/Children of Our Age. *Wislawa Szymborska Poems*. Retrieved from http://www.arlindo-correia.com/wislawa_szymborska.html#Os_filhos_da_epoca_.

Tajfel, H. (1978). *The social psychology of minorities*. New York: Minority Rights Group.

Taylor, D. (1997). The quest for collective identity: the plight of disadvantaged ethnic minorities. *Canadian Psychology, 38* (3), 174–190.

Templeton, D. (1965). The arts: Sources for affective learning. *Educational Leadership, 22,* (7), 465–468.

Thoroski, C. (1997). Adventures in ethnicity: Consuming performances of cultural identity in Winnipeg's Folklorama. *Canadian Folklore Canadien, 19* (2), 105–12.

Thoroski, C. and Greenhill, P. (2001). Putting a price on culture: Ethnic organization, volunteers, and the marketing of multicultural festivals. *Ethnologies, 23* (1), 189–209.

TNN.PL (n.d.). The memory gate—English. *Lublin Pamiec Miejsca*. Retrieved from http://tnn.pl/The_Gate_of_Memory_-_English,3362.html.

Tomaszewski, J. (2005). Why? In J. Ambrosewicz-Jacobs and L. Hońdo (Eds.) *Why Should We Teach About the Holocaust* (pp. 17–21). Kraków: The Jagiellonian Institute of European Studies.

Totten, S. and Feinberg, S. (Eds.). (2001). *Teaching and studying the Holocaust.* Boston: Allyn and Bacon.

Tslil. (n.d.). About the choir. *Jewish Choir Tslil.* Retrieved from http://www.clil.pl/about-the-choir.html.

Tych, F. (2009). A witness and his path to research. In J. Ambrosewicz-Jacobs (Ed.), *The Holocaust: Voices of scholars.* (pp. 173–188). Kraków: Austeria.

Tye, D. (1994). Multiple meanings called Cavendish: The interaction of tourism and traditional culture. *Journal of Canadian Studies, 29* (1), 122–34.

United States Holocaust Memorial Museum. (2012). *Holocaust encyclopedia: Antisemitism.* Retrieved from http://ushmm.org/wlc/en/article.php?moduleId=10005175.

United States Holocaust Memorial Museum. (2012). *Holocaust encyclopedia: Introduction to the Holocaust.* Retrieved from http://ushmm.org/wlc/en/article.php?moduleId=10005143.

Vertovec, S. (2007). Super-diversity and its implications. *Ethnic and Racial Studies, 30* (6), 1024–1054.

Vertovec, S. (2011). The cultural politics of nation and migration. *Annual Review of Anthropology, 40,* 241–56. Retrieved from anthro.annualreviews.org/0.1146/annurev-anthro-081309-145837.

Volenski, L.T. and Grzymala-Moszczynska, H. (1997). Religious pluralism in Poland. *America, 176* (6), 21–23.

Watts, E. (2002). The spectacular consumption of "true" African American culture: Whassup with the Budweiser guys? *Critical Studies in Media Consumption,* 19 (1), 1–20.

Weaver, G. (1997). *Culture, communication and conflict: Readings in intercultural relations*, 2d ed. New York: Pearson.

Weiner, R. (2008). The virtual Jewish history tour: Kraków. Retrieved November 10, 2008, from http://www.jewishvirtuallibrary.org/jsource/vjw/Cracow.html.

Werb, S. (2001). The inclusion of art in a study of the Holocaust. In S. Totten and S. Feinberg (Eds.), *Teaching and studying the Holocaust.* (pp. 239–262). Boston: Allyn and Bacon.

Wieser, P. (2001). Instructional issues/strategies in teaching the Holocaust. In S. Totten and S. Feinberg (Eds.), *Teaching and studying the Holocaust.* (pp. 62–80). Boston: Allyn and Bacon.

Witkowski, R. (2012, July). Jews in Poznań. A historical perspective. Lecture at 22nd Jewish Cultural Festival, Kraków, Poland.

Wygnanski. J. (2011). What are NGOs? Retrieved from http://osektorze.ngo.pl/x/631717;jsessionid=8F1F4F28AC1009B439B30AB471D2EF79.

Zaremba, M. (2012, July). The modern legend of ritual murder—Kielce 1946. Lecture at 22nd Jewish Cultural Festival, Kraków, Poland.

Zatzman, B. (2001). Drama activities and the study of the Holocaust. In S. Totten and S. Feinberg (Eds.), *Teaching and studying the Holocaust.* (pp. 263–279). Boston: Allyn and Bacon.

Zimmerman, L. and Sukovata, V. (2009). Emerging Holocaust Education Programs in Eastern Europe. In K. McSharry (Ed.), *Emerging Issues in Holocaust Education: Selected conference proceedings, Seventh Holocaust Education Conference, November 5–7, 2006* (pp. 115–120). Greensburg, PA: National Catholic Center for Holocaust Education, Seton Hall University.

Zolynia Memorial. (2011). A new Poland. *Zolynia Memorial*. Retrieved from http://www.zolynia.org/poland.html.

About the Contributors

Jolanta **Ambrosewicz-Jacobs**—Director, Center for Holocaust Studies, Jagiellonian University, Kraków, Poland; member, Polish delegation to International Holocaust Remembrance Alliance; Ina Levine Invitational Scholar, USHMM, 2011/2012; Pew Fellow, Center for the Study of Human Rights, Columbia University; visiting fellow, Oxford University, Cambridge University; author and editor of numerous books and articles related to the Holocaust.

Elisabeth **Büttner**—MA, European Faculty of International and Political Studies, Jagiellonian University. PhD candidate, Institute of European Studies/Centre for Holocaust Studies; dissertation topic: the fate of German prisoners of the concentration camp Auschwitz. Trainee and translator with two Polish-German projects; awarded research scholarship by European Holocaust Research Infrastructure in 2013; research interests: anti–Semitism, the history of Auschwitz-Birkenau; Polish-Jewish and Polish-German relations.

Izabella **Goldstein**—MA, choral conducting, F. Chopin Academy of Music of Warsaw; MA, opera singing and performance, Academy of Music of Łódź. PhD candidate, University of Manchester; dissertation topic: Songs of the Jewish underworld in pre–World War II Warsaw. Conductor and artistic director, Tslil Jewish Choir, 2006–2011.

Piotr **Goldstein**—MA, philosophy, University of Łódź; MA, international peace work, University of Trieste. PhD candidate, University of Manchester; dissertation topic: Civil societies of Serbia and Bosnia-Herzegovina. Chairperson of Polish Union of Jewish Students in 1999/2000; founding member, Tslil Jewish Choir.

Katarzyna **Suszkiewicz**—MA, European Studies, Jagiellonian University; PhD candidate, Institute of European Studies/Centre for Holocaust Studies, Jagiellonian University; dissertation topic: Holocaust perception in the political history of Israel. Participated in Polish Israeli Youth Encounter Programme of the Museum of the History of Polish Jews (2009/2010) and seminar for Polish educators in Yad Vashem, Jerusalem (2010); research interests: the Holocaust, Israel, Polish-Israeli relations and issues of heritage, memory and use of cultural space.

Piotr **Trojański**—Assistant professor, Institute of History of the Pedagogical University of Kraków (head of the Division of Ethnic and National Minorities); historian; lecturer, Centre for Holocaust Studies at the Jagiellonian University; academic advisor for the International Center for Education about Auschwitz and the Holocaust at the Auschwitz-Birkenau State Museum in Oświęcim; author of numerous publications on modern Jewish history and Holocaust education.

Lynn W. **Zimmerman**—PhD, professor of education/applied linguistics, Purdue University Calumet, Indiana, and Tischner European University, Kraków, Poland. Peace Corps volunteer, Poland, 1992–1994; Fulbright Scholar, University Wrocław, 2009; recipient: NW Indiana Jewish Federation Community Service Award, 2007; Outstanding Faculty Service Award, Purdue University Calumet, 2012; research interests: intercultural communication, Holocaust education.

Index

Actions Reconciliation/Service for Peace (ARSP) 131
Adam Mickiewicz University, Poznań 51, 52, 75
affective 152, 157, 196
Age of Enlightenment 28
Akademia Polin (Polish Academy), Warsaw 148, 151
Allies 83, 102
Ambrosewicz-Jacobs, J. 58, 61, 63, 64, 65, 78, 109, 112, 113, 119, 121, 137, 191, 193, 194, 196, 197, 198, 201
Anne Frank House, Amsterdam 106, 133
Anti-Defamation League 17, 19, 193
anti-Fascism 35
anti-Judaism 105
antiracist education 79
anti-Semitism 4, 16, 17, 18, 19, 24, 29, 30, 32, 34, 37, 53, 60, 61, 63, 65, 66, 68, 69, 71, 74, 81, 82, 83, 86, 90, 91, 94, 98, 103, 104, 105, 110, 121, 126, 147, 176, 177, 179, 187, 193, 201
the arts 5, 152, 153, 154, 156, 166, 168, 182
Aryans 17
Ashkenazi 27, 153, 159, 183
assimilation 13, 21, 29, 30, 34, 174
Association of European Jewish Museums (AEJM) 141, 142, 143, 144, 146, 147, 150, 151, 193
Auschwitz-Birkenau Memorial and Museum, Oświęcim 107, 113, 115, 143, 144, 151
Auschwitz Jewish Center Foundation, New York 133, 193
Austeria Publishing (Wydawnictwo Austeria) 64, 156, 165
Austria-Hungarian Empire 29, 174

Balfour Declaration of 1917 32
Bauer, Y. 57, 65, 68, 193
Beis-Ya'akov (House of Jacob) 31
Beit Kraków 128, 176, 177, 186
Bełżec 102, 132
Berenbaum, M. 65, 68
Birthright-Taglit 44
Blatt, T. 68

Błoński, J. 98, 113
Bolesław the Pious 27
Borderland Foundation 132, 138
Borderland of Arts, Cultures and Nations Centre, Sejny 132
Bransk 23
Breslau, Germany 24, 56, 141; see also Wrocław, Poland
Breslauer Theologisches Seminar 56, 76
Buchenwald 124, 125
Büttner, E. 58, 201

Canada 65, 78, 79, 81, 167, 193
Cardinal Hlond 32
Catholic Church 18, 22, 23, 25, 27, 29, 32, 63, 174
Center for Holocaust Studies, Jagiellonian University, Kraków 53, 57, 58, 60, 61, 64, 65, 66, 67, 68, 69, 73, 75, 76, 89, 106, 201
Center for Jewish Culture, Kraków (Kraków Jewish Cultural Centre) 51, 104
Center for Jewish Studies, Maria Curie-Skłodowska University, Lublin 54, 76
Central Europe 20, 53, 56, 76; see also Eastern Europe
Central Jewish Historical Commission 50, 54
Centre for Citizenship Education 119, 138
Centre for Education Development, Warsaw 88, 106, 116
Centre for European Studies, Jagiellonian University, Kraków 53, 77, 89, 116
Centre for the Culture and Languages of the Jews, University of Wrocław 56, 76
Centropa 61, 76
Chair of European Studies 60; see also Institute of European Studies
cheder 30, 31
Chief Rabbi of Poland 36, 37
Children of the Holocaust Association, Warsaw 128, 138
children's literature 156
Children's Strike, Września 22
Chmielnik 124, 136, 169, 170, 171, 172, 173, 180, 181, 182, 184, 192, 196

203

Index

Christianity 30, 138, 175
citizenship 29, 174
City Space Association 127
civil society 75, 123, 127, 136, 137
cognitive 13, 14, 80, 152
collective identity 8, 97, 114, 137, 180, 197
collective memory 59, 60, 62, 66, 68, 74, 123, 130, 172
collectivist 10, 12, 16, 20, 21, 26
communication 9, 10, 14, 15, 44, 45, 46, 141, 150, 195, 198
communism 25, 32
Communist period 56, 98, 168
communities of memory 123
community 12, 26, 42, 59, 61, 69, 118, 138, 152, 158, 166, 167, 168, 177, 187, 193
Conference on Jewish Material Claims Against Germany 71, 89
Constitution of May Third, 1792 29
Kraków 58, 59, 68, 71, 75, 92, 104, 106, 113, 114, 115, 174, 198, 201; *see also* Kraków
Cultural and Ecological Education Center (CEKIE), Kraków 127
cultural festivals 3, 4, 5, 38, 158, 159, 166, 167, 168, 180, 181, 184, 185
cultural iceberg 8
cultural markers 7, 8, 12, 26, 34, 152, 158, 166, 180, 181, 183
culture 1, 5, 7, 8, 11, 12, 13, 15, 16, 17, 19, 20, 21, 30, 59, 62, 67, 75, 86, 105, 112, 113, 122, 124, 131, 132, 138, 139, 141, 144, 151, 152, 153, 154, 157, 158, 166, 167, 168, 171, 181, 182, 187, 188, 197, 198

dance 43, 129, 153, 158, 159, 182
Department of Hebrew Studies, Warsaw University 50, 55, 56, 76
Department of Jewish Studies, Jagiellonian University, Kraków 53, 144, 177
deportation 75, 119, 122, 175, 176
diary 84, 156, 191, 192
discrimination 16, 17, 30, 33, 37, 60, 71, 81, 110, 121, 153, 184
drama 84, 132, 152, 157, 165, 177, 198
Działoszyce 4

Eastern Europe 24, 36, 37, 49, 50, 52, 77, 86, 87, 112, 122, 123, 158, 183, 192, 199; *see also* Central Europe
education 3, 4, 5, 7, 17, 21, 31, 34, 42, 43, 50, 52, 60, 61, 62, 63, 64, 66, 70, 74, 77, 79, 80, 85, 86, 87, 88, 89, 92, 93, 94, 100, 103, 104, 107, 108, 110, 117, 119, 120, 123, 125, 126, 128, 132, 140, 148, 149, 150, 154, 155, 160, 166, 167, 168, 169, 171, 175, 179, 184, 185, 187, 188, 189, 194, 195, 196, 197
Elizabeth Morse Genius Charitable Trust 71

Emanuel Ringelblum Jewish Historical Institute, Warsaw 141, 146, 151
Erikson. E. 8, 9, 194
ethical issues 66, 68, 77, 81
ethnocentrism 15, 86, 197
European Association for Jewish Studies 51, 77
European Union 26, 44, 86, 90, 121, 125
European Union Agency for Fundamental Rights 85
European Union of Jewish Students 42
extermination 35, 91, 94, 95, 100, 102, 103, 106
extermination/death camps 23, 63, 68, 83, 86, 87, 96, 102, 107, 125, 128, 130, 157

Fellowships at Auschwitz for the Study of Professional Ethics (FASPE), Museum of Jewish Heritage in New York 66, 77
film 40, 43, 51, 55, 66, 67, 68, 71, 79, 83, 8598, 110, 123, 124, 128, 129, 132, 133, 144, 146, 155, 156, 157, 169, 179
Final Solution 83, 101, 105
Fondation pour la Memoire de la Shoah 61, 122
Forum for Dialogue Among Nations Foundation, Warsaw 130, 138
Foundation for the Preservation of Jewish Heritage (FODZ) 61, 64, 119, 120, 134, 138
Fundacja Civis Polonus, Warsaw 135

Galicia Jewish Museum, Kraków 68, 141, 146, 15, 154, 184
gender 9, 31, 32, 136
genocide 60, 65, 69, 70, 74, 77, 80, 83, 85, 87, 97, 98, 105, 106, 107, 112, 114, 145, 191, 194, 197
German-Polish Youth Office (GPYO) 131
Germany 17, 21, 22, 23, 27, 28, 29, 32, 56, 65, 66, 77, 83, 122, 128, 131, 141, 144, 183, 196
ghetto 13, 23, 41, 59, 66, 83, 90, 98, 100, 119, 127, 160, 162, 163, 164, 172, 175, 192, 197
Goldstein, I. 159, 161, 164, 201
Goldstein, P. 38, 47, 201
graffiti 33, 109, 119, 123, 125, 126, 127, 128, 130
Great Synagogue, Warsaw 146
Grodzka Gate, Lublin 74, 132, 139, 142, 149, 150, 151
Gross, J.T. 35, 99, 111, 113, 132, 192
guidebook 149, 151, 156
Gwoździec Reconstruction project, Warsaw 148, 151

Hall, E.T. 7
Hasidism 28, 30, 33, 40, 57, 129, 170, 182
Hebrew 21, 27, 30, 31, 40, 43, 49, 50, 52, 53, 54, 55, 56, 57, 75, 76, 120, 159, 160, 161, 164, 175, 177, 181

Hillel 41
Historical Institute, University of Warsaw 55
Hitler, A. 17, 23, 32, 66, 82
Hoffman, E. 17, 25, 30, 33, 36, 192, 195
holidays 7, 18, 21, 30, 34, 41, 129, 143, 156, 173, 176
Holocaust 3, 4, 5, 23, 24, 33, 35, 36, 38, 39, 40, 46, 50, 51, 54, 57, 58, 59, 60, 61, 62, 63, 64, 65, 66, 68, 69, 70, 71, 72, 73, 74, 75 ,78, 80, 84, 86, 90, 91, 94, 95, 96, 97, 98, 99, 102, 105, 106, 108, 119, 120, 121, 122, 124, 127, 128, 131, 132, 135, 136, 137, 139, 142, 146, 147, 150, 154, 155, 156, 157, 160, 161, 162, 168, 169, 171, 175, 179, 182, 188
Holocaust awareness 62
Holocaust denial 18, 81, 83, 84, 110
Holocaust education 3, 4, 5, 49, 56, 57, 58, 60, 63, 70, 78, 79, 80, 82, 85, 87, 89, 91, 92, 93, 94, 100, 103, 104, 107, 108, 111, 117, 119, 121, 122, 125, 140, 147, 152, 169, 185, 187, 194, 196, 197, 199, 202
Holocaust Memorial Day 74
Holocaust Museum and Education Center, Skokie, Illinois 71
The Holocaust: Understanding Why 87
The Holocaust: Voices of Scholars 64, 191, 193, 194, 198
homosexuals 23
House of the Wannsee Conference 61, 66, 77, 106

identity 7, 8, 9, 10, 11, 12, 13, 14, 16, 18, 19, 20, 123, 152, 166, 167, 168, 169, 179, 180, 185, 187, 188, 193, 194, 196, 197
Immigration 13, 27, 32, 34, 176
Interfaculty Department of the History and Culture of the Jews in Poland, Jagiellonian University, Kraków 59
International Task Force 62, 104, 122
Internet Guide to Tolerance Education 63
individualist 10, 16
Individualized Interdisciplinary Humanities Study Specializing in Jewish Studies, University of Wrocław 56, 76
ingroup 14, 15, 16
insider 11, 47
insider-outsider 27, 30
Institute of European Studies 60, 68, 116, 131, 201, 202; *see also* Chair of European Studies
Institute of Jewish Studies, Jagiellonian University, Kraków 49, 53, 55, 75
Institute of National Remembrance 70, 71, 88, 106, 116
Institute of Tolerance, Łódź 119, 126, 127, 139
institutional racism 17
intelligentsia 17, 23, 174

International Centre for Education on Auschwitz and the Holocaust 88, 116
International Council of Museums (ICOM) 140, 195
International Monument to Victims of Fascism 96
International Task Force for Holocaust Education, Remembrance, and Research 104, 122
International Youth Meeting Center (IYMC), Oświęcim 31, 133
Internet 39, 44, 45, 46, 63, 69, 74, 84, 85, 127
inter-war period 31, 157
Irena Sendler Memorial Award 178
Israel 18, 24, 34, 36, 40, 44, 45, 54, 55, 62, 65, 66, 67, 69, 70, 71, 96, 102, 126, 127, 128, 129, 130, 131, 139, 144, 154, 156, 173, 175, 176, 177, 180, 182, 183, 196, 201
Izak Synagogue, Kraków 154

Jagiellonian University, Kraków 49, 50, 51, 52, 53, 54, 57, 66, 68, 75, 89, 98, 112, 131, 144, 177, 190, 201
Jagiellonian University's Summer Holocaust Institute for Secondary Teachers 4, 58, 70, 71, 72, 73, 76, 88, 89, 92, 106, 116
Jedwabne 99, 103, 109, 111, 113, 192
Jehovah's Witnesses 23
Jewish Association Czulent 42, 119, 120, 139, 156, 176
Jewish community 21, 24, 27, 29, 31, 33, 34, 36, 37, 38, 40, 42, 43, 44, 45, 46, 54, 68, 103, 113, 121, 126, 135, 139, 140, 143, 149, 154, 161, 170, 171, 174, 175, 176, 178, 192, 197
Jewish Community Center (JCC), Kraków 38, 61, 120, 176, 178, 190
Jewish Cultural Festivals, Poland 3, 4, 51, 159, 166, 168, 178, 180
Jewish Culture Days, Michów 136
Jewish Culture Festival, Kraków 1, 4, 58, 67, 69, 92, 129, 156, 166, 173, 174, 178, 185, 186, 190, 194, 195, 196, 198
Jewish Culture Festival, Singer's Warsaw 2, 120, 139, 186
Jewish Fighting Organization (JFO) 100
Jewish Forum Foundation 128
Jewish Historical Institute (JHI), Warsaw 50, 54, 61, 70, 102, 106, 129, 141, 146, 147, 151
Jewish identity 4, 20, 31, 32, 34, 36, 37, 38, 48, 105, 120, 169, 177
Jewish museums 140, 141, 142, 150, 154, 193, 194, 197
Jewish-Polish issues 50, 97, 99
The Jewish Question 29
Jewish Socialist Bund 32
Jewish Student organizations 38, 42, 43, 44, 45, 46, 47, 201

Jewish Studies 3, 4, 49, 50, 51, 52, 53, 54, 55, 56, 57, 68, 75, 76, 77, 78, 87, 88, 92, 117, 119, 121, 127, 140, 144, 147, 152, 155, 169, 177, 185, 187, 194
John Paul II, Pope 25
Judaica 1, 141, 142, 146, 154

Kazimierz 1, 3, 60, 71, 142, 146, 151, 156, 174, 175, 178, 179, 184, 190
Kazimierz Wielki (Casimir the Great) 27
kehilla 31
Kielce 33, 90, 99, 135, 139, 192, 196, 198
kirkut 135
klezmer 132, 153, 158, 159, 173, 182, 194
Korczak 67, 157
kosher 30, 41, 43, 176, 182
Kraków 1, 2, 3, 33, 42, 51, 53, 61, 104, 120, 126, 127, 128, 133, 140, 141, 142, 143, 146, 154, 155, 156, 158, 166, 169, 172, 174, 175, 176, 177, 178, 179, 180, 182, 183, 185, 192, 194, 195
Kraków ghetto 58, 67, 128

Lauder Foundation 119, 155
Lauder-Morasha School 37, 48
Letters to Henio, Lublin 150, 151
Letters to the Ghetto, Lublin 74, 133
Lieberman, H. 37
literature 7, 22, 38, 50, 52, 53, 54, 55, 56, 57, 75, 84, 87, 98, 105, 110, 138, 155, 156, 160, 184, 194
liturgical music 158, 159, 161, 164
Living History Forum 125
Łódź 40, 41, 42, 43, 51, 76, 90, 119, 120, 1216, 127, 136, 139, 159, 160, 161, 162, 163, 164, 201
Lublin 51, 54, 57, 68, 69, 70, 74, 76, 77, 132, 133, 135, 136, 139, 141, 142, 149, 150, 151, 197

magazines 40, 63, 132, 155, 165
Majdanek Concentration Camp, Lublin 54, 77, 102, 107, 132, 141, 150
Makuch, J. 129, 166, 178, 179, 184, 185, 195, 196
Małopolska (Smaller Poland) 53, 75, 146, 156
maps of memory 135
Maria Curie-Skłodowska University, Lublin 51, 54, 57, 76
Meeting with Jewish Culture, Chmielnik 169, 172, 173
Memorial de la Shoah, Paris 106
memory books 54
Memory Gate Project, Lublin 149, 151, 197
Michael H. Traison Foundation for Poland 71
Midrash Theatre 146, 158, 165, 177

Midrasz 155, 167
Mieszko I 20, 22
Ministry of National Education 70, 100, 101, 104, 108, 112, 130; *see also* Polish Ministry of Education
minority 5, 9, 11, 17, 18, 24, 26, 29, 33, 34, 39, 42, 46, 47, 75, 86, 87, 167, 183, 197
Mordechai Anielewicz Center for the Research and Study of the History and Culture of Jews, Warsaw 55, 76
music 7, 38, 84, 132, 152, 153, 154, 156, 157, 158, 159, 160, 161, 163, 164, 166, 168, 169, 173, 177, 180, 181, 182, 184, 185, 194, 195, 196, 201
museum 1, 3, 5, 38, 60, 61, 68, 73, 74, 85, 94, 107, 125, 140, 141, 142, 143, 144, 147, 149, 150, 154, 178, 190, 195
Museum of the History of Polish Jews, Warsaw 141, 147, 151, 201
Myślenice 75, 135, 136, 137

national identity 8, 9, 11, 12
National In-Service Teacher Training Center in Warsaw (CODN) 70
Nazi 17, 23, 32, 35, 54, 65, 66, 74, 79, 81, 82, 84, 86, 95, 97, 98, 99, 106, 110, 114, 115, 116, 123, 125, 143, 146, 153, 159, 164, 172
Nazi regime 17, 23, 24, 27, 166, 169, 170, 172, 181, 182, 192
Neighbors 99, 113, 132, 192
Non-Governmental Organization (NGO) 5, 38, 39, 42, 43, 44, 45, 46, 59, 62, 167, 70, 71, 73, 74, 75, 78, 106, 108, 117, 118, 119, 121, 126, 128, 129, 134, 140, 187, 198
Nożyk Synagogue, Warsaw 22, 134
Nuremberg laws 17, 83

Office for Democratic Institutions and Human Rights of the Organization for Security and Co-operation in Europe (OSCE) 63
Old Jewish Cemetery, Wrocław 142
Old Synagogue Museum, Kraków 141, 142, 143, 146
Opole University, Opole 51
oral history 66, 128, 132, 135, 149
Ornstein, J. 38, 185
Orthodox Judaism 1, 2, 3, 28, 32, 33, 170, 171, 175, 176, 178, 179, 182
Oświęcim (Auschwitz) Jewish Center, Oświęcim 141, 144, 151
"the other" 13, 14, 15
outgroup 14, 15, 16
outsider 11, 12, 13, 15, 27, 30

Palestine 32, 171
Pan-Slavism 22
Pan Tadeusz 20, 196

pedagogical construct 166, 168, 169, 184
Pedagogical University, Kraków 70, 88, 92, 104, 106, 116, 201
people with disabilities 23
Piast 20, 22, 24, 25
Piłsudski, J. 32
Płaszów 127
Podgórze 71, 175
pogrom 29, 30, 33, 39, 99, 103, 109, 111, 175
Polin 50, 114, 115
POLIN 120, 138
Polin Academy Summer Seminar (PASS), Warsaw 148, 151
Polish Association for Jewish Studies, Kraków 51, 77
Polish Center for Holocaust Research, Warsaw 51, 52, 77, 106
Polish-German-Russian Educational Project 144, 195
Polish Home Army (Armia Krajowa) 95, 101
Polish identity 4, 18, 20, 21, 22, 25, 26, 34, 35, 62, 97, 114, 137, 139, 189
Polish-Jewish heritage 53, 55, 70, 76, 172
Polish-Jewish identity 8, 36
Polish-Jewish relations 98, 99, 101, 103, 111, 144, 179, 187, 192
Polish Ministry of Education 107, 129; *see also* Ministry of National Education
Polish partitions 50
Polish People's Republic 25, 114
Polish Resistance Movement 100
Polish United Workers' Party (PZPR) 101
post–Communist (Soviet) Poland 35, 37, 38, 48, 56, 70, 86, 103, 112, 113, 121, 193, 196
post–Holocaust 48, 50
Poznań 22, 42, 51, 52, 75, 169, 198
pre–Holocaust 36, 154, 156, 157
prejudice 15, 16, 17, 18, 33, 36, 47, 71, 81, 88, 91, 104, 109, 110, 131, 136, 147, 184, 188, 193
presentations of identity 166, 167, 168
print media 155
Progressive Judaism 1, 28, 175
Prussia 29
public memory 97, 114
PUSZ (Polska Unia Studentów Żydowskich, Polish Union of Jewish Students) 42, 44, 45, 46

Rabbi Moses Isserles Remuh Jewish Library, Kraków 177
race 9, 13, 17, 81, 110, 127
racism 69, 71, 81, 82, 86, 103, 104, 134, 202
Radio Maryja 63
Radom 31
Reform Judaism 28, 175, 176, 186
religion 18, 22, 25, 26, 27, 30, 53, 64, 67, 69, 105, 110, 123, 127, 132, 138, 143, 166, 183, 191

remembrance 35, 58, 59, 64, 73, 74, 75, 96, 123, 124, 169, 172, 184
Remuh Synagogue, Kraków 142, 174, 176
Republic of Poland 25
Research Center for Jewish History and Culture in Poland, Jagiellonian University, Kraków 53
Research Centre for the Culture and Languages of the Jews, University of Wrocław 56, 76
Righteous Among Nations/Righteous Gentiles 24, 62, 69, 134, 139, 179, 195
Roma 23, 24, 143, 188
Romantic Period 22, 52
Russia 22, 25, 29, 123, 128, 144, 175, 176, 195

Schindler, O. 67, 191, 192
Schindler's List 66, 79, 192
secondary school 35, 38, 54, 57, 87, 104, 114, 119, 134, 138, 172, 187
secular Jews 29, 30, 33, 175
Segal, Rabbi T. 128, 176, 177
Sephardic 27, 159, 161, 183
Shabbat 1, 31, 41, 42, 43
Shalom Foundation 62, 119, 120, 130, 139, 186
Shavei Israel 176
Shoah 61, 62, 66, 67, 94, 103, 130, 133
shtetl (sztetl) 4, 17, 23, 27, 156, 166, 169, 170, 172, 181, 182, 192, 195
Shudrich, Rabbi M. 36, 37
Sienkiewicz, H. 22
Smolensk 26
Sobibór 68, 102
social class 28
Solidarity 35, 37, 98, 100, 101
Soviet era/period 24, 49, 86, 168
Soviet Union 23, 25, 49, 86, 96
Stalin, J. 34, 96, 110
Statute of Kalisz 27
Stefan Batory Foundation 64
Stowarzyszenie im. Jana Karskiego (Jan KarskiAssociation), Kielce 139
Sukovata, V. 49, 86, 199
survivors 24, 54, 66, 67, 71, 79, 84, 93, 108, 110, 124, 128, 129, 134, 138, 143, 145
Suszkiewicz, K. 58, 201
synagogue 1, 4, 24, 30, 36, 40, 94, 132, 133, 135, 141, 142, 143, 145, 146, 148, 151, 154, 160, 170, 173, 174, 176, 196
Szuchta, R. 64, 91, 92, 104, 112, 114, 115, 130, 197

taboo 35, 36, 61, 74
Talmud 31, 40, 142, 154
Tanakh 30
Tarnów 135
Taube Center for the Renewal of Jewish Life in Poland 37

Tempel Synagogue 1, 2
textbooks 35, 39, 40, 59, 86, 87, 93, 100, 101, 102, 103, 111, 115, 132, 33
theatre 30, 55, 124, 129, 149, 155, 157, 158, 164, 171, 176, 177, 195
Theatre NN Association, Lublin 74, 132
Together and Apart in Brzezany: Poles, Jews and Ukrainians 1919–1945 67, 192
Tour of 5 Shtetls 4
Treblinka 102, 107, 124, 125, 142, 157, 172
Trojański, P. 92, 93, 112, 113, 114, 115, 188, 201
Tslil Jewish Choir of Łódź and Warsaw 5, 42, 43, 45, 46, 159, 161, 162, 164, 198, 201

UNESCO world heritage site 143
Union of Jewish Communities in Poland 120, 134
United Kingdom 78, 79, 83
United States 1, 2, 65, 71, 78, 79, 80, 82, 83, 84, 107, 139, 144, 153, 155, 156, 176, 198
United States Holocaust Museum, Washington, D.C. 144, 156, 198
University of Białystok 51
University of Bydgoszcz 51
University of Gdańsk 51, 76
University of Łódź 51, 76, 127, 201
University of Rzeszów 51, 76
University of Śląsk (Silesia), Katowice 51
University of Warsaw 55, 56, 76, 128
University of Wrocław 51, 55, 56, 57, 76
USSR (United Soviet Socialists Republic) 96

Vaad 27, 29
Vidal Sassoon International Center for the Study of Anti-Semitism (SICSA) 68
visual arts 152

Wajda, A. 67, 157
Warsaw 2, 37, 40, 42, 43, 48, 49, 50, 51, 52, 55, 70, 76, 77, 88, 102, 106, 116, 120, 130, 134, 135, 138, 139, 141, 142, 146, 147, 151, 157, 159, 160, 164, 169, 186, 190, 201
Warsaw Ghetto 52, 142, 147, 157, 162
Warsaw Ghetto Uprising 100, 101, 102, 147
Website Guide to Tolerance Education 77
White Stork Synagogue, Wrocław 141
Why Should We Teach About the Holocaust? 112, 113, 191
Wielkopolska (Greater Poland) 27
World Jewish Restitution Organization 120, 134
World War I 23, 29, 52, 82, 155, 171, 174
World War II 23, 24, 30, 32, 33, 35, 36, 37, 48, 49, 50, 52, 53, 54, 55, 56, 62, 72, 86, 87, 90, 98, 110, 133, 138, 143, 149, 169, 171, 175, 183, 191
Wrocław, Poland 3, 24, 42, 55, 56, 76, 135, 141, 142, 169, 186; see also Breslau, Germany
Września 22

xenophobia 15, 60, 74, 92, 134

Yad Vashem 24, 62, 68, 69, 70, 71, 89, 106, 144, 156, 201
Yalla! 42, 43, 45
yeshiva 30, 31
Yiddish 27, 30, 31, 40, 43, 48, 53, 55, 56, 57, 94, 120, 12, 145, 155, 156, 157, 159, 160, 161, 162, 163, 164, 165, 175, 177, 181, 183
Yiddish literature 57, 156
young adult literature 156

Zagłada 52, 94, 112, 133, 114
Żegota (Council for Aid to Jews) 23, 48, 100, 192
Zionism 18, 32, 96
ŻOB (Żydowska Organizacja Bojowa) 100
ZOOM (Żydowska Ogólnopolska Organizacja Młodzieżowa, yhe Polish Jewish Youth Organization) 42, 43, 45, 119, 120, 139

www.ingramcontent.com/pod-product-compliance
Lightning Source LLC
Chambersburg PA
CBHW032056300426
44116CB00007B/767